Luther W

Cakes-on-the-Go: Chocolate Mound Cake (recipe page 116) and Cherry Crown Cake (recipe page 118). Quick dress-ups make these simple cakes look fancy enough for cake walks and other special occasions.

Cherry-Peach Dumplings (recipe page 153), a quick last-minute dessert, cook in skillet during the first part of meal. Serve it with the hot, bright-color juice spooned over the plump, tender dumplings.

FARM JOURNAL'S TIMESAVING COUNTRY COOKBOOK

1,000 recipes and menus
to help the busy woman
please her family and friends

NELL B. NICHOLS
FIELD FOOD EDITOR

DOUBLEDAY & COMPANY, INC.
GARDEN CITY, NEW YORK

Library of Congress Catalog Card Number 61–17307

Printed in the United States of America
First Edition

CONTENTS

COLOR ILLUSTRATIONS

All photographs created by Farm Journal Food and Art Staffs

* Photographer: Mel Richman, Inc.
† Photographer: Hoedt Studios

[illegible]

[illegible]

[illegible]

[illegible]

[illegible]

[illegible]

What You Will Find in This Cookbook

Every woman is a timesaving cook in her fashion. Not one of you reading this cookbook has all the time you could use in the kitchen. In this book we bring together the best of favorite recipes developed with an eye on the clock. In them, time also is an ingredient, used deftly and purposefully.

What is your definition of a short-cut cookbook? I wish I could chat with you and get your reactions as you turn the pages that follow. I asked the question of 100 women—members of our Family Test Group—and I received about 100 different answers. But the varied points of view and the recipes from our readers picture three types of short-cut cooking.

First come the everything-under-control cooks. They're the make-ahead or two-step cooks who distribute the work in making a dish so that the bulk of it may be done in advance. Their goal is to avoid fuming and fussing the last few minutes before a meal is due on the table. They put salads in the refrigerator to chill, assemble and refrigerate casseroles for quick heating when needed, and store ready-to-go dishes in their freezers. Their motto is: schedule the work.

The second group are the no-pot-watchers. They specialize in dishes that take a few minutes to get ready to cook or chill, but that take long, slow cooking—untended—or hours of chilling. Free from watching over food as it is preparing itself, they gain time to do something beyond the kitchen.

Third, there are the jiffy, last-minute cooks. To them the short-cut dish is one you make quickly and easily, preferably in 30 minutes or less with no advance preparation. They "buy time" in cans, packages, partly prepared foods. Their recipes may be as simple as opening two cans, combining the contents, and adding their own dash of seasoning. These speedy cooks like to fix desserts that chill or bake while the main part of the meal is eaten. They champion skillet specialties. And they rely on well-stocked cupboards and refrigerators. They have expanded what used to be the "emergency shelf" to work for them every day.

So when you glance through this cookbook, you may find recipes that aren't your idea of timesaving. Whether a recipe seems short-cut to you will depend on what type of cooking you do mostly. But don't you agree that most busy cooks are a combination of all three?

So we include in this book recipes that meet these various practices of busy women. If you are one of the thousands of homemakers crowded for cooking time, but who want to serve food your friends and family will praise, this recipe collection is for you. We compiled it especially to help you realize your ambitions and to build your reputation as a superior cook. We turned for inspiration to FARM JOURNAL readers. Hundreds of farm women, just as hurried as you are, share their favorite short-cut recipes with you in this cookbook.

More than two thirds of the recipes, in fact, are contributed by our readers. "I'm sending my recipes for dishes that always bring compliments," one of them wrote. The other one third of the prized recipes that follow came from friends, many of them home economists, who have skill and imagination with foods, from members of the FARM JOURNAL staff and their families, and from our own FARM JOURNAL Countryside Kitchens. All have been tested by home economists and practical homemakers.

Because so many excellent cooks say the right up-to-date equipment makes cooking short-cut, we've adapted wonderful old recipes to new methods.

With time at a premium, menu planning is of prime importance–knowing what you are going to get for a meal before it's time to cook it is a timesaver. We surveyed members of our Family Test Group to find out how they plan meals. Their unanimous answer was: "First I choose the meat or other main dish. Then I select other foods to go with it." This explains the sequence of the chapters in this cookbook–instead of following the traditional alphabetical one, we have updated the order of our chapters. They are based on the system busy women follow in considering the different parts of a menu when they decide what to get for a meal. This explains, for instance, why meat recipes appear in the first chapter in this cookbook.

Most of the recipes in this cookbook make either 4 or 8 servings. Unless otherwise specified, you can double the former and divide the latter in two. All the recipes give good results. Don't you agree with me that the best way of all to save time is to use a reliable recipe that ends up in a wonderful-tasting dish?

NELL B. NICHOLS
Field Food Editor

FARM JOURNAL'S

TIMESAVING COUNTRY COOKBOOK

1,000 recipes and menus
to help the busy woman
please her family and friends

CHAPTER 1

MEATS

Meat is the hub of good country meals—the menu maker's keystone. She selects it and then chooses other foods to complement it. That is how members of FARM JOURNAL's Family Test Group start planning what to have for a meal. And that is why meat recipes come first in this cookbook.

The specialties of farm kitchens appear in this chapter. Here are the meat recipes that bring the most bouquets to the busiest women in the world—those who live on a farm in the middle of a family business.

Ground beef gets top mention in time-saving recipes contributed by our readers. You'll find recipes featuring it in this chapter and under Main Dish Sandwiches. And look for the half dozen meat ball specials.

But busy cooks use many kinds of meat in their best-liked, short-cut recipes—ham, steaks, chops, sausage, frankfurters, canned meats and cold cuts, to name a few.

Ways of cooking speed up meat cookery. Country women fast-broil tender steaks and chops in broiling ovens, but more frequently in heavy skillets. Some of them prefer oven-roasted steaks that cook untended. Slower and longer cooking of meat, in Dutch ovens or foil jackets, has loyal supporters. While the meat cooks, busy farm women go to church, to town, to garden, or to help outdoors—confident they can get a tempting meal on the table double-quick when they return to their kitchens.

You will find tasty meat casseroles, both elegant and homespun, in this chapter. Short-cut cooks often assemble them in advance and freeze or refrigerate them to bake later.

Don't miss the quick tricks in this chapter—such things as meatballs that brown as they bake and a meat loaf that makes its own rich, brown gravy.

Short-cut Ways with Meats

The quick route to good eating.

Beef Dishes to Tote

What to take to covered dish suppers is a question country women frequently have to answer. The two following dishes fill the bill because they're unusual, tasty, portable and not too much work to make. Both are hearty with ground beef and at their best made with lean meat. These good travelers have another common merit —they're seasoned delicately with sour cream. Also serve them at home for special occasions when you want to win compliments on your cooking.

The good farm cook who shares the Beef-Cheese Casserole recipe says it makes her most praised company special. She admits: "It causes a flurry of excitement at potluck suppers, and friends ask me to bring it next time." She often assembles the casserole in the morning, covers and refrigerates it. Then all she has to do at mealtime or before leaving for a neighborhood supper is to bake it half an hour. No wonder she calls it an easygoing main dish.

BEEF-CHEESE CASSEROLE

Everyone who tastes says, "Out of the world. May I have a second helping?"

1½ lbs. ground beef
1 medium onion, chopped (about ¾ c.)
1 tsp. salt
⅛ tsp. pepper
2 (8 oz.) cans tomato sauce
1 c. cottage cheese
1 (8 oz.) pkg. cream cheese
¼ c. dairy sour cream
⅓ c. chopped green pepper
⅓ c. chopped green onion
8 oz. noodles, cooked and drained

Combine ground beef and onion in skillet and cook until beef is browned. Add salt, pepper and tomato sauce and simmer slowly while preparing remaining ingredients.

Combine cottage cheese, cream cheese, sour cream, green pepper and green onion.

Place half the noodles in bottom of greased 3 qt. casserole. Top with cheese mixture, then remaining noodles. Pour meat mixture over top.

Bake in moderate oven (350°) 30 minutes. Makes 8 to 10 servings.

Note: You can use 2 (1½ qt.) casseroles.

GREEN BEAN–BURGER BAKE

Wonderful what an important dish sour cream can make out of beef and beans

4 slices bacon, diced
1 lb. ground beef
1 c. fine bread crumbs
1 tsp. salt
1 c. dairy sour cream
1 egg
2 (10 oz.) pkgs. frozen green beans
1 (1½ oz.) pkg. onion-soup mix
1 can condensed cream of mushroom soup

Cook bacon in skillet; remove and drain.

Combine ground beef, bread crumbs, salt, ½ c. sour cream and egg. Shape into 12 meat balls; brown in bacon drippings.

Cook green beans as directed on package, but do not season.

Combine onion-soup mix, mushroom soup and remaining ½ c. sour cream in greased 2 qt. casserole. Mix in bacon and drained beans. Top with meat balls.

Bake, covered, in moderate oven (350°) 20 minutes. Makes 6 servings.

Meat Balls in Brown Gravy

A Tennessee reader shares her treasured recipe for Meat Balls in Buttermilk Sauce with us. Her specialty is truly delicious, but you need to allow about an hour to shape, brown and bake the balls and to make the sauce. But once the beef nuggets, swimming in smooth, thickened gravy, are tucked in the oven, you can forget them for 30 minutes.

MEAT BALLS IN BUTTERMILK SAUCE

This dish will wait in the oven if dinner is delayed

2 lbs. ground beef
1 c. bread crumbs
½ c. diced onion
1 c. milk
2 tsp. salt
¼ tsp. pepper
⅓ c. butter

Sauce

½ c. butter
½ c. flour
¼ c. sugar
3 tblsp. dry mustard
2 tsp. salt
¼ tsp. pepper
4½ c. buttermilk
2 eggs, beaten

For meat balls: Combine all ingredients, except butter; shape into large balls (about 16). Brown on all sides in butter; remove from skillet; keep hot.

For sauce: Add butter to drippings in skillet. Mix flour, sugar, mustard, salt and pepper; blend into fat. Stir; gradually add buttermilk. Cook over low heat, stirring constantly, until sauce is smooth and thick.

Stir some hot sauce into eggs; return to skillet and cook 2 to 3 minutes more. Pour into greased 3 qt. casserole; add meat balls. Bake in slow oven (300°) 30 minutes. Makes 8 servings.

BAKED MEAT BALLS

They brown as they bake. Serve them with spaghetti sauce, canned, made from a mix or from your freezer

2 eggs
½ c. milk
1 tblsp. instant minced onion
3 slices bread, cut in cubes
2 tsp. salt
¼ tsp. pepper
2 lbs. ground beef

Beat together eggs and milk. Stir in onion, bread and seasonings. Add beef and mix well.

For uniformity in size, measure meat mixture in a ¼ c. measure. Turn out and shape into balls.

Place balls in shallow pan. Bake in moderate oven (350°) 30 minutes. Makes approximately 18 balls.

Two-step Meat Balls

A New Jersey hostess who likes to serve meat balls in gravy to guests divides their preparation in two steps. She browns the meat quickly in the broiling oven and makes a thin brown gravy with the drippings. Then she puts the meat balls in a casserole, pours on the gravy and refrigerates them, covered, for two or three days. She need not watch them while they bake about an hour before the company is due.

SWEDISH MEAT BALLS

Serve with rice, noodles or dumplings

- 1 lb. ground beef
- ½ c. fine bread crumbs
- ⅔ tsp. salt
- ⅛ tsp. pepper
- Dash of nutmeg
- 1 medium onion, finely chopped
- 1 egg
- 2 tblsp. flour
- 2 tblsp. fat
- Water
- 1 beef bouillon cube

Thoroughly mix together beef, bread crumbs, salt, pepper, nutmeg, onion and egg. Shape lightly in 1½″ balls.

Place meat balls on foil-lined baking sheet, turning up edges to catch fat, or on a shallow pan. Brown quickly on all sides in the broiling oven. Remove meat balls to a large casserole.

Make gravy using 2 tblsp. each flour and fat for every cup of gravy desired. Brown flour in fat, add cold water and stir until gravy is smooth and thickened (thin gravy is desirable). Dissolve bouillon cube in gravy and pour over the meat balls. Cover and bake in a slow oven (325°) 1½ hours. Or refrigerate 2 or 3 days, then bake. Makes 6 to 8 servings.

There are fine cooks who hold that old-fashioned Porcupine Meat Balls are the most convenient of all. They make their own gravy or sauce as they bake.

PORCUPINE MEAT BALLS

No shaping of meat balls—you drop mixture from a spoon

- 1 ½ lbs. ground beef
- ½ c. uncooked regular rice
- ⅔ c. milk
- 1 tblsp. instant minced onion (or 1 medium onion, chopped)
- 1 ½ tsp. salt
- ¼ tsp. pepper
- 1 can condensed tomato soup
- ¾ c. water

Combine beef, rice, milk, onion, salt and pepper. Drop rounded tablespoonfuls of mixture into shallow baking pan (13″ × 9″ × 2″).

Combine soup and water. Pour over meat.

Cover pan tightly with foil. Bake in moderate oven (350°) 1 hour. Makes 6 to 8 servings.

BAKED LEMON STEAK

Right for a take-it-easy big meal

- 3 tblsp. butter or margarine, melted
- 3 lbs. sirloin steak, 1 ½″ thick
- 1 tsp. salt
- ¼ tsp. pepper
- 1 lemon, thinly sliced
- 2 onions, thinly sliced
- 1 c. ketchup
- 1 tblsp. Worcestershire sauce
- ¼ c. water

Brush butter on both sides of steak; season with salt and pepper. Place on rack in shallow pan. Lay lemon slices on steak and cover with onions.

Mix ketchup, Worcestershire sauce and water. Pour over steak.

Bake in hot oven (425°) 30 to 45 minutes, depending on degree of doneness desired. Makes 6 to 8 servings.

CALIFORNIA MINUTE STEAKS: Pan-fry minute (cube) steaks quickly in a little butter. Sprinkle one side of steaks lightly with a touch of rosemary or orégano; add a thin slice of tomato and one of Cheddar cheese. Run under broiler just long enough to melt cheese.

Variation: For sandwiches, serve California Minute Steaks on slices of toast or French bread, buttered and sprinkled with parsley.

SWISS STEAK ROYAL

Stewed tomatoes for subtle seasoning

½ c. flour
2 tsp. salt
½ tsp. pepper
3 tblsp. fat
3 lbs. round or chuck steak, 1½" to 2" thick
1 (8 oz.) can stewed tomatoes

Pound mixture of flour, salt and pepper into steak with edge of heavy plate. Brown meat on both sides in hot fat in heavy skillet or Dutch oven. Pour on tomatoes. Cover tightly and bake in moderate oven (350°) until tender, about 1½ hours. Makes 8 servings.

ROUND-STEAK STEW

Rich color, interesting flavor blend

1½ lbs. round steak, ½" thick
3 tblsp. fat
1 can condensed cream of tomato soup
½ c. water
1 (⅕ oz.) pkg. instant minced onion

Lay steak on board and cut in 1" strips; then cut strips in ½" diagonal pieces. Brown in hot fat. Add soup, water and onion and simmer until tender, about 45 minutes. Serve over rice. Makes 6 servings.

SUPREME OF LIVER

Speedy specialty of the CowBelles

1 lb. calf's liver
½ tsp. salt
¼ tsp. pepper
¼ tsp. sage
¼ c. cornmeal
3 to 4 tblsp. salad oil

Slice liver thin.

Mix seasonings and cornmeal. Roll liver in this mixture. Add to oil heated in skillet. Brown on both sides. Serve with Cream Gravy. Makes 4 servings.

Cream Gravy

Drain all but 1 tblsp. fat from skillet. Add ½ c. heavy or dairy sour cream. Season with salt and pepper. Heat, but do not boil. Pour over hot liver slices.

A Dish for Absent Cooks

This tasty pot roast is a made-to-order recipe for the busy cook who needs to be out of the kitchen until just before mealtime.

NO-WATCH POT ROAST

Fix and forget until time to take out of the oven—meat that will wait for the men to come in

3 to 4 lbs. beef pot roast
1 (1½ oz.) pkg. onion-soup mix
1 can condensed tomato soup

Place meat in Dutch oven with tight-fitting lid. Sprinkle with onion-soup mix. Spoon soup over meat.

Bake in slow oven (325°) 3 hours. Makes 6 to 8 servings.

more

Note: If a rump or other lean cut of beef is cooked in this manner, the sauce in the pan will not be too greasy to serve as gravy.

Meat Balls for Two Meals

Some short-cut cooks like to fix enough meat balls for two meals at a time. Half of them cook in a skillet while the other half bake in the oven to freeze for quick reheating later. Here is how they do it.

BEEF BALLS

Enough juicy, brown, tender meat balls for two meals

- 3 lbs. ground beef
- 1 ½ c. fine bread crumbs
- 4 eggs
- 4 tsp. salt or seasoning salt
- 1 c. ketchup
- 3 tblsp. fat

Thoroughly mix together all ingredients except fat. Form into balls about 1½" in diameter. Makes 24 to 28 balls.

Divide into two parts. Brown half the balls on all sides in 3 tblsp. fat. Remove balls to hot platter; make Bean Gravy in same skillet.

At the same time, bake rest of beef balls in large casserole in moderate oven (350°) about 20 minutes. Cool, cover and freeze, or refrigerate. To prepare for serving, use our recipe for Beef Balls with Rice, following.

Bean Gravy

- 3 tblsp. flour
- 1 (8 oz.) can pork and beans in tomato sauce
- 2 c. water
- ¼ c. ketchup (optional)
- 1 tsp. salt

Blend flour with hot drippings. Add beans and mash with fork to blend.

Add water gradually, stirring to keep mixture smooth. Boil 2 or 3 minutes. Add ketchup and salt. Pass with Beef Balls. Makes 1¾ cups.

Note: If you use ketchup in gravy, you may wish to substitute milk for ketchup in meat balls.

BEEF BALLS WITH RICE

A skillet special—thrifty, delicious and praiseworthy. Try it today

- 12 to 14 beef balls
- 2 tblsp. shortening
- ⅓ c. finely chopped onion
- 2 beef bouillon cubes
- 1 tsp. sugar
- 1 ½ tsp. celery salt
- 3 c. tomato juice
- 2 c. precooked rice
- ¼ c. butter or margarine
- ¼ c. finely chopped parsley

If beef balls are frozen (see Beef Balls recipe), thaw over low heat in large skillet containing shortening (about 15 minutes).

Add onion and brown lightly. Add bouillon cubes, sugar, celery salt, tomato juice, rice and butter. Bring to a boil. Cover tightly; place over low heat 10 minutes. Garnish with wreath of parsley snipped with scissors. Makes 6 servings.

Surprise Meat Loaves

Don't miss this trio of meat loaves. They are out of the ordinary. And they are moist and temptingly seasoned. For a quicker loaf than any of the three that follow, use the recipe in this chapter for Baked Meat Balls, which are miniature loaves.

FROSTED MEAT LOAF

Meat loaf at its Sunday best

- 1 slightly beaten egg
- ¼ c. milk
- 2 tsp. salt
- ¼ tsp. pepper
- ¼ c. ketchup or chili sauce
- 1 tblsp. instant minced onion
- 1 ½ c. soft bread crumbs
- 2 lbs. ground beef
- ½ pkg. instant mashed potatoes
- ½ c. shredded Cheddar cheese

Combine egg and milk; stir in salt, pepper, ketchup, onion and bread crumbs. Mix in ground beef. Form into a loaf and place in shallow baking pan (13″ × 9″ × 2″).

Bake in moderate oven (350°) 1 hour.

Prepare mashed potatoes as directed on package. Frost baked meat loaf with potatoes. Sprinkle with cheese. Return to oven until cheese melts. Makes 8 servings.

NO-MIX MEAT LOAF

It makes its own rich, brown gravy

- 2 lbs. ground lean beef
- 1 (1 ½ oz.) pkg. onion-soup mix
- 1 can condensed cream of mushroom soup

Form meat into loaf about 3″ high on large sheet of foil. Sprinkle with soup mix and spread soup over the top. Wrap loosely with foil, but make a tight seal.

Place on baking sheet or in shallow pan and bake in moderate oven (350°) 1 hour and 20 minutes. Serve with mashed potatoes or rice. Makes 8 servings.

Note: Gravy will be greasy unless lean beef is used.

MEAT LOAF WITH VEGETABLES

Cook the meat and vegetables together for an unusual, attractive main dish. Make a well in center of meat loaf and partly bake it. Then add a medley of color-bright frozen vegetables and complete the cooking. You don't have to bother to fix vegetables separately if you do it this way:

BEEF VEGETABLE BAKE

A new way to prepare and serve meat loaf and vegetables

- 2 lbs. ground beef
- 1 ½ c. soft bread crumbs
- 2 eggs
- 2 (8 oz.) cans tomato sauce
- 2 tsp. salt
- 1 ½ tsp. chili powder
- ⅛ tsp. cayenne
- 1 (10 oz.) pkg. frozen carrots and peas
- 1 (10 oz.) pkg. frozen corn
- ¼ tsp. garlic salt
- ½ tsp. salt
- ¾ c. shredded process American cheese

Combine beef, bread crumbs, eggs, 1 can tomato sauce, salt, chili powder and cayenne. Press into a 2 qt. casserole, building up the sides to shape a well in center. Bake in moderate oven (350°) 20 minutes.

Run hot water over vegetables to separate them; drain. Season with garlic salt and salt. Place in center of hot meat. Pour remaining tomato sauce over loaf. Bake in moderate oven (350°) 20 minutes. Sprinkle cheese over top and bake 5 minutes, or until cheese is melted. Makes 6 to 8 servings.

More Ways with Ground Beef

HOMEMADE CHILI CON CARNE

The Michigan woman who shares this recipe says it's the world's best chili con carne. Taste her version of this sturdy dish and see if you don't agree.

CHILI CON CARNE

Thanks to Spanish-Americans, who taught us to use chili powder

1 lb. ground beef
1 (15 oz.) can red beans
1 (1 lb.) can tomatoes
1 (⅕ oz.) pkg. instant onion
1 small garlic clove
2 tblsp. chili powder
½ tsp. salt
¼ tsp. cumin seed

Brown ground beef in skillet. Add beans, tomatoes and onion.

Run toothpick through garlic so it can be removed easily after cooking. Add to meat along with seasonings.

Cover and simmer 15 minutes. Remove garlic. Makes 6 servings.

CHILI WITH HOMINY

Contrast is the thing—spicy, robust chili con carne and mild hominy

1 lb. ground beef
1 medium onion, chopped (¾ c.)
1 (1 lb.) can tomatoes
1 (1 lb.) can hominy
2 tblsp. chili powder
1 tsp. salt

Cook ground beef and onion in skillet until beef is browned. Add remaining ingredients. Simmer, covered, 15 minutes. Makes 6 servings.

BROILED HAMBURGER STEAK

A quick change for hamburgers

2 lbs. ground beef
½ c. milk
1 egg
1 tblsp. Worcestershire sauce
2 tsp. salt
⅛ tsp. pepper
French salad dressing

Thoroughly mix all ingredients except salad dressing. Spread soft mixture in an oval about 1½" thick. Place on preheated broiler rack.

Brush top of meat with bottled French dressing.

Broil 3" from heat source 12 minutes. Turn with broad spatula (or 2 spatulas), brush with salad dressing and broil 12 minutes longer.

Cut in thick slices. Makes 6 servings.

BARBECUED BEEF TARTARE

The ranch way is to serve the beef and raw onion rings in toasted buns

2 lbs. lean ground beef
1 garlic clove, crushed

1 tblsp. minced chives
1 tblsp. minced parsley

Combine meat, garlic, chives and parsley (quickly snipped fine with scissors); shape into thick 4" patties.

Heat greased griddle until very hot; sear meat patties for 15 seconds only on each side. Serve at once. Makes 6 servings.

Note: Authentic Beef Tartare is not cooked. Raw egg, broken over the meat, mixes into it. The beef is served with chopped raw onions. It rates as a favorite treat in the Milwaukee, Wisconsin, area.

BEEF-MACARONI SKILLET

You can thaw frozen ground beef in skillet when making this main dish

1 lb. ground beef
1 medium onion, chopped
3 c. tomato juice
1 tblsp. Worcestershire sauce
1 tblsp. vinegar
1 tsp. salt
⅛ tsp. pepper
1 tsp. dry mustard
1 c. uncooked elbow macaroni

Brown beef and onion in skillet. Add remaining ingredients and cook, covered, until macaroni is done, about 20 minutes. Stir occasionally while cooking. Makes 6 servings.

HAMBURGER PIE

Everyday dish that meat-and-potato men rave over

1 lb. ground beef
1 medium onion, chopped (about ¾ c.)
½ tsp. salt
Dash of pepper
1 can condensed tomato soup
1 (1 lb.) can green lima beans
½ pkg. instant mashed potatoes
½ c. shredded Cheddar cheese

Cook meat and onion in heavy skillet until meat is browned. Add salt, pepper, tomato soup and beans with their liquid. Simmer 5 minutes. Place in a greased 2 qt. casserole.

Prepare potatoes as directed on package. Drop in mounds over hot meat mixture. Sprinkle with cheese.

Bake in moderate oven (350°) 20 minutes. Makes 6 servings.

THRIFTY CASSEROLE

Meat and potatoes get together in this hearty supper dish

1 lb. ground beef
1 medium onion, chopped (about ¾ c.)
1 tsp. salt
Dash of pepper
1 can condensed tomato soup
1 (10 oz.) pkg. frozen mixed vegetables
½ pkg. instant mashed potatoes

Cook ground beef and onion in heavy skillet until meat is browned. Add seasonings and tomato soup; simmer 5 minutes.

Combine mixture with vegetables cooked as directed on package. Turn into a greased 2 qt. casserole.

Top with mounds of mashed potatoes prepared as directed on package.

Bake in moderate oven (350°) 20 minutes. Makes 6 servings.

MEAT-VEGETABLE PIE

Biscuits bake to golden brown on expertly seasoned beef

1 lb. ground beef
1 medium onion, chopped (about ¾ c.)
1 tsp. salt
⅛ tsp. pepper
2 cans condensed vegetable soup
2 c. biscuit mix
⅔ c. milk

Brown beef and onion in skillet. Add seasonings and soup; simmer 5 minutes. Pour into a greased 2 qt. casserole.

Combine biscuit mix with milk as directed on package to make biscuits. Drop by spoonfuls over the hot meat.

Bake in hot oven (425°) until biscuits are browned, 15 to 20 minutes. Makes 8 servings.

CHILI HASH

Another fine way to use ground beef

2½ c. precooked rice
1 medium onion, chopped
2 tblsp. shortening
1 lb. ground beef
2 cans condensed tomato soup
1 tsp. chili powder
1 tsp. salt
¼ tsp. pepper

Prepare rice as directed on package. Keep warm.

Sauté onion in shortening; add beef and brown lightly.

Stir in soup and seasonings; heat to boiling. Add ½ c. rice; cover, remove from heat and let stand 5 minutes. Fluff up with fork. Spoon remainder of rice in ring around hash on platter. Makes 6 to 8 servings.

HEARTY ITALIAN SPAGHETTI

Use of spaghetti-sauce mix adds expert seasoning in a jiffy

1 (½ oz.) pkg. Italian spaghetti-sauce mix
1 (8 oz.) can tomato sauce
1 lb. ground beef
12 oz. spaghetti
½ c. shredded pizza cheese
1 tsp. instant parsley flakes (optional)

Prepare sauce as directed on package. Meanwhile brown beef in skillet. Add spaghetti sauce and simmer.

Cook spaghetti as directed on package. Place drained, cooked spaghetti on platter or in large, shallow bowl. Top with sauce. Sprinkle with cheese and parsley. Makes 8 servings.

LASAGNE CASSEROLE

Mixed herbs season expertly

8 oz. broad noodles
1 tblsp. salad oil
1 (8 oz.) pkg. heat-and-serve sausages
1 (1 lb.) can tomatoes
1 (6 oz.) can tomato paste
1 tblsp. instant minced onion
1 tsp. mixed Italian herbs
1 c. drained cottage cheese
¼ c. grated Parmesan cheese
1 (6 or 8 oz.) pkg. Mozzarella cheese, cut in ½" strips

Cook noodles as directed on package and drain. Return to same saucepan. Toss with salad oil to prevent sticking.

Meanwhile, dice sausages and brown, stirring often, in medium skillet. Stir in tomatoes, tomato paste, onion and herbs. Heat to boiling and simmer, stirring occasionally, 5 minutes.

Layer half the noodles, cottage cheese, Parmesan cheese, tomato mixture and Mozzarella cheese in greased 2 qt. casserole. Repeat, trimming the top by crisscrossing Mozzarella cheese strips.

Bake in moderate oven (350°) 30 minutes, until bubbling at edges and cheese is browned. Makes 6 servings.

Note: Double the recipe to serve 10 to 12.

BEEF-MACARONI CASSEROLE

In the morning you may assemble beef and macaroni mixtures in casserole and refrigerate. In evening add colorful tomato slices and bake

1 lb. ground beef
2 eggs
½ c. ketchup
⅓ c. milk
¼ c. chopped onion
1 ½ tsp. salt
8 oz. elbow macaroni, cooked
2 tsp. prepared mustard
¼ c. chopped green pepper
½ c. mayonnaise
1 c. grated American cheese
½ c. dry bread crumbs
2 tblsp. melted butter or margarine
6 slices tomato

Mix beef, eggs, ketchup, milk, onion and salt.

Mix macaroni, mustard, green pepper and mayonnaise; spread in greased 2 qt. baking dish. Spread beef mixture over top; sprinkle with cheese; top with mixture of crumbs and butter.

Bake in moderate oven (350°) 20 minutes; place tomatoes on top and bake 10 minutes. Makes 6 servings.

Sizzling Steaks—Broiler-fast

Broiling is a speedy way to cook meat. And almost everyone agrees that a hot, tender steak, browned on the outside, juicy and pink within, has few peers on the platter. When steaks are less than 1″ thick, pan-broiling gives the best results. Here are the directions for broiling beef successfully.

BEEF CUTS TO BROIL: Club, porterhouse, rib, sirloin, T-bone and tenderloin (filet mignon). Hamburger patties and liver also may be broiled.

THICKNESS OF STEAKS: 1″ to 2″.

HOW TO BROIL: Preheat broiler 10 minutes, or as directed by range manufacturer. Rub heated broiler rack with piece of suet.

Slash fatty edges of steaks with a knife or scissors at 1″ intervals, but do not cut into meat. Lay steak on heated rack 3″ to 5″ from heat–5″ for well-done, 3″ to 5″ for medium to rare. If the distance in your broiler must be less, reduce temperature accordingly.

Broil steak on one side; turn and broil on the other side. Season with salt and pepper and serve at once on warm platter.

HOW LONG TO BROIL: The time depends on many factors like thickness of steak, its size and shape and the amount of bone and fat. All timetables for broiling are an approximate guide. The test for doneness is to cut a slit in the steak near the bone and observe the color–gray for well-done, pink for medium-rare and red for rare. Broil 1″ steak from 5 to 7 minutes, 1½″ steak from 8 to 12 minutes, and a 2″ steak from 15 to 20 minutes on each side.

more

SEASONINGS FOR BROILED STEAKS: Salt and pepper may be the only seasonings desired. Bottled meat sauces may be sprinkled over the hot steak. Other toppings to add just before serving are: dabs of butter, butter blended with prepared mustard, a squeeze of lemon juice or a little mashed Roquefort or blue cheese mixed with butter or margarine. Or mix ⅛ lb. Roquefort or blue cheese with 1 tblsp. heavy cream and 1 tblsp. Worcestershire sauce. Spread on broiled steak before removing it from rack. Broil close to heat for 2 minutes.

For a barbecued flavor, brush the steak before broiling and as it broils with bottled French dressing. Or brush both sides of the steak before broiling with salad oil; when cooked to desired doneness, sprinkle with garlic salt and seasoning salt.

PAN-BROILED STEAKS

CUTS TO PAN-BROIL: Same as for broiling but cut ½″ to ¾″ thick—up to 1½″ if you like steak pink inside.

HOW TO COOK: Place in preheated heavy skillet. Rub skillet with a little suet, but do not add fat. Do not cover; do not add water. Brown on both sides. Reduce heat and cook to the desired degree of doneness, pouring off fat as it accumulates in pan. Turn occasionally to insure even cooking. It takes about 12 minutes to pan-broil a rare steak and 18 to 24 minutes for a well-done steak. Season and serve.

MINUTE STEAKS: These are thin steaks from the round that are scored by a special machine to cut the connective tissue. Rub a hot, heavy skillet with a little fat. Cook the steaks quickly, about 1 or 2 minutes on each side. Season with salt and pepper.

TENDERIZED STEAKS: Chuck, round, rump, flank and any less tender steak may be broiled if tenderizer is used. Sprinkle tenderizer on all surfaces of the steak, ½ tsp. per pound of meat. Do not season tenderized steaks with salt.

After adding the tenderizer, deeply pierce all surfaces of the meat with a sharp-tined fork, at 1″ intervals. Then cover loosely and place in refrigerator in the evening to use the next day. Broil like any other steak. Since tenderized meats tend to cook more quickly than other steaks, be careful not to overcook.

Instead of refrigerating meat after tenderizer has been added, you can let it stand at room temperature. It requires no attention until time for broiling. Let it stand 30 to 40 minutes if the steak is 1″ thick, about an hour for thicker steaks.

OTHER BEEF CUTS TO BROIL

HAMBURGER PATTIES: Broil 1″ patties like steak about 5 minutes on each side.

LIVER (calf's and young beef): Brush ½″ slices with soft butter or margarine and broil on rack in shallow pan 3″ or 4″ from heat, 2 to 4 minutes on each side. Broil until delicate pink inside or well-done, but use care not to overcook, for that toughens it.

LONDON BROIL: Use only top-quality flank steak scored lightly, crisscross fashion on both sides. Salt both sides of the steak and brush generously with French dressing. Broil 3″ from heat 4 to 5 minutes on each side. Slice diagonally in thin slices. For 6 servings, use flank steak weighing 2½ lbs.

OVEN-ROASTED STEAKS: Place ½″ steaks on rack in shallow oven. Place in preheated slow oven (300°) and cook 30 minutes for medium-rare steaks. Steaks 1″ to 1¼″ take 45 to 60 minutes to reach the medium-rare stage. There's no spattering, no turning and no watching during cooking.

Ham—Easy-on-the-Cook

EASY-SERVE BAKED HAM

A famous FARM JOURNAL *recipe. Cut the string and presto—the ham falls apart in even slices. A natural for church and club suppers*

1 (6 lb.) canned ham
1 (1 lb.) jar apricot preserves
(about 1 ½ c.)
Whole cloves

Slice ham and tie together with string. Or have your meat dealer slice the ham on his slicer and tie it up for you.

Place ham, fat side up, on rack in shallow baking pan. Spread apricot preserves over the top. Stud with cloves.

Heat in slow oven (325°) 15 minutes per pound. Baste with pan juices 3 or 4 times while baking.

Place on platter to serve. Cut and remove string. Makes 15 to 20 servings.

Variation: Substitute peach, cherry or pineapple preserves, orange marmalade or apple, cranberry or currant jelly for the apricot preserves.

SPICY HAM SLICE

Something different, something good

1 thick slice precooked ham,
1 ½″ thick
2 tblsp. prepared mustard
3 tblsp. finely chopped onion
1 c. ketchup
½ tsp. anise seed
5 triangles American cheese
Onion rings

Place ham in shallow baking dish.

Spread with mustard; sprinkle with onion. Bake in hot oven (400°) 15 minutes.

Remove from oven; pour ketchup over ham; sprinkle with anise seed.

Arrange cheese triangles on top.

Bake 10 minutes longer, or until cheese melts. Serve with onion rings. Makes 4 servings.

HAM BALLS WITH PEACHES

Makes a cheerful platter and good eating. Cooks in 16 minutes

1 (1 lb. 13 oz.) can peach halves
1 beaten egg
½ c. quick-cooking oats
1 tsp. prepared mustard
2 tsp. Worcestershire sauce
¼ tsp. pepper
1 lb. ground cooked ham
¼ c. chopped green pepper
(optional)

Drain peaches.

Combine ¼ c. syrup from peaches, egg, oats, mustard, Worcestershire sauce and pepper. Stir in ham and green pepper. Shape into 18 balls.

Broil in preheated broiler until browned, about 8 minutes. Turn balls.

more

Place peach halves in broiler and broil about 8 minutes. Serve a peach half with 3 ham balls. Makes 6 servings.

Note: Green pepper adds a crisp-tender texture.

HAM-ASPARAGUS CASSEROLE

Just the ticket for a spring supper

- 1 can condensed cream of mushroom soup
- ⅓ c. light cream
- 2 c. diced cooked ham
- 1 c. cooked or canned cut asparagus
- Buttered bread crumbs

Blend soup with cream; add ham and asparagus. Pour into 4 individual ramekins, or a small, shallow baking dish. Top with crumbs.

Bake in moderate oven (375°) about 20 minutes. Makes 4 servings.

Variation: Use 1 c. diced ham and 2 c. asparagus pieces.

BROILED HAM: Slash edge of 1″ ham slice in several places. Broil 2″ from heat, about 8 minutes per side, if the ham is ready-to-eat or cooked, and 12 minutes per side if ham is uncooked.

SPICY BROILED HAM: Place center-cut, ready-to-eat or cooked slice of ham in shallow pan. (A center cut weighs around 2 lbs. and makes 4 servings.) Mix ¼ c. brown sugar, 2 tblsp. cider vinegar and 1½ tsp. dry mustard and spread over top of ham. Broil under moderate heat until lightly browned, baste with drippings, turn and brown other side.

COMPANY BROILED HAM: Broil or pan-fry a slice of ham. Spread top to within ½″ of outer edge with mixture made by combining ⅓ c. mayonnaise, 3 tblsp. grated Parmesan cheese and ½ tsp. prepared mustard. Broil until bubbly and tinged with brown.

SUPPER HAM AND EGGS: Lay thin slices of cooked ham on warm platter. Top with sliced hard-cooked eggs and heated cooked or canned asparagus spears or broccoli. Pour warm Nobby Cheese Sauce (see Index) over eggs.

POTLUCK HAM CASSEROLE

A main dish you'll be proud to take to the party or to serve guests

- ½ c. milk
- 1 can condensed cream of mushroom soup
- 1 c. dairy sour cream
- 2 tsp. prepared mustard
- 1 tsp. instant minced green onion
- ⅛ tsp. pepper
- 4 oz. noodles, cooked and drained
- 2 c. thin pieces cooked ham
- ¼ c. toasted slivered almonds

Gradually add milk to mushroom soup, stirring over low heat to make smooth sauce. Blend in sour cream, mustard, onion and pepper.

Arrange half of noodles, ham and sauce in greased 2 qt. casserole. Repeat layers. Top with toasted almonds.

Bake in slow oven (325°) 25 minutes. Makes 6 servings.

Fork-tender Pork Chops

PORK CHOPS WITH APPLE JELLY

Dish has blend of three superlative flavors—rich browned pork, apple jelly and caraway seeds

6 pork chops, ½" thick
2 tblsp. fat
½ tsp. salt
⅛ tsp. pepper
¼ c. apple jelly
½ tsp. caraway seeds
¼ c. water

Brown chops in hot fat. Sprinkle with salt and pepper. Spread jelly on chops; sprinkle with caraway seeds. Add water, cover and simmer 30 minutes or until pork chops are done. Makes 4 to 6 servings.

BAKED PORK CHOPS

Chops brown themselves—require no attention while cooking

4 pork chops
1 tblsp. onion-soup mix
2 tblsp. French salad dressing
¼ c. water

Place pork chops in skillet. Top with soup mix and pour in the salad dressing and the water. Bake covered in moderate oven (350°) 1 hour. Makes 4 servings.

RANCHO PORK CHOPS

Lemon and onion add flavor—requires almost no pot watching

8 pork chops
1 tsp. salt
8 thin slices onion
8 thin slices lemon (1 lemon)
½ c. brown sugar
½ c. ketchup

Trim fat from chops; place in shallow pan; sprinkle with salt.

Top each chop with onion slice, lemon slice, sugar and ketchup.

Cover; bake in moderate oven (350°) 1 hour; uncover and bake 15 minutes longer, or until tender and well done. Makes 8 servings.

BARBECUED PORK CHOPS

You can make the sauce ahead—store in refrigerator for quick use

8 loin or shoulder pork chops, 1" thick
1 (8 oz.) can tomato sauce
½ c. ketchup
½ c. water
¼ c. vinegar
1 tsp. salt
1 tsp. celery seeds
⅛ tsp. cloves
½ tsp. Tabasco sauce
1 tblsp. prepared mustard
1 medium onion, sliced
1 clove garlic, crushed (optional)

Cut a little fat from pork chops, heat in skillet, then brown meat in it (about 10 minutes). Place meat in shallow baking dish (13" × 9" × 2") one layer deep.

Pour fat from skillet. Combine remaining ingredients; mix with browned particles in skillet. Pour over chops.

Bake uncovered in moderate oven (350°) 1 hour and 15 minutes. Turn once during baking. Adjust time for thicker or thinner chops. Makes 8 generous servings. If someone is late to dinner, these chops will taste good re-warmed.

Note: If your family likes more "bite" in sauce, sprinkle chops with a little red pepper before baking.

COMPANY PORK CHOPS

Savory pork cooks to succulent tenderness with no watching

8 pork chops, ½″ thick
2 tblsp. fat
1 can condensed chicken with rice soup

Brown pork chops on both sides in hot fat. Pour soup over pork chops. Simmer, covered, over low heat until pork chops are cooked, about 45 minutes. Makes 6 servings.

Note: The left-over broth makes excellent gravy to serve on rice.

Meat and Potatoes

Many busy women resist giving up some of the great all-American dishes even if they do require considerable time for proper cooking. Hearty pork chops and scalloped potatoes are a splendid example.

In the recipe for this favorite that follows, the spuds and pork bake 1½ hours for perfection. But you need pay no attention to them while they cook. And when you take them, hot and neatly browned on top, from the oven, getting the rest of the meal is quick.

There are short cuts in fixing the dish. The pork chops are browned only on one side. Canned soup provides seasoning as well as liquid and eliminates adding flour. It also prevents curdling of the cheese sauce that makes itself around the meat and potatoes.

Here's a dish to fix when you want to give your attention to work about the house, but not in the kitchen.

SCALLOPED POTATOES WITH PORK CHOPS

Add a green vegetable, salad and dessert—and dinner's ready

6 pork chops, ½″ thick
1 tblsp. fat
5 c. sliced, peeled raw potatoes
6 (1 oz.) slices process American cheese
1 tsp. salt
¼ tsp. pepper
½ c. chopped green onions
1 can condensed cream of celery soup
1 ¼ c. milk

Brown chops on one side in hot fat.

Place half of potatoes in greased baking pan (13″ × 9″ × 2″). Top with cheese slices. Add remaining potatoes. Place pork chops, browned side up, on potatoes. Sprinkle with salt and pepper.

Cook onions in drippings in skillet until tender, but do not brown. Add soup and milk. Heat; then pour over the pork chops.

Cover with foil or a baking sheet and bake in moderate oven (350°) 1 hour. Remove cover and continue baking 30 minutes. Makes 6 servings.

Variations: Use condensed cream of mushroom soup for the celery soup and slices of ham for the pork chops. Or use process pimiento cheese instead of American cheese.

Fast-fix Pork Sausage

PORK SAUSAGE WITH FRIED APPLES

Country food—fragrant, tasty, quick

2 lbs. pork sausage
8 c. sliced, unpeeled red apples
½ c. brown sugar
¼ tsp. cinnamon
Dash of ground cloves

Shape sausage into 18 patties. Pan-fry over low heat until no trace of pink color shows. Drain once during cooking. Keep hot.

Place ½ c. sausage drippings in skillet with tight-fitting lid. Add apples, sprinkle with sugar, cover and cook slowly until apples are almost tender, 15 to 20 minutes. Remove cover. Cook until apples are glazed. Sprinkle with cinnamon and cloves.

Serve sausage and apples on a large platter. Makes 6 servings.

SAUSAGE-APPLE SKILLET

Let your Junior Cooks try this when it's their night to fix supper

4 (½ lb.) pkgs. brown-and-serve sausages
2 tblsp. butter or margarine
1 c. sugar
1 tsp. cinnamon or nutmeg
2 (1 lb. 4 oz.) cans pie-sliced apples, drained
1 c. flour

Brown sausages in skillet—about 3 minutes if thawed, 4 to 5 minutes if frozen. Remove sausages; add butter to drippings in skillet.

Combine sugar and cinnamon. Sprinkle over apple slices. Dredge slices in flour. Brown in skillet. Serve sausages and apples together on platter. Makes 8 servings.

POTATO-SAUSAGE SKILLET

Big breakfast eaters like to start the day with this hearty dish

½ (9 oz.) pkg. hash-brown potatoes
½ lb. pork sausage
1 c. chopped onion
½ tsp. salt
¼ tsp. celery salt
¼ tsp. ground sage
⅛ tsp. pepper

Prepare potatoes as directed on package; drain well.

Cook sausage and onion together in skillet until sausage browns. Drain off fat if more than ¼ c. Add potatoes and seasonings.

Cook, stirring occasionally, until golden brown. Makes 6 servings.

SAVORY SAUSAGE RICE

Soup mix adds seasoning—packaged slivered almonds simplify preparation

2 lbs. bulk sausage
1 c. finely chopped green pepper
¾ c. chopped onion
2½ c. coarsely chopped celery
2 (2⅛ oz.) pkgs. chicken-noodle-soup mix
4½ c. boiling water
1 c. uncooked rice
½ tsp. salt
¼ c. melted butter or margarine
1 c. blanched almonds, slivered (optional)

Brown sausage in large skillet; pour off excess fat. Add green pepper, onion and 1 c. celery; sauté.

more

Combine soup mix and water in large saucepan; stir in rice. Cover and simmer 20 minutes, or until tender. Add sausage mixture and salt; stir well.

Pour into greased baking dish (about 12″ × 8″ × 2″). Sprinkle remaining celery over top; drizzle with melted butter. Bake in moderate oven (375°) 20 minutes. Makes 10 servings.

If almonds are used, sauté all celery with green pepper and onion. Mix most of almonds with other ingredients; save a few to sprinkle on top. Omit melted butter.

SPEEDY PANCAKE ROLL-UPS

The cook can sit down and eat when she bakes pancakes this way

2 lbs. link pork sausages
2 c. biscuit mix
2 c. milk
2 eggs

Pan-fry link sausages.

Combine biscuit mix, milk and eggs. Beat with rotary beater until smooth. Bake 5″ pancakes on hot griddle.

As cakes come off the griddle, roll each around a cooked sausage. Place in shallow baking pan, rolled side down.

Bake pancake rolls in hot oven (400°) about 5 minutes, or just long enough to heat. Serve with butter and syrup or with Buttered Applesauce (recipe follows). Makes 20 to 24 pancake rolls.

BUTTERED APPLESAUCE

Heat together 2 c. applesauce and ¼ c. butter, stirring together. Makes about 2 cups.

Bring on the Bacon

THREE WAYS TO COOK BACON

An ideal way to cook bacon for a crowd is to bake it. There's no turning, draining or watching, and the browning is even. Here's how to do it.

BAKED BACON: Lay bacon slices with fat side overlapping lean side of the next slice, on rack in shallow pan. Set pan on top shelf in hot oven (400°) and bake 10 to 12 minutes, or until bacon is of desired crispness. (Bacon cooked at its best is crisp, never brittle.)

Broiling also is a fine way to cook bacon, but you need to keep an eye on it. That's because it cooks so fast. Turn only once and do not preheat broiler. BROILED BACON: Lay bacon slices on rack of broiler pan. Broil 3″ to 5″ from heat. Turn once.

Many cooks prefer to fry bacon even if they have to stand over it. For perfect results every time, do it this way. PAN-FRIED BACON: Lay bacon slices in an unheated, heavy skillet. Cook over moderately low heat, 6 to 8 minutes, turning often. Drain. If you like bacon crisp, pour off the fat during cooking.

TIPS FOR FLAVORING WITH BACON

Sprinkle crumbled crisp-fried bits over: macaroni-and-cheese casseroles, pizza, creamed soups, vegetables.

Combine bits with: sandwich fillings —egg, chicken, tuna salad, cucumber, peanut butter, cream cheese; stuffings–meat, fowl and fish; scrambled eggs.

Wrap raw strips around and broil: hamburgers, frankfurters, asparagus spears, prunes, olives, pineapple chunks.

Lay raw strips over and bake: meat loaves, lean roasts, fish, poultry.

BACON-POTATO SKILLET

Bacon and eggs join potatoes for a hearty dish that men praise

½ (9 oz.) pkg. hash-brown potatoes
6 slices bacon
½ tsp. salt
⅛ tsp. pepper
4 eggs, slightly beaten
¼ c. milk

Simmer potatoes as directed on package; drain well.

Pan-broil bacon until crisp. Drain on paper toweling and crumble.

Remove all but ¼ c. bacon fat from skillet. Stir in potatoes. Add salt and pepper. Cook, turning occasionally, until golden brown.

Reduce heat to low. Combine eggs and milk; add, with bacon, to potatoes. Cook, stirring occasionally, until eggs are set. Makes 6 servings.

Note: Bacon seasons many dishes so delightfully that the best country cooks use it extensively. It is an ingredient in many recipes in this cookbook (look in Index under Bacon). Among them are: Bacon-Spinach Salad, Green-Bean–Burger Bake, Corn Chowder and several sandwiches–Tomato-Bacon, Bacon-Soup, Bacon-Egg, Peanut-Butter–Bacon and Mushroom-Bacon Supreme.

Lamb—Hot from the Grill

LAMB BALLS IN RED SAUCE

Shape balls lightly, brown deeply and simmer tenderly in the sauce

1 lb. ground lamb
½ c. fine bread crumbs
⅓ c. milk
1 egg yolk
1 tsp. salt
⅛ tsp. poultry seasoning
1 tblsp. fat
1 c. Basic Red Sauce (see Index)

Combine lamb, bread crumbs, milk, egg yolk, salt and poultry seasoning. Work together to blend ingredients. Form into 16 balls 1½″ in diameter.

Brown meat balls on all sides in hot fat. Drain off fat. Add Red Sauce. Cover and simmer 10 to 15 minutes. Makes 4 servings.

Variation: To make Beef Balls in Red Sauce, substitute ground beef for the lamb.

LAMB-SAUSAGE GRILL

Broil the meat for a special-occasion, hurry-up meal. A mixed grill is especially attractive and good. Excellent teammates are lamb chops, little pig sausages and canned pineapple rings. It's easy to fix such a combination of foods this way.

MIXED GRILL: Slash fat edges of rib lamb chops. Lay on broiler rack with pork-sausage links. (There are 12 to 16 sausages in a pound.) Broil 5″ to 6″ from source of heat, 7 to 8 minutes. Turn chops and season; turn sausages. Place well-drained, canned pineapple slices on rack and dot with butter or margarine. Broil 7 to 8 minutes longer.

Note: Cook frozen lima beans while meats broil; toss a green salad. While taking up the meats and pineapple, warm hard rolls in the oven. Presto! your dinner menu will be: Mixed Grill, buttered lima beans, green salad, hard rolls and chocolate cake for dessert.

BROILED LAMB

CUTS TO USE: Loin, rib or shoulder chops and leg steaks, cut 1″ thick.

HOW TO BROIL: Place on rack in preheated broiler 3″ from heat. Brown on one side, 6 to 7 minutes. Season with salt and pepper and turn. Brown on the other side another 6 to 7 minutes. To test for doneness, cut a slit along the bone and note if color is that of rare, medium-rare or well-done meat. Serve at once on a hot platter.

SEASONINGS: Rub the lamb before broiling with a cut garlic clove. Or sprinkle broiled lamb with a little dry salad mix, garlic flavor. Or serve broiled lamb topped with lemon juice and butter, mixed. Cream ¼ c. butter with spoon and gradually stir in 1 tblsp. lemon juice (fresh, frozen or canned) and add ½ tsp. salt. If available, add 1 tblsp. chives or parsley, snipped fine with scissors, to the butter mixture.

PAN-BROILED LAMB: Use loin, sirloin, rib or shoulder chops or leg steaks ½″ to ¾″ thick. Trim piece of fat from meat and rub over surface of a heated, heavy skillet. Remove fat. Cook meat in greased skillet over moderate heat until well browned; turn and continue cooking. Turn occasionally while cooking. Test for doneness by cutting a slit near bone and observing color.

BROILED LAMB PATTIES: Mix 1½ lbs. ground lamb with 1½ tsp. salt and ¼ c. or 6 tblsp. milk. Shape lightly into 6 patties. Score both sides with spatula. Place on broiler pan and broil 4″ to 5″ from heat, 10 to 12 minutes. Turn and broil 5 to 8 minutes longer or until patties are cooked. Serve plain or topped with dabs of Garlic Butter (see Index). A little marjoram added to the uncooked ground lamb adds flavor.

Delicate, Delicious Veal

MUSHROOM BREADED VEAL

A new route to superlative flavor

2 lbs. veal steak, ½″ thick
1 (1 ½ oz.) pkg. mushroom-soup mix
1 c. cracker crumbs
2 eggs, slightly beaten
2 tblsp. water
⅓ c. hot fat
½ c. water

Cut veal in serving pieces.

Roll mushroom-soup mix in unopened package with rolling pin to crush large pieces. Combine with cracker crumbs.

Dip veal in crumbs, then in egg mixed with water, then in crumbs again. Brown on both sides in hot fat until golden. (Do not over-brown.)

Add water, cover and bake in moderate oven (350°) 45 minutes. Uncover during last 10 minutes of cooking. Makes 6 to 8 servings.

Variation: Substitute pieces of broiler-fryer chickens for the veal steaks. An easy way to fix Mushroom Fried Chicken.

VEAL PATTIES

Crusty on the outside, moist within

1 ½ lbs. ground veal
½ c. melted fat (chicken fat if available)
½ tsp. lemon juice, fresh, frozen or canned
Salt
Pepper
1 egg, beaten
2 tblsp. water
1 c. cracker crumbs

Combine meat, fat, lemon juice, salt and pepper. Shape into 6 patties.

Mix egg with water.

Dip patties in egg mixture and then into cracker crumbs. Brown on both sides in hot fat. Cook about 15 minutes. Makes 6 servings.

Note: Gravy may be made with drippings and half-and-half milk and cream. Season delicately with nutmeg if desired.

Variations: Brush patties with French dressing before dipping them in the egg mixture and cracker crumbs. Heat dairy sour cream (do not let come to a boil) and serve over veal patties.

VEAL IN SOUR CREAM

Simple way to fix this famous dish

1 ½ lbs. cubed veal steaks, cut in serving-size pieces
2 tblsp. fat
1 (10 oz.) can mushroom gravy
½ c. water
½ c. dairy sour cream
Parsley

Cook veal over medium heat in hot fat about 5 minutes on each side, or until tender. Lift to warm platter and keep warm.

Pour fat from skillet. Add gravy and water and stir, heating to boiling and simmering 3 minutes.

Stir in sour cream, but do not cook. Pour around veal, garnish with parsley and serve. Makes 5 to 6 servings.

Favorite Frankfurters

PENNY PANCAKES

Serve with your favorite barbecue sauce—pennies are sliced franks

1 ½ c. milk
2 eggs, beaten
2 tblsp. salad oil
2 c. buckwheat pancake mix
8 frankfurters, cut in ¼" slices

Combine milk, eggs and oil; add pancake mix; stir lightly. Arrange frankfurters in clusters of six on hot griddle; pour 2 tblsp. batter over each cluster; brown. Makes 15 cakes.

SAUERKRAUT AND FRANKFURTERS

It looks out for itself in the oven

2 (1 lb.) cans sauerkraut
1 (1 lb.) pkg. frankfurters (about 10)
1 large apple, cored and sliced
½ tsp. caraway seeds (optional)

Place 1 can sauerkraut in bottom of 2 qt. casserole. Top with frankfurters, then with remaining sauerkraut. Spread apple slices on top. Sprinkle with caraway seeds.

Bake covered in moderate oven (350°) 1 hour. Makes 5 servings.

Note: Serve with instant mashed potatoes prepared as directed on package.

QUICK BARBECUED FRANKS

Peeled, sliced, cooked onions come from a can ready-to-go

1 lb. frankfurters
½ c. ketchup
2 tblsp. prepared mustard
½ tsp. cloves
2 tblsp. salad oil
1 (3 ½ oz.) can French-fried onions

Drop frankfurters into boiling water; cover, heat 5 to 8 minutes; drain.

Add ketchup, prepared mustard, cloves and oil to frankfurters. Simmer about 5 minutes.

Heat onions as directed on can.

Remove frankfurters to platter. Garnish with onions. Makes 6 servings.

ARIZONA WAGON WHEEL

Homey family dish just right to get for dinner when time is short

½ c. chopped onion
2 tblsp. butter or margarine
⅔ c. chili sauce
1 (1 lb.) can kidney beans
1 (1 lb.) pkg. wieners, cut in ¼″ slices
⅛ tsp. black pepper
⅛ tsp. cayenne pepper
1 tsp. chili powder
2 c. shredded Cheddar cheese

Cook onion in butter until soft. Add chili sauce, kidney beans, wieners and seasonings. Simmer 10 minutes.

Add cheese and simmer, stirring frequently, until cheese is melted and blended. Makes 6 servings.

Note: To make dish to take to a potluck supper, pour hot bean mixture into greased 2 qt. casserole. Trim top with extra strips of cheese to represent spokes in wheel. Bake in hot oven (400°) to melt cheese.

WIENER-SUCCOTASH SKILLET

Good summertime main dish when you don't want to use the oven

6 wieners
⅓ c. chopped onion
⅓ c. chopped green pepper
2 tblsp. butter or margarine
¾ c. chili sauce
1 (12 oz.) can whole-kernel corn
1 (10 oz.) pkg. frozen lima beans
½ tsp. salt
Dash pepper

Slice wieners diagonally in ¼″ slices. Cook wieners, onion and green pepper in butter in skillet until onion is soft.

Add remaining ingredients to mixture and simmer, covered, until lima beans are cooked, about 20 minutes. Stir occasionally to separate frozen limas. Makes 5 to 6 servings.

CURRIED FRANKFURTERS

East and West meet deliciously in this dish—22 minutes to the table

1 large onion, chopped
1 medium apple, peeled and chopped
1 small garlic clove, minced
3 tblsp. butter or margarine
1 tblsp. flour
1 tblsp. curry powder
1 tsp. salt
1 c. water
1 lb. frankfurters, cut in thirds
Rice

Cook onion, apple and garlic in butter until onion is soft. Stir in flour,

Skip work with Beef Vegetable Bake (recipe page 17). Meat and vegetables cook together in same pan. Double recipe if you like — fill one loaf with frozen vegetables and freeze for later use.

Saucy Chicken Bake (recipe page 39) gets its red-gold color and wonderful seasoning from Basic Red Sauce. Keep a jar of this sauce in your refrigerator or freezer for other tasty recipes in this book.

curry powder and salt. Add water and cook, stirring constantly, until mixture comes to a boil. Add frankfurters and cook, covered, over low heat 10 minutes. Serve over rice. Makes 6 servings.

POTATO-STUFFED FRANKS

A come-again recipe—easy and good with just plain sauerkraut any time

12 frankfurters (1 ½ lbs.)
3 c. seasoned mashed potatoes (about 6 medium potatoes)
1 c. grated Cheddar cheese
Paprika

Split frankfurters lengthwise; lay cut side up in shallow baking pan.

Spoon potatoes over frankfurters in light, fluffy peaks. Sprinkle on cheese and paprika. Bake in hot oven (425°) 15 to 20 minutes. Serve immediately with sauerkraut. Makes 6 servings.

For the short-cut cook: Use packaged instant mashed potatoes, made according to package directions, for stuffing.

Variation: Fold ½ c. chopped chives or green onion into the potatoes before arranging them on frankfurters.

10-MINUTE MAIN DISH. Heat canned beans with franks in tomato sauce as label on can directs. Serve over toast or corn chips with a hot-dog relish alongside.

BOY-SCOUT SPECIAL

FAST-FIX STUFFED FRANKFURTERS: Split each frankfurter, but not quite through. Stuff with 1 tsp. canned spaghetti sauce and 1 tsp. pickle relish. Wrap with bacon slice and fasten with toothpick. Broil cut side down 2″ to 3″ from heat in preheated broiler, about 3 minutes. Turn and continue broiling until bacon is cooked, about 3 minutes. Serve in split long bun if desired.

BLACK-EYE PEAS WITH FRANKS

Serve with Baked Tomato Casserole

1 tblsp. finely chopped onion
2 tblsp. bacon fat
1 (1 lb.) can black-eye peas and pork
¼ c. ketchup
2 tblsp. molasses or brown sugar
1 tsp. dry mustard
Frankfurters

Cook onion in fat until soft. Combine in casserole with peas, ketchup, molasses and mustard. Lay frankfurters, two for every person, on top.

Cover and bake in moderate oven (350°) 30 minutes. Makes 3 servings.

Variation: Substitute canned pork and beans for black-eye peas.

Double-quick Meat Dishes

MEAT-AND-BEANS BAKE

An easy way to satisfy big appetites

1 (1 lb. 15 oz.) can pork and beans
1 tblsp. instant minced onion
3 tblsp. molasses
1 tsp. prepared mustard
1 (12 oz.) can luncheon meat, sliced

Combine beans, onion, 2 tblsp. molasses and mustard in saucepan. Simmer 10 minutes, stirring occasionally.

Pour into greased 1½ qt. casserole.

more

Spread luncheon meat lightly with remaining molasses. Place on top of beans, molasses side up.

Bake in moderate oven (350°) 30 minutes. Makes 6 servings.

JIFFY MEAT PIE

Double-quick main dish

1 (1 ½ lb.) can beef stew
1 pkg. refrigerator biscuits

Heat stew in saucepan until boiling. Pour into greased 1½ qt. casserole. Top with biscuits.

Bake in very hot oven (450°) until biscuits are brown, 12 to 15 minutes. Makes 4 servings.

DEVILED CORNED-BEEF HASH

A he-man favorite every time

1 (1 lb.) can corned-beef hash
½ c. mayonnaise
1 tsp. prepared mustard
2 tblsp. chopped onion

Cut chilled corned-beef hash in 4 slices and place in shallow baking pan. Top with mayonnaise, mustard and onion, mixed. Bake in hot oven (400°) until lightly browned, 15 to 20 minutes. Makes 4 servings.

CHILI-MAC CASSEROLE

Garlic bread is good with this. Heat it in the oven with the casserole

1 c. macaroni
2 (16 oz.) cans chili with beans
Dill-pickle slices

Cook macaroni as directed on package.

Heat chili to boiling point.

Drain cooked macaroni and combine with chili. Place in a 1½ qt. casserole. Top with pickle slices.

Bake in moderate oven (375°) 20 minutes. Makes 4 servings.

QUICK BEEF STROGANOFF

Here's what to have for supper the afternoon you arrive home late

1 medium onion, chopped (¾ c.)
2 tblsp. butter or margarine
2 (12 oz.) cans roast beef
1 (2 oz.) can mushroom pieces
1 can condensed tomato soup
½ tsp. salt
Dash pepper
¼ c. dairy sour cream
12 slices toast

Cook chopped onion in butter until lightly browned. Add roast beef, cut in chunks, mushrooms with liquid, soup and seasonings. Cover and simmer 10 minutes. Stir in sour cream. Serve over toast. Makes 6 servings.

CHEESE-MEAT LOAF

Bright red cherry sauce makes this hurry-up dish appealing

2 (12 oz.) cans luncheon meat
¼ tsp. ground cloves
4 tsp. prepared mustard
16 slices process American cheese
1 (1 lb. 8 oz.) jar cherry-pie filling

Cut each can of meat into 9 slices, cutting almost through to bottom of loaf. Spread between slices mixture of cloves and mustard; put 1 cheese slice into each slash in loaf.

Place meat in baking dish; pour cherries around it. Bake in hot oven

(400°) 15 minutes, or until cheese melts. To serve, slice loaf at right angle to cuts. Makes 8 servings.

Variation: Instead of cherries, use thick applesauce or drained crushed pineapple, lightly sprinkled with cinnamon.

SPANISH-RICE DINNER

Last-minute main dish—from cupboard shelf to table in 15 minutes

- 1 1/3 c. precooked rice
- 1 (45 grams) pkg. Spanish-rice seasoning mix
- 1 (12 oz.) can luncheon meat

Prepare rice as directed on seasoning-mix package.

Cut luncheon meat in small cubes. Add to rice mixture the last 5 minutes of cooking. Makes 6 servings.

MEXICAN CASSEROLE

Set before a hungry man who arrives between meals—sure way to please

- 1 (15 oz.) can tamales
- 1 (15 oz.) can chili con carne
- 1/2 c. grated sharp Cheddar cheese
- 1 (3/4 oz.) pkg. corn chips (3/4 c.)

Remove husks from tamales and add to chili con carne. Cover and heat thoroughly. Place in serving dish. Sprinkle with cheese and corn chips. Makes 3 servings.

BOLOGNA CUPS: Buy unsliced bologna and slice twice as thick as ready-to-buy slices. Heat in a little hot fat until slices form cups. Fill with scrambled eggs or Hot Potato Salad (see Index).

20-*Minute Main Dishes*

When you are late starting a meal, try these main dishes. If you keep the ingredients for making at least one of them on hand, you'll find they come in handy.

EGG–CORNED-BEEF STACK

Your men folks will like this

- 2 (12 oz.) cans corned beef
- 2 cans condensed cream of mushroom soup
- 1/4 c. instant minced onion
- 8 slices bread, toasted
- 8 eggs, poached
- Paprika

Combine corned beef with soup and onion; heat thoroughly.

Pour over slices of toast; top each with a poached egg. Sprinkle with paprika. Makes 8 servings.

HAMBURGER SHORTCAKE RING

Looks fancy, but it's simple—and extra good

- 1/4 c. shortening
- 2 c. biscuit mix
- 2 tsp. caraway seeds
- 2/3 c. milk
- 2 lbs. ground beef
- 1 tblsp. instant minced onion
- 1 can condensed cream of celery soup
- 1/4 c. ketchup
- 1/2 tsp. chili powder
- 1/2 c. sliced olives
- 1/2 tsp. salt

To make ring: Cut shortening into biscuit mix; mix in caraway seeds.

more

Add milk; stir with fork to make soft dough; beat 15 strokes. Drop tablespoonfuls of dough onto greased baking sheet to form circle. Bake in very hot oven (450°) 10 to 15 minutes.

Brown beef in skillet. Add remaining ingredients; simmer gently until thoroughly heated. Spoon into center of biscuit ring. Garnish with pimiento-stuffed olives. Makes 8 servings.

BEAN-AND-CORN BAKE

Colorful as confetti and inexpensive

- 2 (1 lb.) cans baked beans
- 8 frankfurters, cut in 1″ pieces
- 1½ tsp. dry mustard
- 2 (12 oz.) cans Mexicorn, drained
- 1 tsp. salt
- 8 thin slices process American cheese

Combine beans, frankfurters and mustard in 2 qt. casserole. Mix corn and salt; spread in layer over beans; top with cheese.

Bake in hot oven (400°) 15 minutes, or until cheese is melted and casserole is heated through. Makes 8 servings.

Variations: Omit corn and salt; mix 2 (13½ oz.) cans pineapple chunks, drained, with baked-bean mixture.

Omit corn; combine 2 (1 lb.) cans lima beans, drained, with salt and baked-bean mixture.

Substitute 1 (15½ oz.) can kidney beans, drained, for 1 can baked beans; omit corn. Add 1 tblsp. instant minced onion. Mix well. Makes 6 servings.

DOUBLE-QUICK COMBINATIONS

CHILI-SPAGHETTI: Combine 1 (15½ oz.) can chili with beans with 1 (15½ oz.) can spaghetti in tomato sauce. Simmer gently until thoroughly heated. Serve over toast or with toast on the side; add a lettuce-cucumber salad and cantaloupe à la mode for dessert. Makes 6 servings.

BEEF-CORN: Sauté 2 medium onions, chopped, in 2 tblsp. butter or margarine. Add 1 (12 oz.) can corned beef, shredded, and 1 (16 oz.) can cream-style corn. Simmer gently until thoroughly heated. Try this over canned chow-mein noodles. Makes 6 servings.

HAM-CHICKEN: Spread 6 slices of toast with deviled ham—you'll need about 3 (2¼ oz.) cans. Heat 3 (10½ oz.) cans chicken à la king. Pour ½ c. mixture on each toast slice. Makes 6 servings.

CHAPTER 2

CHICKEN AND TURKEY

Ask anyone about the most unforgettable country meals he has eaten. Nine chances out of ten he will describe a chicken or turkey dinner. And no wonder! These homey feasts are as much a part of farm life as wheat rippled by the wind or the rustle of corn on a starlit summer night. But these famous chicken and turkey dinners take more work and time than many busy cooks can spare, except for special occasions.

Smart short-cut cooks, therefore, meet the challenge of chicken and turkey dinners by cooking and freezing them ahead for handy use. They heap platters with country-fried chicken—their children have a full quota of drumsticks and wishbones in true farm style. Hurried cooks also oven-fry the chicken because it takes almost no attention.

There are many ways to obtain variety in this quick-fried chicken, however: rolling the chicken pieces in different coatings, for example. Golden Fried Chicken gets its rosy-golden glow from cheese-cracker crumbs. Crispy Fried Chicken, a famous FARM JOURNAL recipe, derives its name and crust from corn-flake crumbs. Then there are the pour-on cooks (pouring is quicker than brushing) who add barbecue sauces when the chicken is brown. There's almost no end to the sauces they use. Mayonnaise Chicken, for instance, owes its glazed and flavorful brown crust to salad dressing kept in the refrigerator.

Look also in this chapter for intriguing casseroles, the kind that meet all needs—parties, covered-dish suppers, Sunday dinners and everyday family meals. You can use either cooked chicken or turkey from the freezer or canned chicken or turkey to make these praiseworthy dishes. And in one elegant casserole, Chicken Crunch, tuna fish and chicken combine their flavors. Do try this specialty of a busy country hostess when you are having guests.

Chicken and Turkey Dinners

They're tops in good eating

Skillet and Oven-fried Chicken

Smart short-cut cooks know how to keep good chicken and turkey dinners coming to country tables. They use recipes like the ones that follow—recipes they share with us.

COUNTRY FRIED CHICKEN

Company delicious—curry powder adds a surprise many people like

1 (2 ½ to 3 lb.) frying chicken, cut in serving pieces
½ c. flour
1 ½ tsp. salt
⅛ tsp. pepper
¼ tsp. curry powder
Salad oil or fat
1 tblsp. water

Toss chicken in paper or plastic bag containing flour, salt, pepper and curry powder. Dry on rack or paper towels.

Heat oil (about ½″) in heavy skillet. Add chicken pieces, the meatier ones first. Do not crowd chicken. Brown on all sides, about 20 minutes.

Drain off fat. Add water and cover tightly. (If lid fits snugly, omit water.) Cook until tender, about 30 to 40 minutes. Uncover the last 10 minutes for extra-crisp crust. Keep warm while you make gravy. Makes 4 to 5 servings, depending on size of chicken.

Chicken Gravy

Measure 2 tblsp. fat drained from chicken into skillet in which chicken cooked (to make 1 c. gravy). Leave crusty bits in skillet. Add 2 tblsp. flour. Blend and brown on very low heat, using care not to scorch. Remove from heat; add 1 c. cold milk. Season with salt and pepper. Return to low heat and simmer until smooth and thickened, stirring constantly. Makes 3 to 4 servings.

Variation: Omit curry powder from chicken recipe. Add a touch of marjoram to the gravy.

CRISPY FRIED CHICKEN

A famous FARM JOURNAL *recipe for oven-fried chicken*

1 (2 ½ to 3 lb.) frying chicken, cut in serving pieces
3 tblsp. melted fat
2 tsp. salt
¼ tsp. pepper
1 c. corn flake crumbs

Rub chicken with 1 tblsp. fat, salt and pepper.

Roll chicken in corn flake crumbs until well coated.

Place in greased, shallow baking pan and sprinkle with remaining fat. Bake in moderate oven (375°) until browned and tender, 45 to 60 minutes. Makes 4 to 5 servings.

Variation: Instead of rubbing chicken with fat, dip it in ½ c. evaporated milk. Do not use regular milk.

OVEN-FRIED CHICKEN

Pour on zesty sauces for a change of pace and to win compliments

1 (2 to 3 lb.) frying chicken, cut in serving pieces
1 c. flour
2 tsp. salt
¼ tsp. pepper
2 tsp. paprika
½ c. butter

Shake chicken pieces, a few at a time, in plastic or paper bag containing mixture of flour, salt, pepper and paprika.

Melt butter in shallow baking pan in moderate oven (375°). Add chicken and turn pieces to coat. Then arrange them in pan in one layer, skin side down.

Bake in moderate oven (375°) about 30 minutes. Turn chicken. Bake 20 to 30 minutes longer. If chicken cannot be served immediately, brush with melted butter and leave in oven, heat reduced to 300°. Makes 4 to 5 servings.

VARIATIONS

BARBECUED CHICKEN: When chicken is turned, after cooking 30 minutes, pour ¾ c. of your favorite barbecue sauce over it. Complete cooking like Oven-fried Chicken.

ORIENTAL CHICKEN: Pour a mixture of ¼ c. each melted butter, honey and lemon juice and 1 tblsp. soy sauce over chicken after turning it. Complete cooking like Oven-fried Chicken.

MAYONNAISE CHICKEN: When chicken pieces are hot, brush with mayonnaise. Brush other side of chicken with mayonnaise after turning it. Complete cooking like Oven-fried Chicken.

GOLDEN FRIED CHICKEN

Requires no turning as it cooks—crust is crisp, rosy-gold in color

2 (2½ to 3 lb.) frying chickens, cut in serving pieces
⅔ c. salad oil
2 c. cheese-cracker crumbs
2 tsp. salt

Dip chicken pieces in oil, then in cracker crumbs, with salt added, to coat. Bake in a foil-lined, shallow baking pan or on baking sheet in moderate oven (375°) 45 to 60 minutes. Makes 6 to 8 servings.

SAUCY CHICKEN BAKE

You just pour the bright sauce over chicken and vegetable—then bake

2 to 3 medium zucchini
1 (2½ to 3 lb.) frying chicken, cut in pieces
½ tsp. orégano
1 c. Basic Red Sauce (see Index)
2 to 3 tblsp. grated Parmesan cheese

Slice unpeeled squash in ½" slices. Arrange in bottom of 3 qt. baking dish. Place chicken, skin side up, over zucchini.

Add orégano to Basic Red Sauce; pour evenly over the chicken and zucchini.

Bake uncovered in hot oven (400°) 30 minutes. Baste chicken and zucchini with drippings; bake another 30 minutes, or until chicken is tender. Sprinkle with cheese and return to oven for a few minutes. Makes 4 to 6 servings.

Extra-good Chicken Casseroles

CHICKEN-ASPARAGUS CASSEROLE

Add a big fruit salad and cake and you have a company luncheon

1 can condensed cream of mushroom soup
⅓ c. milk
Dash of nutmeg
1 c. diced cooked or canned chicken
1 (14½ oz.) can asparagus spears, drained
½ c. crushed corn chips

Combine soup and milk. Mix in nutmeg and chicken. Pour into a 1½ qt. casserole. Top with asparagus, attractively arranged. Sprinkle with corn chips. Heat in moderate oven (375°) 15 to 20 minutes. Makes 4 servings.

Variations: Substitute diced cooked ham for the chicken. Use buttered bread crumbs for the corn chips.

BAKED CHICKEN WITH DRESSING

Stuffing mix and canned gravy provide skillful seasoning—quick

¼ c. butter or margarine
⅓ c. hot water
2 c. herb-seasoned stuffing mix
1 (10¾ oz.) can chicken gravy
1 (6 oz.) can boned chicken, cubed, or ⅔ c. cooked chicken
1 (10 oz.) pkg. frozen peas

Melt 3 tblsp. butter in water; toss lightly with 1 c. stuffing mix; place half in 1 qt. casserole.

Mix gravy, chicken, cooked peas, unsalted, and 1 c. dry stuffing mix; pour over mixture in casserole; top with rest of stuffing; dot with 1 tblsp. butter.

Bake in moderate oven (350°) 20 minutes. Makes 6 servings.

CHICKEN CASSEROLE

Noodles add pleasant crunchy texture

1 can condensed cream of mushroom soup
1 can condensed chicken with rice soup
⅔ c. cubed, cooked chicken or 1 (5 oz.) can boned chicken
1 (3 oz.) can chow mein noodles
¾ c. corn flake crumbs

Mix soups together in greased 1½ qt. casserole. Stir in chicken and noodles. Top with corn flake crumbs.

Bake in moderate oven (350°) 30 minutes. Makes 4 to 5 servings.

CHICKEN CASSEROLE SUPREME

Exceptionally good—a dish for company luncheons or to tote to covered-dish suppers. Assemble it in the morning, if you like, cover and refrigerate until time to bake

1 can condensed cream of vegetable soup
1 (14½ oz.) can asparagus spears
1 (8 oz.) pkg. noodles, cooked and drained
1⅓ c. cooked chicken or 2 (5 oz.) cans boned chicken
⅓ c. sliced, stuffed green olives
½ c. corn flake crumbs
1 tblsp. butter

Heat soup blended with liquid drained from asparagus.

Place thick layer of noodles in bottom of a greased 2 qt. casserole. Top with half the chicken, asparagus and olives. Repeat layers ending with noodles. Pour heated soup mixture over noodles.

Top with corn flake crumbs. Dot with butter.

Heat in moderate oven (350°) 20 minutes. Makes 6 to 8 servings.

CHICKEN-CORN CASSEROLE

A fast-fix casserole if there's cooked chicken in the freezer

⅓ c. butter or margarine
⅓ c. flour
¾ tsp. salt
¼ tsp. pepper
½ tsp. celery salt
2 c. milk
2 c. cooked chicken, cut up
1 (1 lb.) can cream-style corn
¼ c. bread or cracker crumbs
1 tblsp. butter

Melt butter over low heat. Stir in flour, salt, pepper and celery salt; cook until smooth and bubbly. Remove from heat. Add milk; boil for 1 minute.

Combine sauce, chicken and corn. Pour into 1½ qt. casserole. Top with crumbs; dot with butter.

Bake in moderate oven (350°) 25 to 30 minutes, until browned on top. Makes 6 to 8 servings.

Note: It's a good idea to keep cooked chicken in the freezer for use in this dish. Or use canned chicken to make it.

CHICKEN CRUNCH

A superb dish for the buffet supper

½ c. chicken broth or milk
2 cans condensed cream of mushroom soup
3 c. diced cooked chicken
1 (7 oz.) can tuna, drained and flaked
¼ c. minced onion
1 c. diced celery
1 (5 oz.) can water chestnuts, thinly sliced
1 (3 oz.) can chow mein noodles
⅓ c. toasted almonds (optional)

Blend broth into soup in 2 qt. casserole. Mix in remaining ingredients except almonds.

Bake in slow oven (325°) 40 minutes. Just before serving, sprinkle with almonds. Makes 8 servings.

Variation: Omit water chestnuts and use ⅓ c. more celery.

CHICKEN-NOODLE HOT DISH

Superior casserole—olives add color and piquant flavor

4 oz. broad noodles
1 can condensed cream of chicken soup
1 c. milk
1 (5 oz.) can boned chicken, chopped, or ⅔ c. cooked, chopped chicken
½ c. shredded Cheddar cheese
½ c. pimiento-stuffed olives
½ tsp. salt
½ c. toasted, slivered almonds

Cook noodles in boiling, salted water as directed on package.

Blend together soup and milk. Add chicken and cheese and heat to boiling. Add olives, salt and noodles. Place in greased 1½ qt. casserole. Top with almonds.

Bake in moderate oven (350°) 30 minutes. Makes 6 servings.

CASSEROLE À LA KING

All the makings come off the cupboard shelf and out of the refrigerator

- 1 (15¼ oz.) can macaroni with cheese sauce
- 1 (10½ oz.) can chicken à la king
- 3 tblsp. bread crumbs
- 2 tblsp. butter or margarine, melted
- ¼ c. shredded Cheddar cheese
- Paprika

Heat macaroni and chicken à la king on top of range in separate saucepans.

Place half of heated macaroni in bottom of greased 1 qt. casserole. Top with chicken mixture, then remaining macaroni. Combine bread crumbs and butter; sprinkle on top. Scatter on cheese and dust with paprika.

Broil until top is bubbly and brown, about 5 minutes. Makes 4 servings.

CHICKEN QUEEN

Out of the cupboard to the table—quick. Keep the makings on hand

- 1 can condensed cream of mushroom soup
- 3 tsp. instant minced onion
- 1 tblsp. mayonnaise
- 1 (5 to 6 oz.) can boned chicken, (about ⅔ c. cooked chicken)
- 1 c. crushed potato chips
- 1 c. drained canned peas
- 1 (4 oz.) can or jar pimientos

Combine soup, onion and mayonnaise in greased 1½ qt. casserole. Add liquid from canned chicken, chicken, cut in pieces, ¾ c. potato chips, peas and pimiento, cut in strips. Mix gently. Sprinkle remaining potato chips on top.

Bake in moderate oven (350°) about 30 minutes. Makes 4 servings.

CHICKEN-RICE CASSEROLE

A family dish that makes left-over chicken welcome

- 1 (10 oz.) pkg. frozen peas and carrots
- 1 can condensed cream of mushroom soup
- 1⅓ c. water
- ½ c. milk
- ½ tsp. salt
- 1⅓ c. precooked rice
- 1½ c. diced cooked chicken or 2 (5 oz.) cans chicken
- ½ c. grated Cheddar cheese

Combine peas and carrots, soup, water, milk and salt in saucepan. Bring to a boil and simmer 3 minutes.

Pour half of soup mixture into greased 2 qt. casserole. Top with rice, chicken and remaining soup mixture. Sprinkle with cheese.

Bake in moderate oven (350°) 20 minutes. Makes 6 servings.

CHOW MEIN HOT DISH

Suitable for a potluck supper—uses left-over chicken or turkey

- 1 can condensed cream of chicken soup
- 1 can condensed cream of mushroom soup
- 1 c. milk
- 1 c. cubed cooked turkey or chicken
- 1 (1 lb.) can chow mein vegetables, drained
- 1 (8 oz.) can chow mein noodles

Blend soups and milk in a greased 2 qt. casserole. Stir in turkey, vegetables and two thirds of the noodles. Top with remaining noodles. Bake in moderate oven (350°) 50 minutes. Makes 8 servings.

Short-cut Chicken Dishes

BROILED CHICKEN

Today and tomorrow recipe—fix the chicken one day, cook it the next

2 (2 to 2½ lb.) broiler-fryer chickens
Italian salad dressing
1½ tsp. salt
⅛ tsp. pepper

Cut chickens in halves. Break wing, hip and drumstick joints so chicken will stay flat while cooking. Brush both sides generously with salad dressing. Cover and chill in refrigerator overnight (or 4 to 5 hours).

Season chicken with salt and pepper. Place skin side up on rack in broiling pan.

Broil 5" to 7" from heat 25 minutes, or until lightly browned, basting occasionally with Italian salad dressing. Turn, brush again with salad dressing and continue broiling 15 minutes longer, or until chicken is golden brown. (Chicken is cooked when drumstick cuts easily and no pink color shows.) Makes 4 servings.

CHICKEN WITH BRAN BISCUITS

Chicken cooks while you're at church. Add biscuits when you get home

2 (3 lb.) broiler-fryer chickens
1 can condensed cream of celery soup
1 can condensed cream of chicken soup
1 can condensed tomato soup
½ c. milk
½ tsp. turmeric (optional)
1½ c. biscuit mix
¾ c. whole-bran cereal
¼ tsp. baking soda
⅔ c. buttermilk
⅛ tsp. poultry seasoning

Cut chickens in serving pieces; remove small breast bones and skin (cook skin with back, neck and giblets for soup).

Arrange chicken pieces in buttered 2½ qt. casserole. Blend soups, milk and turmeric; pour over chicken; cover.

Bake in slow oven (325°) 1½ hours or until chicken is tender. Reset oven to 450°.

For biscuits, combine remaining ingredients; stir to make soft dough.

Remove casserole from oven; uncover. Drop dough by spoonfuls in a ring on top of bubbling-hot chicken mixture.

Return to oven (450°) and bake about 15 minutes, or until biscuits are brown. Makes 6 to 8 servings.

Variation: Substitute plain biscuits made with 2 c. biscuit mix for the bran biscuits.

CHICKEN FOR SUNDAY DINNER

Divide the work between Saturday and Sunday. It's easier that way

What to do on Saturday: Cook chicken. You will cut cooking time in half by using a pressure cooker. Electric ones are handy. Assemble casserole of chicken (recipe follows), cover and refrigerate it.

PRESSURE-COOKED CHICKEN: Disjoint and cut up a 5½ lb. (dressed weight) stewing fowl. Place in pressure pan. Add 2 c. water, 4 tsp. salt, 1 small onion, quartered, 1 small carrot, quartered, 3 celery tops, 1 whole clove and 2 peppercorns. Place lid on pressure pan and secure. Cook at 10 lbs. pressure, 40 to 50 minutes. Reduce pressure and remove cover as manufacturer of pressure pan recommends. Remove chicken, strain broth, cool; remove meat from bones in large pieces. If meat and broth will not be used immediately, cover and refrigerate at once. If you have no pressure pan, simmer chicken until thickest pieces are fork-tender in water to cover. This takes 2½ to 3½ hours. Use broth and meat in Chicken-Noodle Casserole.

CHICKEN-NOODLE CASSEROLE

Country food at its best

1 (8 oz.) pkg. broad noodles
3 qts. boiling water
1 tblsp. salt
4½ c. chicken broth
Salt and pepper
½ c. chicken fat (or part butter or margarine)
½ c. flour
¼ c. cold water
2 (10 oz.) pkgs. frozen peas
4 to 5 c. cooked chicken, cut in large pieces
1 (3 oz.) can chow mein noodles
2 cooked carrots (optional)

Cook broad noodles 5 minutes in boiling salted water. Drain; cover with paper towel to prevent drying.

Heat broth; season with salt and pepper. Blend fat, flour and cold water. Add to broth, stirring. Boil 2 to 3 minutes.

Pour boiling water over peas to separate them; drain. Reserve ½ c. peas for garnish.

Arrange noodles, peas, chicken and gravy in layers in a 4 qt. greased casserole for buffet service (or covered-dish supper) or in two 2½ qt. casseroles for easy passing at sit-down family meal. Mound peas in center of casserole and cover. Refrigerate overnight.

Bake casserole in moderate oven (375°) 40 to 50 minutes or until bubbly hot (15 minutes less for casseroles not refrigerated).

Sprinkle band of chow mein noodles around rim of casserole. Slice carrots on the slant for flower petal; arrange around peas on casserole. Return to oven and bake 5 minutes. Serve at once. Makes 8 to 10 servings.

What to do on Sunday: Take casserole from refrigerator, bake and add garnish.

CHICKEN NEWBURG

Wonderful way to use cooked chicken from freezer or canned chicken

6 tblsp. butter or margarine
2 tblsp. flour
1 tsp. salt
⅛ tsp. nutmeg
Dash red pepper
2 egg yolks (slightly beaten)
1 c. undiluted evaporated milk
1 c. milk
1 tblsp. lemon juice
2 c. diced cooked chicken
6 toast slices

Melt butter in saucepan; blend in flour and seasonings.

Combine egg yolks and milks; stir into flour mixture. Place over medium heat, stirring constantly, until mixture comes to a boil and thickens.

Gently stir in lemon juice and chicken. Serve at once on toast. Makes 6 servings.

Tip from a Smart Country Cook

QUICK ONION STUFFING FOR A CHICKEN OR TURKEY: Spread a slice of bread with butter or margarine. Lay three or four paper-thin onion slices on bread; sprinkle with ½ tsp. poultry seasoning. Fold half of bread over on other half, buttered side in. Tuck into body cavity of bird. Repeat until the body cavity is filled. The stuffing tastes good, flavors the chicken, and you have only a knife to wash after making it. There is no adding of liquid or chopping of onion. An especially good method to use when a small amount of stuffing is desired.

DELICIOUS TURKEY TREATS

You can substitute cooked turkey for the chicken in any of the chicken casseroles. Or you can use canned boned turkey. A 5-ounce can of turkey or chicken makes about ⅔ cup of poultry meat.

Look in Chapter 5 for Grilled Turkey Sandwiches and Turkey and Gravy Sandwiches, in Chapter 7 for Turkey Salad Supreme.

BARBECUED TURKEY: Heat slices of cooked turkey in your favorite barbecue sauce, bottled or from freezer. Serve on platter or in toasted buns.

TURKEY DIVAN

A quick main dish when you have turkey on the shelf or in the freezer

12 large slices cooked turkey
2 (10 oz.) pkgs. frozen broccoli or asparagus, cooked and drained
1 can condensed cream of chicken soup
¾ c. shredded sharp cheese

Arrange sliced turkey on bottom of greased shallow baking dish (about 7″ × 11″); cover with layer of broccoli. Add soup. Sprinkle with cheese.

Bake in moderate oven (375°) 20 to 25 minutes or until lightly browned. Makes 6 servings.

Variation: Blend 1 c. mayonnaise with 1 beaten egg white; use for soup.

TURKEY AND HAM PLATTER: Arrange overlapping thin slices of cooked turkey on one side of platter, ham on the other. Lay slices of canned jellied cranberries or Spicy Peach Pickles (see Index) down the center of the platter. Serve with hot rolls and vegetables.

TURKEY SHORTCAKES

A snap to fix

½ lb. process American cheese
2 tblsp. chicken broth or milk
2 c. cooked turkey, cubed, or 3 (5 oz.) cans boned turkey
1½ tsp. instant minced onion
Salt
Pepper

Place cheese and broth in double boiler. Cook over boiling water until cheese is melted, stirring occasionally to blend. Add remaining ingredients, seasoning to taste.

more

Serve over toast, hot biscuits or corn bread. Makes 4 servings.

Variations: For Chicken Shortcakes, use cooked or canned chicken instead of turkey. For Superlative Burgers, serve the cheese sauce, with the onion added, over cooked hamburger patties on toasted bun halves.

TURKEY TETRAZZINI

Just the treat to make with left-over turkey from freezer or refrigerator

4 c. cream sauce
2 c. grated process American cheese
6 c. cooked spaghetti (12 oz. uncooked)
4 c. boned cooked turkey, diced
½ c. mushrooms or toasted almonds (optional)
½ c. grated Parmesan cheese
Dash paprika

Make Cream Sauce (see Index) and blend in process cheese. Mix with spaghetti, turkey and mushrooms. Turn into greased shallow baking dish (about 7½" × 12"). Sprinkle top with Parmesan cheese and paprika.

Bake in moderate oven (350°) until bubbly and browned, about 30 minutes. Makes 8 to 10 servings.

To save time: Substitute for cream sauce 1 can each condensed cream of mushroom and chicken soup and blend of 1 c. turkey stock and milk.

Note: Many country cooks believe the best flavor of turkey and chicken is in its skin. Or as one of them says, "It's the skin that makes turkey and chicken taste better than rabbits." A trick in making turkey and chicken salads is to add a little finely ground skin. But this takes time and most busy women skip using the food chopper whenever they can.

See Chapter 7 for Turkey Salad Supreme.

CHAPTER 3

FISH AND SEA FOOD

Fish and sea food are made to order for busy women. They are at their best cooked for only a few minutes. In fact, overcooking makes fried, broiled and baked fish and sea food dry and tasteless, makes fish cooked in sauces and liquids mushy and tasteless. The test for doneness is easy on last-minute cooks. Fish is ready for the platter when the flesh flakes easily with a fork.

Fish is neglected in many country kitchens that are not located in areas where rivers and lakes furnish a local supply. But in some communities farms now have their own ponds. And with frozen fish and sea food widely available today, their prestige and popularity are going up.

Of all sea foods, oysters and shrimp are valued most highly by farmers. Steaming oyster stew suppers with crackers and celery are a gathering point in many neighborhoods on midwinter evenings. The preference for oysters and shrimp again is due primarily to their availability in frozen form. It explains why most of the recipes in this chapter call for them.

Cupboard shelves in most country kitchens always hold a few cans of tuna. It is the most used canned fish. Canned salmon has long been a traditional farm food, but in recent years dwindling supplies and higher prices have somewhat curtailed its use.

The recipes that follow show how women rushed for time cook fish and sea foods. All the dishes are quick. And if you are looking for a delightful, attractive and unusual main dish for a women's luncheon, do try Party Crab Bake. It is extra delicious and appealing. Red tomato slices and yellow cheese on top contribute bright color and a blend of flavors that glorify the crab meat.

Timesaving Fish and Sea Food

They're coming up in popularity

Fast-fix Fish

BAKED FISH FILLETS

No need to thaw fish completely—cut it with a saw-edged freezer knife

1 (1 lb.) pkg. frozen fish fillets
1 egg white
¼ c. mayonnaise
1 tblsp. prepared mustard
½ tsp. salt
⅛ tsp. pepper

Thaw fish slightly. Cut in 4 pieces. Place skin side down in greased shallow baking dish.

Beat egg until stiff. Fold in mayonnaise, mustard, salt and pepper. Spread on fish. Bake in hot oven (425°) 20 minutes or until fish flakes with fork and topping is brown. Makes 4 servings.

DEVILED FISH FILLETS

Into the oven and out in a jiffy

1 lb. fish fillets
¼ c. mayonnaise or salad dressing
2 tsp. prepared mustard
2 tsp. minced onion

Place fish in greased shallow baking dish. Mix remaining ingredients and spread mixture on fish.

Bake in extremely hot oven (500°) 15 minutes. Makes 3 servings.

Note: Sprinkle with paprika or snipped parsley to add color.

FISH POACHED IN SHRIMP SOUP

A gourmet dish to fast-fix

1 (10 oz.) can frozen cream of shrimp soup, thawed
1 ¼ c. water
½ tsp. salt
1 tsp. instant parsley flakes
1 (1 lb.) pkg. frozen fish fillets, thawed to separate

Blend soup and water in skillet. Add salt and parsley. Bring to a boil. Add fish fillets, separated, and simmer, covered, until fish flakes easily with fork, about 10 minutes.

Serve fish from skillet, as it breaks very easily if transferred to platter. Makes 4 servings.

Note: Serve soup mixture around fish over rice.

FISH ROLL-UPS

Takes a few minutes to roll the fish, but well worth the time spent

¼ c. chopped onion
¼ c. butter
1 qt. day-old bread crumbs
¼ c. diced celery
1 tsp. poultry seasoning
¼ c. chopped parsley (optional)
¼ tsp. pepper
2 tsp. salt
8 fish fillets, fresh or frozen
8 bacon slices

To make stuffing, sauté onion in melted butter until tender. Add crumbs, celery and seasonings; mix well. Heat slowly; add water to moisten slightly.

Place ¼ c. stuffing on each fillet. Roll up, wrap slice of bacon around each, and secure with toothpick. Bake in moderate oven (350°) about 35 minutes, or until fish is tender and bacon crisp. Makes 8 servings.

BARBECUED SALMON STEAKS

Fish cooked this way looks out for itself in the oven

6 (1") salmon steaks
⅓ c. butter or margarine
½ tsp. salt
2 tsp. Worcestershire sauce
2 tblsp. finely chopped onion

Place salmon in greased shallow baking pan. Combine butter, salt and Worcestershire sauce. Brush mixture over salmon. Sprinkle on onion.

Bake in moderate oven (350°) about 30 minutes. Serve with Tartar Sauce (see Index). Makes 6 servings.

FISH PIQUANT

Try this for Friday's supper—it's a winner, and fish cooks fast

2 lbs. frozen fish fillets (haddock, flounder or perch)
½ c. French dressing
2 tblsp. butter or margarine
1 small onion, chopped
1 lemon
Tartar Sauce

Thaw fish as directed on package.

Dip pieces in French dressing.

Heat butter in skillet. Add fish; sprinkle onion over top.

Cook over moderate heat 7 to 8 minutes on each side, turning once.

Serve with lemon wedges and Tartar Sauce (see Index). Makes 6 servings.

OVEN-FRIED FISH

Heat frozen French-fried potatoes in oven with fish

¼ c. evaporated milk
½ c. water
2 tsp. salt
2 lbs. fish fillets
1 c. corn flake crumbs
Lemon slices

Mix milk and water; add salt. Dip fish in milk mixture and roll in corn flake crumbs. Arrange on a greased baking sheet.

Bake in extremely hot oven (500°) about 15 minutes. Serve garnished with lemon slices. Makes 6 servings.

Sea-food Specialties

POTATO-CLAM SCALLOP

Marvelous-tasting potato dish direct from Maine to you

3 tblsp. butter or margarine
2 tblsp. flour
3 c. milk
2½ tsp. salt
¼ tsp. pepper
8 medium potatoes, sliced thin
2 tblsp. chopped onion
1 (7 oz.) can minced clams, drained

Melt butter; stir in flour and cook until smooth and bubbly. Remove from heat; add milk (you can substitute clam juice for equal amount of milk), 1½ tsp. salt and pepper. Boil 1 minute.

Arrange half the potatoes in bottom of 2 qt. casserole. Sprinkle with ½ tsp. salt and half of onion, clams and sauce. Repeat for top layer. Bake, uncovered, in moderate oven (350°) 50 to 55 minutes. Makes 8 servings.

PARTY CRAB BAKE

Tomatoes and cheese make bright topping for this superior casserole

6 oz. shell macaroni
1 (8 oz.) pkg. cream cheese
½ c. dairy sour cream
½ c. cottage cheese
¼ c. sliced green onions and tops
1 (7½ oz.) can crab meat, flaked
2 medium tomatoes, peeled and sliced
¼ tsp. salt
1½ c. shredded sharp Cheddar cheese

Cook macaroni as directed on package.

Combine cream cheese, sour cream, cottage cheese and onions.

Arrange half of macaroni in bottom of greased 2 qt. casserole. Dip half of cream-cheese mixture by spoonfuls over macaroni. Spread to cover. Top with half of crab meat. Repeat these layers. Top crab meat with sliced tomatoes. Sprinkle with salt and with shredded cheese.

Bake in moderate oven (350°) 30 minutes. Makes 6 to 8 servings.

OVEN-FRIED OYSTERS: Drain 24 large oysters; dry between paper towels. Roll in 1½ c. flour seasoned with 1¼ tsp. salt and ¼ tsp. pepper. Dip in 2 slightly beaten eggs mixed with 3 tblsp. cold water. Roll in dry bread crumbs or cracker crumbs. Sprinkle crumbed oysters on both sides with salad oil. Bake in a single layer in an oiled shallow pan in hot oven (400°) about 15 minutes. Good served with lemon wedges or Tartar Sauce (see Index).

OVEN-FRIED SCALLOPS: Substitute scallops for oysters in recipe for Oven-fried Oysters.

SCALLOPED OYSTERS

Secret to success: bake only 2 layers of oysters

2½ c. coarse cracker crumbs
1 pt. oysters
¼ c. oyster liquor
¾ c. light cream
1 tsp. Worcestershire sauce
½ tsp. salt
⅛ tsp. pepper
⅓ c. butter or margarine

Arrange ⅓ cracker crumbs in well-buttered shallow 1 qt. baking dish. Cover with ½ of oysters; repeat layers of crumbs and oysters. Blend liquids and seasonings; pour over oysters. Top with remaining crumbs. Dot with butter.

Bake in moderate oven (350°) about 45 minutes. Makes 5 servings.

FARMHOUSE OYSTER STEW

Garnish hot soup with dabs of butter and sprinkle with paprika

2 tblsp. flour
1½ tsp. salt
Few drops Worcestershire sauce
2 tblsp. cold water
1 pt. oysters
1 qt. milk or half-and-half milk and cream, scalded

Combine flour, salt, Worcestershire sauce and water. Blend to a smooth paste. Stir in oysters and their liquor.

Simmer over very low heat until edges of oysters ruffle. Remove from heat, pour in the hot milk, cover and let stand 10 to 15 minutes to mellow.

Reheat stew and serve in warm bowls. Makes 3 to 4 servings.

SHRIMP ALMOND

A party casserole—make it in two steps to reduce work at serving time

1 (6 to 7 oz.) pkg. shell macaroni
1 (3 oz.) can chopped mushrooms
⅓ c. slivered almonds
¼ c. butter
1 tblsp. chopped pimiento
2 tblsp. flour
1 tsp. salt
⅛ tsp. pepper
1 can condensed cream of vegetable soup
2 c. milk
1 lb. shrimp, cooked and cleaned
1 c. bread crumbs
3 tblsp. butter, melted

Cook macaroni as directed on package.

Cook mushrooms and almonds in ¼ c. butter about 1 minute. Stir in pimiento, flour and seasonings. Add soup and milk gradually. Cook over medium heat, stirring constantly, until sauce comes to a boil.

Combine macaroni, shrimp and sauce in a greased 2 qt. casserole.

Toss bread crumbs with 3 tblsp. melted butter. Sprinkle over shrimp mixture. Cover and refrigerate.

When preparing meal, bake casserole, uncovered, in moderate oven (350°) 30 minutes. Makes 6 servings.

SHRIMP BISQUE

Canned soup and shrimp give the cook a head start on this hearty dish

1 can condensed cream of celery soup
1 ½ c. milk
1 (5 oz.) can shrimp
¼ c. chopped green pepper
3 drops Tabasco sauce

Dilute soup with milk in saucepan.

Chop shrimp, reserving some whole for garnish.

Add shrimp, green pepper, and Tabasco sauce to soup.

Heat and pour into soup bowls. Makes 6 servings.

SHRIMP CREOLE

Keep sauce on hand to make this New Orleans special extra-quick

1 lb. raw shrimp in the shell
½ c. chopped green pepper
½ c. chopped celery
1 tblsp. salad oil
1 c. Basic Red Sauce (see Index)

Cook shrimp, remove shells and veins.

Cook pepper and celery in hot oil until just soft. Add Red Sauce and shrimp. Serve with rice. Makes 4 servings.

To Cook Shrimp: Add just enough boiling water to cover shrimp, about 1 qt. to 1 lb. of shrimp. To every quart of water add 1 tsp. salt and 3 slices of onion. Cook 3 to 5 minutes, depending on size of shrimp. Drain at once and rinse in cold water to cool. Remove shells and the dark intestinal veins along the backs.

Tuna and Salmon for Supper

DUMP-IN TUNA BAKE

Couldn't be easier—no peeling, cleaning, measuring or pot-watching

2 (7 oz.) cans tuna, chunk style
3 (2 ¼ oz.) cans shoestring potatoes (4 ½ c.)
1 (14 ½ oz.) can evaporated milk
1 can condensed cream of mushroom soup
1 (3 oz.) can mushroom pieces
1 (4 oz.) can chopped pimientos

Dump all the ingredients into a greased 2 qt. casserole and mix.

Bake in moderate oven (375°) about 45 minutes. Makes 6 to 8 servings.

Variation: Substitute 1 (1 lb.) can salmon for the tuna.

COMPANY TUNA CASSEROLE

The celery is tender-crisp, Oriental style—adds a crunchy note

1 (3 oz.) can chow mein noodles
1 can condensed cream of mushroom soup
¼ c. water
1 (6 ½ oz.) can tuna
1 (¼ lb.) pkg. salted cashews, chopped
1 c. finely chopped celery
¼ c. minced onion
1 tblsp. soy sauce

Combine one-half can noodles with remaining ingredients in greased 1½ qt. casserole. Sprinkle on noodles.

Bake in moderate oven (350°) 40 minutes. Makes 5 servings.

TUNA-CORN BREAD CASSEROLE

Keep makings for this tasty main dish in cupboard and freezer

1 (10 oz.) pkg. frozen mixed vegetables
1 tblsp. instant minced onion
1 (6 ½ to 7 oz.) can tuna
¼ tsp. salt
Pepper
1 can condensed cream of celery soup
¾ c. milk
1 (8 oz.) pkg. corn-muffin mix

Cook vegetables in boiling salted water until barely tender. Drain. Add onion, tuna, salt, pepper, soup and milk. Heat to boiling.

Meanwhile, prepare corn bread batter as directed on package. Pour hot tuna mixture into greased 2 qt. casserole. Top with batter.

Bake in hot oven (400°) until top is golden brown, 25 to 30 minutes. Makes 6 servings.

TUNA-POTATO PIE

Double quick and very rewarding

1 (6 ½ to 7 oz.) can tuna
1 can condensed cream of vegetable soup
½ c. milk
½ pkg. instant mashed potatoes

Combine tuna, soup and milk. Pour into greased pie pan (9").

Prepare potatoes as directed on package. Drop by spoonfuls on top of tuna mixture.

Bake in very hot oven (450°) until potatoes are lightly browned, about 15 minutes. Makes 4 servings.

HOT TUNA SALAD

Individual baking dishes cut down on cooking time—only 10 minutes

2 (7 oz.) cans tuna, drained and flaked
2 c. chopped celery
¼ c. chopped sweet pickles
2 tsp. grated onion
2 tblsp. lemon juice
½ tsp. salt
1 c. mayonnaise
½ c. shredded sharp cheese
1 c. crushed potato chips

Combine ingredients except cheese and potato chips. Pile lightly in individual bakers.

Top with layer of cheese and then potato chips. Bake in very hot oven (450°) 10 minutes. Makes 6 servings.

MACARONI-TUNA TREAT

Tastes as good as if you spent an hour instead of 30 minutes making it

1 (7 ¼ oz.) macaroni-and-cheese dinner
1 (7 oz.) can tuna, flaked
2 tblsp. cream
1 tsp. instant green onion

Prepare macaroni and cheese as directed on package. Add remaining ingredients. Cook over low heat, stirring occasionally and gently, until thoroughly heated. Makes 4 servings.

TUNA BISQUE

Also have tossed green salad, crackers and a fruit dessert

1 can condensed cream of tomato soup
1 can condensed pea soup
2 (6 to 7 oz.) cans tuna
2 c. milk
½ c. light cream
1 ½ tsp. lemon juice
Thin lemon slices

Mix soups until smooth. Add drained, flaked tuna, milk and cream. Heat. Add lemon juice. Simmer a few minutes before serving. Float lemon slices on top. Makes 6 to 8 servings.

SALMON LOAF

Salmon and vegetable flavors make a wonderful-tasting loaf

1 can condensed cream of celery soup
⅓ c. mayonnaise or salad dressing
1 egg, beaten
½ c. chopped onion
¼ c. chopped green pepper
1 tblsp. lemon juice
1 (1 lb.) can salmon, drained, boned and flaked
1 c. cracker crumbs

Mix together all ingredients. Place in a greased loaf pan (9″ × 5″ × 3″).

Bake in moderate oven (350°) 1 hour. Unmold and slice. Makes 6 to 8 servings.

LIGHTNING SALMON PIE

Puffs of cheese-sprinkled potatoes, delicately browned, ring the salmon

1 (1 lb.) can salmon, drained
½ pkg. instant mashed potatoes
2 tblsp. milk
½ c. grated process American cheese
1 tblsp. butter or margarine

Break salmon into pieces with fork; pile in center of greased pie pan (9″).

more

Prepare potatoes as directed on package. Place ring of hot potatoes around salmon.

Sprinkle milk over salmon, and cheese over potatoes. Dot with butter.

Bake in very hot oven (450°) until potatoes are lightly browned, 15 to 20 minutes. Makes 4 servings.

SALMON SCALLOP

Mix and bake this rewarding main dish in the same casserole

1 (1 lb.) can salmon
3 eggs
1 c. milk
1 ¼ c. coarse cracker crumbs
½ tsp. salt
Dash of pepper
1 tblsp. instant onion
¼ c. butter or margarine
½ c. cracker crumbs
2 tblsp. butter or margarine, melted

Empty salmon (including bones and liquid) into greased 1½ qt. casserole. Break up with fork. Add eggs and stir with fork until thoroughly mixed. Stir in milk, 1¼ c. cracker crumbs, salt, pepper and onion. Dot with butter, stirring it in.

Toss ½ c. cracker crumbs with 2 tblsp. melted butter. Sprinkle on top.

Bake in moderate oven (350°) 50 minutes. Makes 6 servings.

SOUR CREAM-SALMON

It's the blend of flavors that exalts this quick dish and makes it unusual

2 (1 lb.) cans salmon, drained
2 cans condensed clam chowder
1 tsp. instant minced onion
2 tblsp. dry bread crumbs
1 ½ c. dairy sour cream
2 tblsp. chopped chives

Combine salmon, chowder, onion and crumbs in greased baking dish (8″ × 8″); spread cream over top; sprinkle with chives (or green onion tops, chopped, or instant green onions).

Bake in moderate oven (375°) 20 to 25 minutes. Makes 6 to 8 servings.

CHAPTER 4

CHEESE AND EGG MAIN DISHES

Cheese and eggs are near the top of the list of foods that serve busy women well. They reach perfection with little cooking and little heat. Overcooking and high heat toughen them. They are protein foods and deserve the important place country cooks give them in hot main dishes for lunch and supper.

Cheese is the diplomat of the kitchen; it gets along well when combined with a fascinating variety of foods—desserts, salads, bread, sandwiches, sauces, vegetables, fruits, meat, fish, poultry and sea food, for example.

Eggs, like cheese, are good mixers. They are important for any course in a meal. And they are the neatest, most convenient food package designed by Nature. Scrambled eggs, of course, always have been the busy cook's closest friend. We have recipes for them in this chapter. Then there are recipes for dishes in which eggs and cheese support each other: Cheese-Bread Casserole, Baked Swiss Fondue, Eggs in Potato Pockets and Eggs Baked in Tomatoes. Many taste triumphs in which eggs and cheese contribute flavor and appearance are sprinkled throughout other chapters in this cookbook. (Look in the Index under Eggs and under Cheese.)

The egg main dishes that follow divide into two families. In one, you break the eggs and cook them in a jiffy. In the other, refrigerated hard-cooked eggs are the short-cut ingredient. Many busy cooks keep a supply of them on hand ready to use when the time to get a meal is short.

Take a tip from hurried country cooks and rely on a puffed omelet or a meltingly rich, French-type Cheese-Bacon Pie to please family and friends.

Hurry-up Cheese and Eggs

They give suppers a lift

First-choice Egg Dishes

EGGS BAKED IN TOMATOES: Place thin slices of tomatoes, peeled, in bottom of greased, large muffin-pan cups. Top each with an egg. Season with salt and pepper and sprinkle with shredded process American cheese. Bake in slow oven (325°) until eggs are set, about 25 minutes. Serve on rounds of buttered toast.

EGGS FOO YOUNG

A speedy version of a famous Chinese dish—just right for supper

- 4 eggs, beaten
- 1 (1 lb.) can bean sprouts, drained
- ½ c. cooked or canned chicken, chopped
- 1 small onion, chopped
- ½ tsp. salt
- ⅛ tsp. pepper
- 1 tblsp. soy sauce (optional)
- 2 tblsp. salad oil

Combine all ingredients except oil. Drop by spoonfuls into hot oil in skillet; spread bean sprouts gently with tip of spoon to cover egg mixture.

Cook until little cakes set and brown on edges. Turn and brown on the other side. Add more oil to skillet if necessary as you cook additional patties. Place on hot platter and serve at once with Chinese Sauce. Makes 10 patties.

Chinese Sauce

Combine 1½ c. chicken broth (or 1½ c. hot water with 2 chicken bouillon cubes added) with 1 tsp. molasses and 1 tsp. soy sauce. Blend 2 tblsp. cornstarch and 2 tblsp. cold water; add to chicken broth and cook, stirring constantly, over low heat until mixture comes to a boil.

OMELET SQUARES

A Spanish-type potato omelet

- 6 eggs, beaten
- ⅔ c. milk
- 1 c. instant mashed potatoes
- ½ tsp. instant minced onion
- ½ tsp. salt
- ⅛ tsp. pepper
- 1 tsp. mustard
- ½ c. crumbled, cooked bacon
- ¼ c. pickle relish
- 1 tblsp. butter or margarine

Combine eggs and milk; beat in rest of ingredients except butter.

Melt butter in 10″ electric skillet; add egg mixture; cook over low heat (280°) 30 minutes or until set (occasionally make cuts in omelet to let uncooked egg run down). Cut in squares; serve hot with Tomato Sauce. Makes 6 servings.

Tomato Sauce

Combine in saucepan 1 can condensed tomato soup, 1 tsp. brown sugar, 1 tsp. parsley flakes, ½ tsp. Worcestershire sauce and ¼ tsp. orégano; heat, do not boil.

OMELET PANCAKES

Best invitation to early breakfast

- ¾ c. sifted flour
- 1 tsp. salt

¼ tsp. pepper
¾ c. milk
6 large eggs, beaten

Combine flour, salt and pepper in mixing bowl. Stir in milk slowly and beat to form a smooth batter.

Stir in beaten eggs, blend well.

Pour ½ cup of batter on very hot, greased 10″ griddle; spread batter to edges.

Cook about 20 seconds until browned. Turn, brown on other side.

Remove to warm plate. Spread with cooked bulk sausage, cranberry sauce, jam or cinnamon and sugar. Roll up if you wish.

Keep warm in oven while cooking other pancakes. Makes 6 pancakes.

PUFFY OMELET

Failure-proof—adding the sauce makes the omelet sturdier

¼ c. butter or margarine
3½ tblsp. flour
1 tsp. salt
1 c. milk
4 eggs, separated
2 tblsp. shortening
Chopped parsley

Melt butter in small saucepan over low heat. Blend in flour and salt; cook 1 minute, stirring constantly.

Remove from heat; gradually stir in milk; return to heat. Cook, stirring constantly, until white sauce is thick and smooth. Cool.

Beat egg whites until stiff enough to hold firm peaks. Then beat the yolks.

Blend egg yolks into white sauce. Then fold in beaten egg whites.

Heat shortening over low heat in a 10″ skillet. Pour in the omelet mixture. Cover with a close fitting lid.

Cook over low heat 15 to 20 minutes, or until a light brown crust is formed on bottom and top is firm.

Loosen the omelet from the sides of skillet and cut through the center down to crust in bottom. Tilt pan; fold one half over the other. Slide onto platter.

Sprinkle with chopped parsley. Makes 4 servings.

Variation: Just before folding omelet, sprinkle lower half with ⅓ c. shredded cheese.

SCRAMBLED EGGS

Cook them in a double boiler—they take less watching

3 tblsp. butter or margarine
12 eggs
½ c. milk
1 tsp. salt
⅛ tsp. pepper

Melt butter in top of double boiler.

Beat eggs slightly; add milk and seasonings. Pour into double boiler and cook over simmering, not boiling, water, scraping the cooked portions from bottom and sides of the pan until the eggs are thick and creamy flakes, but moist. Serve at once. Makes 8 servings.

Note: For a Spanish touch, serve eggs on buttered toast with hot Tomato Sauce (see Index) spooned over.

SCRAMBLED EGGS, SANTA FE STYLE: Season scrambled eggs with a dash of chili powder. Spoon on thin slices of avocado arranged on buttered toast. Serve with bacon or ham for breakfast or with a tossed green or fruit salad for supper.

CHEESE SCRAMBLED EGGS

"Old faithful"—that's what farm short-cut cooks call scrambled eggs. This time they're cheese-flavored

6 eggs
6 tblsp. light cream
Salt
Pepper
3 tblsp. butter
½ c. coarsely shredded process American cheese

Combine eggs, cream, salt and pepper. Stir with fork to mix.

Melt butter in a 12" skillet. Add eggs and cook over low heat, gently lifting egg mixture with a spoon so uncooked eggs will flow to bottom of skillet. Add cheese just before eggs are cooked; mix in lightly. Cook eggs until set, but remove from heat while they are moist. Makes 4 servings.

Variation: Add 2 tblsp. chopped chives or crumbled crisp bacon just before serving.

MUSHROOM-EGG SCRAMBLE

Border platter of eggs with baked tomatoes for a gay summer special

8 eggs
1 can condensed cream of mushroom soup
¼ c. milk
⅛ tsp. pepper
2 tblsp. butter
½ c. shredded yellow cheese
Parsley

Beat eggs slightly. Add soup and beat gently with rotary beater. Blend in milk and pepper.

Melt butter in skillet. Pour in egg mixture. Cook slowly until eggs are set, stirring occasionally. Sprinkle with cheese and chopped parsley just before serving. Makes 6 servings.

EGGS IN POTATO POCKETS

A pleasing version of the famous farm team—eggs and potatoes

8 c. instant mashed potatoes
1 tsp. instant minced onion
2 tblsp. chopped pimiento
½ tsp. pepper
8 eggs
½ tsp. salt
2 c. grated process American cheese
⅓ c. crumbled cooked bacon

Prepare potatoes as directed on package. Mix in onion, pimiento and pepper; spread in greased shallow 2½ qt. baking dish.

Break eggs into ½" depressions in potatoes. Sprinkle with salt, cheese and bacon. Bake in slow oven (325°) 35 minutes or until eggs are consistency you desire. Makes 8 servings.

POTATO-EGG SUPPER

Here's what to have for supper if you have cooked eggs and potatoes on hand

4 c. diced cooked potatoes
6 hard-cooked eggs, sliced
1 can condensed cream of chicken soup
1 c. milk
½ tsp. salt
⅛ tsp. pepper
1 c. shredded sharp Cheddar cheese

Place potatoes and eggs in greased 2 qt. casserole. Blend soup, milk and seasonings. Pour over potatoes. Top with cheese.

Bake in moderate oven (375°) until hot and bubbly, about 25 minutes. Makes 6 servings.

EGGS IN SPINACH CUPS

No need to cut up spinach—buy the frozen chopped kind

2 (10 oz.) pkgs. frozen chopped spinach, cooked and drained
1 can condensed cream of mushroom soup
¼ tsp. onion salt
8 eggs
Paprika

Mix spinach with soup and onion salt. Butter 8 (6 oz.) baking cups; line with spinach; break one egg into each cup. Bake in slow oven (325°) 15 minutes. Sprinkle with paprika. Makes 8 servings.

TUNA-EGG SCRAMBLE

Five-minute main dish from ingredients kept on hand

6 eggs
⅓ c. light cream or milk
½ tsp. salt
1 (6½ oz.) can tuna
2 tblsp. butter or margarine

Blend together eggs, cream and salt. Stir in tuna. Pour into hot skillet with butter. Cook over low heat, stirring occasionally until eggs are thickened, but still moist. Makes 6 servings.

EGGS BENEDICT

Serve with a green vegetable to complete the main course

6 thin, small ham slices
6 eggs
3 hamburger buns, split

Score fat edges of ham slices. Place on broiler rack, 3" from heat. Broil 3 minutes; turn.

Poach eggs; keep warm.

Place bun halves on broiler. Broil until light golden, but broil ham 3 minutes longer.

Place ham on buns. Top with poached eggs. Pour Hollandaise Sauce (see Index) over all. Makes 6 servings.

Made with Hard-cooked Eggs

CREAMED EGGS

A country main dish to serve over many foods—we give you six

½ c. butter or margarine
6 tblsp. flour
1 qt. milk
1½ tsp. salt
½ tsp. paprika
⅛ tsp. pepper
¼ tsp. Tabasco
2 tsp. finely grated onion
12 hard-cooked eggs, coarsely cut

Melt butter over low heat. Add flour, stir until bubbly (do not let brown) and add milk. Cook, stirring constantly, until mixture thickens. Add remaining ingredients. Heat thoroughly.

Serve over split hot biscuits, toast, rice, baked potatoes, broccoli or asparagus. Makes 6 to 8 servings.

Note: Peel the hard-cooked eggs and cut in halves. Remove yolks. Chop whites and cut yolks in halves to decrease breaking during the heating.

CREAMED EGGS WITH PEAS

Quick-as-a-wink supper dish

1 (10 oz.) pkg. frozen peas
6 hard-cooked eggs, sliced
2 c. Medium Cream Sauce (recipe follows)
1 (6 oz.) can fried noodles

Cook peas as directed on package; drain. Add eggs and peas to Cream Sauce. Heat. Serve over noodles. Makes 6 servings.

MEDIUM CREAM SAUCE

Melt 4 tblsp. butter or margarine over low heat. Add 4 tblsp. flour, blend together and add 2 c. milk, stirring constantly. Cook until thick and smooth. Add ¾ tsp. salt. Makes 2 cups. To hasten cooking, heat 1 c. of milk and stir it in after blending in cold milk.

Variation: Instead of Cream Sauce use 1 c. condensed cream of celery soup and ⅓ soup can of milk. Serve over fried noodles, hot biscuits or toast.

DEVILED EGGS

Make these in the morning and chill them until suppertime

1 doz. hard-cooked eggs
2 tsp. vinegar
¾ tsp. salt
⅛ tsp. pepper
1 tsp. prepared mustard
2 tblsp. melted butter or margarine
3 tblsp. mayonnaise

Cut eggs in halves lengthwise. Remove yolks; put through sieve, or mash with fork.

Add remaining ingredients to yolks; whip until smooth and fluffy. Heap into white halves. Crisscross tops with tines of fork. Refrigerate. Makes 24 halves.

Variations: Follow egg-yolk recipe above and add 3 or 4 tblsp. of cream or grated cheese, deviled or chopped ham, mashed cooked chicken livers or crisp bacon bits. Or, put bits of any of these in hollow of egg white halves before adding yolk mixture.

HOT DEVILED EGGS

A country main dish for supper

¼ c. butter or margarine
¼ c. flour
½ tsp. salt
¼ tsp. pepper
2 c. milk
12 deviled-egg halves
½ c. dry bread crumbs
½ c. grated sharp cheese

Make medium white sauce with butter, flour, salt, pepper and milk. Pour over eggs, arranged in rows in greased baking dish (8″ × 8″). Top with crumbs, then cheese. Bake in moderate oven (350°) until cheese melts. Makes 6 servings.

SUNDAY-SUPPER DEVILED EGGS

You can get this ready to bake in the morning and refrigerate. Cook eggs while you're getting breakfast

½ c. chopped onion
¼ c. butter or margarine
2 c. precooked rice (or 4 c. cooked regular rice)
1 tsp. salt
2 c. boiling water
1 (12 oz.) can pork luncheon meat
⅛ tsp. pepper

3 tblsp. chopped parsley
⅔ c. mayonnaise
2 tblsp. light cream
3 tblsp. ketchup
12 deviled-egg halves

Sauté onion in melted butter over low heat until golden. Add rice, salt and water. Cover; let stand 5 minutes.

Cut meat into 3 or 4 slices; mash with fork. Add to rice mixture with pepper and parsley.

Blend together mayonnaise, cream and ketchup. Add half this sauce to rice mixture. Spread in bottom of greased shallow baking dish (12″ × 7½″).

Cut eggs in lengthwise halves.

With back of spoon make depressions in rice to hold eggs. Spoon remaining sauce over indentations. Put eggs in place. Cover; bake in moderate oven (350°) 20 minutes. Makes 6 servings.

Change-of-Pace Cheese Specials

BAKED SWISS FONDUE

A puffed-up main dish

8 slices bread
6 (1 oz.) slices process Swiss cheese
3 eggs, beaten
2 c. milk
½ tsp. salt
⅛ tsp. white pepper
½ tsp. instant minced green onion

Trim crusts from bread; cut in halves diagonally. Arrange 8 halves in pinwheel pattern in greased round pan (or in 1½ qt. casserole). Cover bread with cheese slices cut in halves for easy placement. Top with remaining bread like first layer.

Combine beaten eggs, milk, salt and pepper with rotary beater. Pour over bread and cheese. Sprinkle with onion.

Bake in slow oven (325°) until puffy and golden brown, about 1 hour. Serve at once. Makes 6 servings.

CHEESE-BREAD CASSEROLE

Fluffy, yellow pudding with curried sauce spooned over

5 slices bread
Butter or margarine
3 eggs, separated
1 c. milk
¼ tsp. salt
½ tsp. prepared mustard
½ lb. grated sharp cheese

Trim crusts from bread; spread bread generously with butter; cut into cubes. Place in greased 1½ qt. casserole.

Beat egg yolks until foamy; add milk, salt, mustard and cheese.

Beat egg whites until stiff; fold into yolk mixture; pour over bread.

Bake in moderate oven (375°) about 35 minutes or until puffed and brown. Serve hot, topped with Curried Dried Beef (recipe follows) or creamed vegetables. Makes 6 to 8 servings.

CURRIED DRIED BEEF

Melt ¼ c. butter in saucepan; stir in ¼ c. flour, ¼ tsp. curry powder and ⅓ c. chopped green onions. Cook 1 minute.

more

Gradually add 2½ c. mixture of half-and-half milk and cream; cook until thickened, stirring constantly. Shred 1 (4 oz.) pkg. dried beef and mix into sauce. Serve hot. Makes 3 cups.

CHEESE-BACON PIE

A good way to use the unbaked pastry shell you keep in freezer

- 10 slices bacon
- 1¼ c. chopped onion
- ¾ lb. grated Cheddar cheese
- 2 eggs, beaten
- 1 c. milk
- 1 tblsp. flour
- ½ tsp. salt
- ⅛ tsp. pepper
- Dash cayenne pepper
- 1 (9") unbaked pie shell

Fry bacon until crisp; drain. Cook onion in 2 tblsp. bacon drippings until just transparent.

Blend onion and crumbled bacon with remaining ingredients; pour into pie shell.

Bake in very hot oven (450°) about 25 minutes. Cut in wedges. Serve warm. Makes 8 servings.

Note: To cut down on time, cook enough extra bacon while getting breakfast, for this main dish.

HASTY-TASTY RAREBIT

Favorite cheese dish with a taste adventure in every forkful

- 2 cans condensed cream of celery soup
- 2 (6 oz.) links smoke-flavor cheese
- 8 slices toast
- Stuffed green olives
- Parsley

Blend together soup and cheese over hot water. Serve immediately on toast. Garnish with pimiento-stuffed green olives and parsley. Makes 8 servings.

MACARONI AND CHEESE

Busy mothers favor this top-stove main dish. Children ask for it

- 8 oz. elbow macaroni
- ¼ c. butter or margarine
- 1 (8 oz.) pkg. process American cheese, shredded
- ½ c. milk
- ¼ c. grated onion
- 1 tsp. salt
- ⅛ tsp. pepper

Cook macaroni as directed on package. Drain, but do not remove from saucepan. Add remaining ingredients. Cook over low heat, stirring frequently, until cheese melts, about 5 minutes. Makes 8 servings.

STUFFED GREEN PEPPERS

Speed up this favorite main dish with a quick stuffing—a package of Spanish rice and a can of tomato sauce or a can of macaroni and cheese. You can get the peppers ready for stuffing in 10 minutes. But fix Spanish rice first and then cut 4 medium peppers in halves. Remove seeds and cook in boiling, salted water until barely tender, about 8 minutes. Drain.

SPANISH-RICE STUFFING

- ½ lb. ground beef
- 2 c. water
- 1 beef bouillon cube
- 1 (6 oz.) pkg. Spanish-rice mix
- 2 tblsp. butter or margarine

1 (8 oz.) can tomato sauce
½ c. grated Cheddar cheese

Brown beef in skillet over low heat. Add water and bouillon cube and bring to a boil.

Remove from heat and stir in Spanish-rice mix and butter. Cover and let stand 20 minutes. Prepare peppers.

Fill peppers with rice mixture and place in baking pan (13″ × 9″ × 2″). Spoon tomato sauce over rice in peppers; sprinkle with cheese. Broil until cheese melts, about 5 minutes. Makes 4 to 6 servings.

MACARONI AND CHEESE STUFFING

2 (15¼ oz.) cans macaroni and cheese
½ c. shredded or grated Cheddar cheese
Paprika

Heat macaroni and cheese. Fill peppers with mixture. Top with cheese, sprinkle lightly with paprika. Broil to melt cheese, about 5 minutes. Makes 4 to 8 servings.

CHAPTER 5

MAIN DISH SANDWICHES

Substantial sandwiches have been a lunchtime favorite in the country for years. Children carried them to school in their lunch boxes. Bread and butter with meat or a sweet filling gave men in the field quick energy in midmorning and afternoon. And picnic baskets were heaped with sandwiches.

Then the hot school lunch came along and changed the children's noonday fare. Tractors and pick-up trucks make it easier for men to come to the house for their coffee break. And the vogue for outdoor cooking has brought a new kind of "build your own" sandwich.

Regardless of these changes, sandwiches are as much of a family standby as ever, but with a difference and more variety. In many homes they go to the table almost every day. Good cooks, crowded for minutes, make hearty main-dish lunch-and-supper sandwiches. These have caught on. Short-cut cooks sent us main-dish sandwich recipes as prized quick-and-easy dishes.

One observing farm woman explains the evolution like this: "Hamburger, hot dog and grilled sandwiches gave the main-dish sandwich its start. Their immediate popularity prodded busy cooks to look for others that would stick to the ribs."

Mothers will want to try the Boys' Breakfast Sandwiches. If your children greet the day's first meal without enthusiasm, set a Frankfurter-Egg Sandwich before them and watch a miracle take place. This type of sandwich often tempts youngsters to meat and eggs, the combination that research shows effective. Like most sandwiches in this chapter, they are served piping hot. And many of them are open-faced, to be eaten with a fork. All are easy to fix. All have won blue-ribbon praise for country cooks from their appreciative families.

Main-dish sandwiches like this Hamburger-Hot-Dog Bake (recipe page 66) are hearty supper favorites. You can get them ready to bake and refrigerate them. Require no attention while they bake and brown in oven.

Quick Pizza (recipe page 181) bakes in an electric skillet with controlled heat — no pot watching. Ideal refreshment for the hungry young crowd. Chapter 12 also has "from-scratch" pizza to bake in oven.

Speedy Substantial Sandwiches

They're hot and satisfying

Best-ever Burgers

BETTER BURGERS

New version of spoon-on burgers—sauce adds tang

1 lb. ground beef
1 tblsp. fat
½ tsp. salt
1 c. Basic Red Sauce (see Index)

Brown beef in hot fat. Add salt and sauce; cover and simmer 10 minutes. Serve on hamburger buns, split and toasted. Makes 4 to 6 servings.

Cheeseburgers—Three Ways

CowBelles put ground beef and cheese together in many appetizing dishes. The following three sandwich recipes from their Roundup of Beef Cookery indicate how imaginative these women are in using ground beef in their ranch kitchens.

TOMATO CHEESEBURGERS

Tomatoes, onions and cheese get together in a typical Southwestern way

1½ lbs. lean ground beef
1 small onion, chopped
2 tblsp. salad oil
1½ tsp. salt
¼ tsp. pepper
1 (1 lb.) can tomatoes
½ lb. sharp Cheddar cheese, chopped
Hamburger buns

Brown beef and onion in hot salad oil. Pour excess fat from skillet. Season beef with salt and pepper; add tomatoes. Cook 15 to 20 minutes, or until mixture has absorbed most of the juice. Add cheese; cook about 5 minutes.

Serve on heated soft buns. Makes about 8 servings.

WEST COAST CHEESEBURGERS

Long burgers for a change

1 tblsp. instant minced onion
¼ c. bread crumbs
1 egg
⅓ c. milk
1 tsp. salt
1 tsp. prepared mustard
1 lb. lean ground beef
6 sticks process American cheese (¼" × ¼" × 5")
6 frankfurter buns
Butter or margarine

Combine onion, crumbs, egg, milk, salt and mustard. Add beef and mix thoroughly. Divide into six portions. Shape into logs around the cheese sticks, covering cheese.

Place meat-cheese logs in shallow pan. Bake in hot oven (400°) about 20 minutes or until well browned.

Split buns and toast; spread with butter. Place a cheeseburger in each bun and serve at once. Makes 6 servings.

OLIVE CHEESEBURGERS

A touch of Spain in a Western main-dish sandwich—a ranch favorite

1 ½ c. soft bread crumbs
3 tblsp. olive brine
3 tblsp. water
1 tsp. Ac'cent
⅛ tsp. pepper
1 ½ lbs. lean ground beef
Prepared mustard
12 large pimiento-stuffed olives
8 slices Swiss cheese (½ lb.)
8 hamburger buns

Combine first five ingredients; mix well. Add beef; form into 8 patties.

Broil meat on one side about 7 minutes, with patties about 3″ below heat source. Turn, spread with mustard and top with olive slices. Top each patty with a cheese slice. Broil 5 minutes longer or until cheese melts and browns.

Serve in split buns. Makes 8 servings.

CORNBURGERS

Hearty hamburgers with south-of-the-border seasonings

1 lb. ground beef
¼ c. finely chopped onion
¼ c. finely chopped green pepper
1 tblsp. flour
1 tsp. salt
⅛ tsp. pepper
½ c. ketchup
½ c. milk
1 (1 lb. 1 oz.) can whole-kernel corn
8 sandwich buns

Cook beef, onion and green pepper in skillet until meat browns. Sprinkle on flour, salt and pepper and stir to blend. Add remaining ingredients, except buns.

Cook over low heat 5 to 10 minutes to blend flavors. Serve between split sandwich buns. Makes 8 servings.

Note: For a flavor change add ½ tsp. chili powder and a dash of orégano.

HAMBURGER–HOT-DOG BAKE

Put these two-meat sandwiches together, refrigerate until baking time

12 slices bread
Butter or margarine
1 lb. lean ground beef
¼ c. ketchup
1 tsp. salt
6 frankfurters
2 medium onions, sliced
6 slices process American cheese
2 eggs, beaten
1 c. milk

Spread 6 bread slices with butter; arrange in bottom of greased pan (13″ × 9″ × 2″). Toast in moderate oven (350°) about 15 minutes.

Combine beef, ketchup and salt; spread over toast (⅓ c. per sandwich). Top with frankfurters, cut almost in half lengthwise, onion and cheese slices. Cover with remaining bread slices.

Combine eggs and milk; pour over bread.

Bake in moderate oven (350°) about 50 minutes. Makes 6 servings.

VARIATIONS

BAKED TUNA SANDWICHES: Omit ground-beef mixture and frankfurters. Spread toast with mixture of 2 (7 oz.) cans tuna, flaked, ¼ c. chopped celery, ¼ c. chopped apple and ¼ c. mayonnaise. Bake as directed.

BAKED LUNCHEON-MEAT SANDWICHES: Omit frankfurters. Substitute 1 (12 oz.) can luncheon meat, ground, for beef. Bake as directed.

BAKED HAM AND CHICKEN SANDWICHES: Omit ground-beef mixture, frankfurters and onions. Spread toast with mixture of 2 c. diced cooked chicken and ¼ c. mayonnaise. Top with 6 slices boiled ham and 6 process American cheese slices. Bake as directed.

ITALIAN HAMBURGERS

Ideal refreshments for teen-agers

1 lb. ground beef
1 tblsp. instant minced onion
1 can condensed minestrone soup
⅓ c. ketchup
⅓ c. water
⅛ tsp. orégano
1 (6 oz.) pkg. sliced Mozzarella cheese
6 hamburger buns

Brown ground beef in skillet. Pour off excess fat. Add onion, soup, ketchup, water and orégano. Simmer 5 to 10 minutes.

Spread mixture on split, toasted buns; top with cheese and broil until cheese melts. Makes 12 open-faced sandwiches.

SPOONBURGERS

One pound of ground beef makes eight burgers seasoned just right

1 lb. ground beef
1 can condensed chicken-gumbo soup
⅓ c. ketchup
8 sandwich buns

Brown ground beef in skillet over medium heat. (If meat is frozen, thaw it in skillet.) Pour off fat. Stir in soup and ketchup. Simmer 5 minutes to blend ingredients. Serve between split hamburger buns. Makes 8 servings.

ONION HAMBURGERS

Another typically American way to fix ground beef

1 lb. ground beef
4 tsp. onion-soup mix

Divide ground beef into 8 equal portions. Flatten each into thin patty. Top each of 4 patties with 1 tsp. onion-soup mix; then with remaining beef patties, pressing edges together to seal.

Broil or pan-fry. Serve plain or in buttered buns. Makes 4 servings.

Boys' Breakfast Sandwiches

Why not have hearty, hot sandwiches for a breakfast surprise? Boys especially like them. Mothers report that fast-fix, hot sandwiches are as well received for the first meal of the day as for lunch, supper and substantial snacks. Serve them morning, night or noon—whenever you have youngsters to feed.

FRANKFURTER-EGG: Cut hot frankfurters in round slices; arrange these "pennies" on buttered toast. Top with scrambled eggs and hurry to the table.

EGG-CHEESE WITH HELP-YOURSELF TOPPINGS: Toast hamburger buns, split in halves. Top with hot scrambled eggs.

more

Pass bowls of grated cheese and crumbled crisp bacon to sprinkle on top.

HAM-CHEESE IN FOIL: Split and butter hamburger buns. Insert a thin slice of boiled or baked ham and a slice of process American cheese in each. Wrap in foil. If you do this in the evening, store sandwich bundles in refrigerator. Put sandwiches on a baking sheet and bake in moderate oven (350°) 20 minutes, 5 minutes longer if sandwiches have been chilled. Serve in foil, opened at the top.

WAFFLED HAM: Spread bread slices on both sides with soft butter, a bit of prepared mustard folded in; put together in pairs with sliced cooked ham or luncheon meat. Toast sandwiches in waffle iron until browned, about 1 minute. Children like to brown their own.

PEANUT-BUTTER–BACON: Spread peanut butter on bread slices; drizzle on a little honey. Add crumbled, crisp bacon. Heat in the broiler until edges of bread are crisp. An all-boy favorite. Make it with raisin bread for a change they'll like.

BACON-EGG: Butter 2 bread slices. Cook 1 bacon slice in heavy skillet; remove and keep warm. Pour off excess fat. Break an egg into a measuring cup, season with salt and pepper and beat lightly with a fork. Pour egg into skillet; do not stir. When it is set on bottom, turn like a pancake and remove skillet from heat. Lift egg with spatula to one of the bread slices. Dot with ketchup. Top with other bread slice and serve immediately. You can make three egg-sandwich fillings at a time.

Oven Cheese Sandwiches

BAKED DEVILED-CHEESE SANDWICHES

They stay in the oven 5 minutes

½ c. butter or margarine
12 slices bread
1 (3 oz.) can deviled ham
6 slices process American cheese

Cover large baking sheet with brown paper, cut to fit. (Or use paper sack.)

Melt butter in skillet. Dip one side of bread slices *very quickly* in butter.

Place 6 slices, buttered side down, on paper-lined baking sheet. Spread bread with deviled ham. Top each slice with cheese; then with remaining bread, buttered sides up.

Bake in extremely hot oven (500°) until golden brown, about 5 minutes. Makes 6 servings.

CHEESE RYE LOAF

New way to make hot sandwiches

1 round loaf rye bread
⅓ c. soft butter or margarine
1 (8 oz.) pkg. process pimiento cheese (8 slices)

If bread is unsliced, slice in ¾″ slices almost to bottom crust. If sliced, place loaf in a 9″ round layer pan. Spread each cut surface with butter. Insert cheese slices in every other slit. Cut up a few cheese slices to add extra cheese to fill wider slices.

Wrap loaf in foil and bake in hot oven (425°) until cheese is melted, about 20 minutes.

To serve, cut through slits that have no cheese to make hot cheese sandwiches. Makes 6 servings.

Note: You can use same idea with long rye loaf.

Variation: Substitute Garlic Butter (see Index) for plain butter.

CHEESE-SANDWICH FILLING

At its finest when spread on bread slices and toasted in hot oven (400°) for 5 minutes or until the bread browns around edges

- 1 (3 oz.) pkg. cream cheese
- ⅓ c. shredded smoked cheese
- ¼ c. soft butter

Mix all the ingredients. Makes about 1 cup.

Tempting Hot Dogs

CONEY ISLAND HOT DOGS

Milder than most "Coneys" with a peppy, tomato-chili flavor

- 1 (15 oz.) can chili con carne
- 1 (6 oz.) can tomato paste
- 1 tsp. prepared mustard
- 10 frankfurters
- 10 frankfurter buns

Combine chili con carne, tomato paste and mustard in saucepan; heat.

Heat frankfurters in hot water, but do not boil.

Toast split buns. Place a frankfurter in each bun and spoon sauce over. Makes 10 servings.

HOT DOGS IN BREAD JACKETS: Spread fresh bread slices lightly with butter. Lay a frankfurter diagonally on each slice. Fold opposite corners of bread slice over frank and secure with toothpick. Brush top of sandwiches at fold with butter. Broil 6″ from heat to brown bread without burning and to heat frankfurter. Serve hot-dog relish at ends of sandwiches.

Note: A clever, thrifty cook invented these sandwiches to please her sons and to come out even—buns come in packages of 8, and a 1 lb. package contains 10 frankfurters. Be sure to use fresh bread so it will fold without breaking.

More Sandwich Selections

TOMATO-BACON SANDWICHES: Split buns in half, toast and butter. Lay a slice of peeled tomato on each bun half. Pour your favorite cheese sauce, heated, over tomatoes and top each sandwich with 2 slices (crisscross fashion) of crisp bacon.

BACON-SOUP SANDWICHES

A new hot sandwich, broiler-quick

- 8 slices white or whole-wheat bread
- 1 can condensed cream of mushroom soup
- 12 bacon slices, crisp-fried

Toast bread on one side under broiler. Remove from oven. Spread untoasted side with 2½ tblsp. soup. Top with bacon, crumbled or in strips.

Broil a few seconds until bacon is crisp, soup bubbly and bread slightly browned on edges. Makes 8 servings.

Variations: Try other condensed soups. Tomato sprinkled with Parmesan cheese makes a pizza-like treat.

BROWN BEAN SANDWICHES

Don't bother to measure ketchup—just shake it on from bottle

1 (9 oz.) can brown bread
1 (about 1 lb.) can New England-style baked beans
Ketchup

Cut bread in 10 slices; top each slice with baked beans. Shake ketchup on sandwich tops, as much as you like.

Bake on ungreased baking sheet in moderate oven (375°) 8 to 10 minutes. Makes 5 servings.

ROAST-BEEF SANDWICHES: Cover 4 buttered toast slices with thin slices of left-over roast beef. Top with thin tomato slices and sprinkle with seasoned salt. Combine ½ c. mayonnaise with 1½ c. grated Cheddar or Parmesan cheese and brush on sandwich tops. Broil just long enough to brown.

EASY-DO BARBECUED SANDWICHES

Have for lunch with hot soup and pineapple or other fruit salad

1 (12 oz.) can luncheon meat
½ c. ketchup
½ c. bottled barbecue sauce
8 hamburger buns

Chop luncheon meat. Combine in saucepan with ketchup and barbecue sauce. Bring to boiling and simmer 5 minutes.

Serve between split hamburger buns. Makes 8 sandwiches.

BOLOGNA SANDWICHES: Buy unsliced bologna, cover with water and bring to boiling. Serve hot, sliced, in toasted, buttered buns. Pass ketchup and prepared mustard. Excellent with Hot Potato Salad (see Index).

CORNED-BEEF SANDWICHES

Men give this sandwich top rating

1 small onion, chopped
3 tblsp. butter or margarine
1 (12 oz.) can corned beef, shredded
1 c. ketchup
8 sandwich buns

Cook onion until soft in butter. Stir in corned beef and ketchup. Cook over low heat, stirring frequently, 15 minutes. Serve in hot, split buns. Makes 8 sandwiches.

HAM-EGG SANDWICHES: Spread toast with deviled ham. Top with hard-cooked egg slices. Heat canned cream of mushroom soup, adding milk for the consistency you desire. Spoon over toast and serve at once.

BARBECUED STEAK SANDWICHES

Easy way to get the barbecued flavor

4 minute steaks
1 tblsp. hot fat
1 (10¾ oz.) can beef gravy
4 slices buttered toast
¼ c. barbecue pickle relish
¼ c. finely chopped onion

Brown steaks in hot fat. Pour gravy over steaks and heat.

Place each steak on a slice of toast. Spoon gravy over steaks.

Top with relish and onion. Makes 4 servings.

DEVILED DENVER SANDWICH FILLING

Shake up and cook this sandwich filling at the last minute

2 eggs
1 tblsp. instant or fresh minced onion
1 tblsp. minced green pepper
1 tblsp. milk
1 (2 ¼ oz.) can deviled ham
1 tblsp. butter or bacon drippings

Put ingredients, except butter, in jar. Cover and shake to blend. Pour into skillet containing butter, melted, and brown on both sides. Makes filling for 2 sandwiches.

Note: Serve on split buns or between buttered bread slices.

DEVILED HAM AND EGG SANDWICHES: Spread toast slices with deviled ham. Cover with slices of hard-cooked eggs. Spoon on a hot sauce like Speedy Cheese Sauce (see Index) or a can of condensed cream of mushroom soup with ⅓ c. milk and a pinch of herbs added.

BUTTER-BROWNED PEANUT SANDWICHES: Make sandwiches with peanut butter and raisin bread. Spread outside of sandwiches (both sides) with soft butter or margarine. Brown in heavy skillet.

WOMEN'S LUNCHEON SANDWICHES

Main-dish sandwich. To simplify, bake corn bread in advance

1 (10 oz.) pkg. corn-bread mix
6 thin slices baked ham
6 slices Swiss cheese
2 tblsp. flour
½ c. water
½ tsp. instant onion flakes
¼ tsp. salt
1 (8 oz.) can tomato sauce

Prepare batter of corn bread as directed on package. Spread in foil pan in mix package; bake in hot oven (425°) 20 minutes. Cool. Open corner folder of pan for easy cutting. Cut corn bread in 3 pieces, lengthwise. Then cut in half, making 6 finger-shaped pieces. Split each finger crosswise in halves.

Roll slices of ham in thirds and put with slices of cheese in fingers of corn bread to make 6 sandwiches. Fasten with toothpicks.

Bake on ungreased baking sheet in hot oven (400°) until cheese melts, about 10 minutes.

Meanwhile, make smooth paste of flour and water. Add onion flakes, salt and tomato sauce. Cook, stirring constantly until mixture thickens. Serve sauce over hot sandwiches. Makes 6 servings.

Friday Sandwiches

GLAZED CRAB SANDWICHES

Delicious for an evening-company snack or a family supper. You can stir up the crab mixture in advance

1 c. crab meat or 1 (7 ½ oz.) can
2 tblsp. chopped green onion
1 tblsp. lemon juice
2 tblsp. ketchup or chili sauce
6 slices toast
½ c. mayonnaise
¼ c. grated Cheddar cheese

Combine crab, onion, lemon juice

and ketchup; mix well. Spread mixture on toast slices.

Frost top of each sandwich with mayonnaise and cheese, mixed together.

Run under broiler a few minutes or until crab mixture is heated and glazed by topping. Makes 6 sandwiches.

Variations: Put a thin slice of tomato on each slice of toast before adding crab mixture. Or top crab on each sandwich with 2 slices of avocado before adding the mayonnaise and cheese.

SKILLET TUNA SANDWICHES

Try these for supper—you brown them quickly in a skillet

1 (6½ oz.) can flaked tuna
¼ c. chopped celery
3 tblsp. mayonnaise
2 tsp. lemon juice
1 tsp. finely chopped onion
8 slices bread
1 to 2 tblsp. shortening or salad oil
2 eggs
½ tsp. salt
½ c. milk

Drain tuna and empty into bowl. Add celery, mayonnaise, lemon juice and onion. Mix with fork. Spread on 4 slices bread; top each with another slice of bread. Cut each sandwich in half to make triangles.

Heat shortening over medium heat in large skillet.

Beat eggs; add salt and milk; mix. With slotted pancake turner, dip one side of each sandwich in egg mixture. Turn, and dip second side; place in hot skillet. Brown quickly. Turn and brown other side (quick browning makes the best sandwiches). Serve immediately. Makes 8 sandwiches.

TUNA-CHEESE BUNS

Serve for a hurry-up supper, and your reputation as a good cook will go up

1 (9¼ oz.) can tuna
5 hard-cooked eggs, chopped
3 tblsp. sweet pickle relish
2 tblsp. chopped onion
1 tsp. seasoned salt
½ c. mayonnaise
1 (8 oz.) pkg. sliced process American cheese
8 long buns, split and buttered

Combine tuna, eggs, pickle relish, onion, salt and mayonnaise. Spread between split buns. Cut each cheese slice in half. Put 2 halves, end to end, in bun on top of tuna filling.

Place buns on large sheet of foil and wrap. Arrange on baking sheet.

Bake in moderate oven (350°) 20 minutes. Makes 8 servings.

Note: You can make and wrap sandwiches in advance and store in refrigerator to heat just before serving. Bake chilled sandwiches 25 minutes.

TUNA-CHEESE SANDWICHES

Especially tasty when made with whole-wheat bread

2 tsp. lemon juice
1 (3¼ oz.) can tuna, drained and flaked
1 (12 oz.) carton onion-chive cottage cheese
14 slices buttered bread
Lettuce

Sprinkle lemon juice on tuna (finely flaked) and toss lightly. Gently stir in cottage cheese.

Spread tuna-cheese mixture over 7 bread slices. Top with lettuce leaves and remaining bread slices. Makes 7 sandwiches.

Variation: Use plain cottage cheese instead of onion-chive cottage cheese and add 1 tblsp. finely chopped onion.

Chicken and Turkey Sandwiches

SAUCY CHICKEN-CHEESE SANDWICH

Couldn't be easier and it's delicious

- 1 can condensed cream of chicken soup
- ⅓ c. milk
- ⅓ c. shredded sharp Cheddar cheese
- 1 (5 to 6 oz.) can chicken, cubed, or ⅔ c. cooked cubed chicken
- 1 (14½ oz.) can cut asparagus, drained
- 6 slices toast

Blend soup and milk in saucepan. Add cheese, chicken and asparagus. Heat until cheese is melted, stirring occasionally.

Serve over toast. Makes 6 servings.

Note: Add ¼ c. sliced pimiento-stuffed green olives for additional flavor and color.

FRENCHED CHICKEN SANDWICH

The best reason to hope there will be left-over chicken in the freezer

- 1 egg, beaten
- 2 tblsp. milk
- 4 slices bread, day old
- 8 slices cooked chicken
- 1 can condensed cream of chicken soup

Blend together egg and milk.

Cut bread slices diagonally. Dip in milk-egg mixture. Brown lightly on both sides in small amount of hot fat in heavy skillet. Arrange in baking pan.

Cover with chicken. Pour on soup. Bake in moderate oven (375°) 20 minutes. Makes 4 servings.

GRILLED TURKEY SANDWICH

Melted cheese bubbles atop turkey and spicy ham on bread

- 8 slices bread
- 1 (4½ oz.) can deviled ham
- 8 to 12 slices cooked turkey
- 8 slices process American cheese (8 oz. pkg.)

Toast bread lightly on one side under broiler. Turn over and spread untoasted side with deviled ham. Cover with turkey; top with cheese slice.

Broil until cheese is delicately browned and bubbly. Serve hot. Makes 8 sandwiches.

TURKEY AND GRAVY SANDWICH

No left-over gravy? Open a can

- 6 slices buttered toast
- 6 thick slices cooked turkey
- 2 (10¾ oz.) cans chicken gravy

Lay turkey slices on toast. Heat gravy and spoon over turkey. Serve at once with buttered asparagus or Mexicorn. Makes 6 open-faced sandwiches.

Knife and Fork Sandwiches

A fast-fix, hearty sandwich that's almost a meal in itself comes in handy. Serve it with hot coffee or tea to a hungry man who arrives too late for supper. Have it for lunch at noon or any time of the day. It satisfies.

These substantial, invitingly thick sandwiches are favorite fare in Denmark. You can borrow the Danish way of stacking tempting foods on buttered bread slices, using favorite American foods. You need no recipes. Just look in your refrigerator and freezer for tasty tidbits and left-overs.

The next three open-faced sandwiches, made in our Countryside Kitchens, are typical examples, but you need not follow the recipes to the letter to get good results. They are not the finger kind and neither are they dainty. Serve them with knives and forks. You will find they are eye-catching and that they appease lively appetites. Each sandwich is pretty as a picture.

COMPANY SANDWICH: Spread rye bread with butter. On right side of each slice, lay two cheese slices; on left side of same slice, pile your favorite potato salad. Top cheese with crisp bacon slices; add cheerful topknot of red-ripe tomato slices to potato salad.

HAWAIIAN FAVORITE: Cover buttered white bread with two or three layers of sliced corned beef. Mix crushed pineapple with cottage cheese; spread on top. Garnish with thin carrot curls.

SOUTHERN SPECIAL: Spread buttered whole wheat bread with thin layer of peanut butter. Cover with slices of ham, then chicken or turkey. Mix hard-cooked eggs, cubed, with mayonnaise, salt, pepper, pimiento and parsley. Spread over meat. Top with thin, unpeeled cucumber slices, sliced pickles or olives.

CHAPTER 6

VEGETABLES

The past and the present meet harmoniously in this chapter. Grandmother's garden peas in cream and her thick tomato slices spread with heavy cream share honors with frozen and canned vegetables.

Among the hundreds of short-cut vegetable recipes sorted out by FARM JOURNAL readers for their ease of preparation and their tastiness, potatoes and canned baked beans received the most mention, with green beans coming in third. Corn and tomatoes were next in line.

You will find three ways to make French-fried potatoes, for example. And if you help plan church and community suppers, you will want to profit from the experience of a group of Minnesota farm women. They find packaged mashed potatoes not only convenient and economical, but much praised when served hot. We tell you how they do it.

Favorite baked-bean dishes are on the sweet side. Be sure to note the Boston Baked Beans from the New England kitchen of a busy woman famed in her neighborhood for baked-bean suppers. Canned beans are laced with maple syrup.

Luck is on the busy woman's side in preparing fresh vegetables. They are most delicious cooked a few minutes and only until tender-crisp—tender, but never soft. And on farms people pick vegetables young, when they cook fastest and taste their succulent best.

Canned vegetables are quick cookers. Often a touch of seasoning and speedy heating do the trick. Some of them come seasoned and pep up other foods as quickly as you pour out the contents. Many of the best short-cut cooks use canned soups to season and sauce their vegetable dishes—they are a favorite short-cut ingredient.

Country Vegetable Alphabet

Tasty and quick from A to Z

Many country cooks find that color-bright vegetables boost their cooking fame. They substitute imagination for time and come up with tempting dishes. The recipes that follow show how they do it.

ASPARAGUS WITH BACON

Old country saying: run to house after cutting asparagus and cook it pronto

24 asparagus stalks
1 c. dairy sour cream
¼ c. mayonnaise
1 tblsp. lemon juice
4 slices toast
¼ c. crisp bacon, crumbled

Cook tender part of stalks, scales removed if sandy, in just enough salted water to cover, until tender, about 15 minutes.

Meanwhile combine sour cream, mayonnaise and lemon juice.

Drain asparagus and arrange on toast. Top with cream mixture. Run under broiler until top bubbles. Scatter bacon on top; serve. Makes 4 servings.

Variation: Substitute Speedy Cheese Sauce (see Index) for the cream-mayonnaise mixture.

Note: Country cooks believe thin asparagus stalks are more tasty than thick ones—that they cook more quickly.

NEW-STYLE CREAMED ASPARAGUS

Run it in the oven to cook without a bit of attention

1 can condensed cream of mushroom soup
½ c. milk
2 (1 lb.) cans whole asparagus, drained
⅔ c. cheese-cracker crumbs
1 tblsp. butter

Blend together soup and milk in saucepan. Heat to boiling.

Place half of asparagus in bottom of greased 1½ qt. casserole. Top with half of soup and cracker crumbs. Repeat layers. Dot with butter.

Bake in moderate oven (350°) 20 minutes. Makes 6 to 8 servings.

CREAMED ASPARAGUS ON TOAST

Off-the-shelf dish gives a spring touch to meals the year round

1 can condensed cream of asparagus soup
¼ c. milk
1 (14½ oz.) can cut asparagus
4 slices toast

Combine soup and milk in saucepan. Add asparagus and heat. Serve on toast. Makes 4 servings.

Note: If you have hard-cooked eggs in refrigerator, garnish servings with egg slices. For a heartier dish, lay cheese slices on toast before spooning on hot asparagus.

ASPARAGUS WITH HERBS: Cook 2 (10 oz.) pkgs. frozen asparagus as directed on package. Drain. Meanwhile cream ¼ c. butter; add a dash each of rosemary and thyme. Blend in juice of ½ lemon. Serve on the hot asparagus. Makes 4 to 6 servings.

BEETS IN CREAM: Heat 24 small canned or cooked beets, drained. Season with salt and add 1 c. dairy sour cream to hot beets. Serve at once. Makes 6 servings.

GREEN BEANS—18 WAYS

TO COOK GREEN BEANS: Place 2 lbs. beans in kettle containing ½″ to 1″ boiling salted water (¾ tsp. salt to 2 c. water) with 1 tsp. sugar added. Cook, covered, until barely tender, 10 to 30 minutes. Usually much of the water evaporates in cooking, but if it doesn't, cook it down to 2 or 3 tablespoonfuls after the beans have been removed from the kettle. Add to beans. Makes 6 to 7 cups, or 6 servings.

Let imagination be your guide in seasoning. Here are 17 ways to dress up the cooked beans; 1 for raw beans.

PLAIN BUTTERED: Add ¼ to ½ c. melted butter.

DEVILED: Add 2 tsp. prepared mustard mixed with ¼ to ½ c. butter.

WITH MUSHROOMS: Sauté 1 (3 oz.) can chopped mushrooms (or ½ c. fresh mushrooms) in ½ c. melted butter.

WITH BACON AND ONIONS: Sauté 4 cut-up bacon slices with 3 tblsp. chopped onion until bacon is crisp and onion is soft.

WITH BACON AND PEPPER: Add ¼ to ½ c. bacon drippings and 1 small red-pepper pod; top with ½ c. crumbled crisp bacon. Or cook beans as directed, adding 6 slices bacon cut up, and 1 small red-pepper pod.

WITH ALMONDS: Lightly sauté ½ c. blanched, slivered almonds (or pecans or Brazil nuts) in ¼ to ½ c. butter.

WITH BREAD CRUMBS: Sauté ½ c. bread crumbs in ½ c. butter until delicately browned.

WITH SAVORY: Add ½ tsp. dried summer savory or a few leaves of the fresh savory (known in Europe as the "bean herb") to ¼ to ½ c. butter.

WITH WATER CHESTNUTS: Add ½ c. thinly sliced water chestnuts (canned) to ¼ to ½ c. butter.

WITH CHEESE: Sprinkle hot, buttered beans liberally with grated cheese.

WITH CHEESE SAUCE: Pour your favorite cheese sauce over beans.

WITH EGGS: Put 2 hard-cooked egg yolks through sieve. Add ¼ c. soft butter, 1½ tblsp. lemon juice and salt to taste. Beat with electric mixer or rotary beater until fluffy. Serve on hot beans.

WITH MUSHROOM SAUCE: Heat cream of mushroom soup, thinned with milk as you like it. Pour over beans.

WITH QUICK HOLLANDAISE: Blend 2 tblsp. hot water into ½ c. mayonnaise in measuring cup. Set cup in hot water to heat sauce, stirring occasionally. Spoon sauce on hot beans.

IN BROILER: Place cooked beans in broiler pan. Broil ham slices on rack above. Drippings season beans.

BUNDLES: Cook small whole beans and season as you like. Arrange in bundles with band of pimiento over each. Or circle beans with lemon rings. (Save lemons after juice is extracted and cut in slices.) Garnish platter of meat or chicken with bundles.

SALAD: Add 1 tsp. prepared horse-radish to ½ c. French dressing and 3 tblsp. chopped onion. Add to hot beans; cool, cover and chill several hours. Serve on 6 lettuce-lined salad plates; garnish with hard-cooked egg slices and white or red onion rings.

ORIENTAL: Add raw beans to ¼ c. butter or margarine melted in a heavy skillet. Add ¼ c. water, salt and pepper. Cover and cook on high heat until they steam. Then reduce heat and cook slowly 20 to 25 minutes. Add more water during the cooking if necessary to prevent burning. When crisp-tender, add ½ c. light cream.

ELEGANT GREEN BEANS

Bake this along with your oven meal

2 (1 lb.) cans green beans, drained
1 can condensed cream of mushroom soup
½ c. grated Cheddar cheese

Combine beans and soup. Place in greased 1½ qt. casserole. Top with cheese.

Bake in moderate oven (350°) 30 minutes. Makes 6 to 8 servings.

TANGY GREEN BEANS

Gives an early summer taste to canned beans. Good with steaks

1 tblsp. butter or margarine
1 tsp. vinegar
1 tblsp. crumbled blue cheese
1 (1 lb.) can green beans

Melt butter and add vinegar and cheese. Heat, stirring, to melt cheese.

Heat beans; drain. Pour cheese mixture over beans and toss lightly. Makes 4 servings.

CREOLE BEANS

Seasoned expertly in a jiffy with stewed tomatoes and soup mix

8 slices bacon
2 (1lb.) cans green beans
1 tblsp. onion-soup mix
1 (1 lb.) can stewed tomatoes
1 tsp. sugar

Sauté bacon until crisp; drain on paper toweling. Pour off all but 3 tblsp. drippings.

Empty beans carefully into skillet; add onion-soup mix; heat thoroughly.

Snip bacon into small pieces; add half to beans; also add stewed tomatoes and sugar. Top with remaining bacon. Makes 8 servings.

PEPPY GREEN BEANS: Heat canned green beans in their own liquid; drain. Serve topped with whipped cream, unsweetened, with prepared horse-radish folded in. Taste for salt.

PIMIENTO GREEN BEANS

Salad dressing gives a tangy taste—pimiento adds flashes of color

2 (10 oz.) pkgs. frozen green beans
½ c. French or Italian salad dressing
1 pimiento, chopped
¼ tsp. salt

Cook beans as directed on package. Drain; add pimiento and salt. Toss to mix and serve piping hot. Makes 6 servings.

SOUTHWESTERN BEANS: Cook a little diced bacon and chopped onion in a heavy skillet until bacon is crisp and onions are soft. Toss into hot canned, or cooked fresh, or frozen green beans, drained. Serve at once.

ITALIAN GREEN BEANS WITH SOUR CREAM

To add to your collection of first-rate bean dishes. It's unusual and good

3 (9 oz.) pkgs. frozen Italian green beans
1 (3½ oz.) can mushroom pieces
¼ c. sliced green onion
2 tblsp. butter or margarine
2 tblsp. flour
½ tsp. salt
1 c. dairy sour cream
Pimiento (optional)

Cook green beans as directed on package; drain.

Drain mushrooms, reserving liquid.

Cook mushrooms and onion in melted butter 1 minute. Stir in flour and salt. Add mushroom liquid and sour cream and heat to boiling, but do not boil.

Add cream mixture to green beans and toss gently. Serve hot, garnished with pimiento strips. Makes 8 servings.

Note: You can prepare this dish in advance. Store it in refrigerator in a 2 qt. casserole. Heat, covered, in moderate oven (350°) just until hot, about 20 to 30 minutes. You can substitute regular green beans for the broad Italian ones.

Smart Country Cooks Say:

"If you have green beans in your garden, cook small ones when you are in a hurry. Cook them whole in salted water–no breaking, chopping or cutting into short lengths. Serve them buttered. For special occasions, delicately brown ¼ c. slivered almonds (you can buy them slivered) in the melted butter and pour over the hot beans. Or serve the hot, crisp-tender baby green beans with cheese sauce."

BROCCOLI CASSEROLE

Easy way to glamorize broccoli

1 (12 oz.) pkg. frozen broccoli
1 can condensed cream of celery soup
⅔ c. shredded Cheddar cheese
2 slices bread
2 tblsp. butter or margarine, melted

Cook broccoli as directed on package until barely tender. Place in greased 1 qt. casserole. Top with soup, then cheese. Quickly tear bread in tiny pieces, toss in melted butter and sprinkle over top.

Bake in moderate oven (350°) 30 minutes. Makes 4 to 5 servings.

Variations: Substitute green beans, lima beans, cauliflower or asparagus for broccoli.

CALIFORNIA BROCCOLI

Slitting the stems speeds cooking

2 lbs. fresh broccoli
½ c. mayonnaise
2 tblsp. tarragon vinegar
2 hard-cooked eggs, cut fine

Wash broccoli and trim off ends from stems. Cut stems lengthwise almost to the florets. (Stems will cook almost as quickly as florets.) Drop into a small amount of boiling salted water.

Cover and cook until just tender, 12 to 15 minutes. Drain.

Meanwhile heat mayonnaise in double boiler with vinegar and eggs. Serve broccoli topped with mayonnaise mixture. Makes 6 servings.

Note: Another way to cook broccoli quickly is to chop it before dropping it into the boiling salted water.

BROCCOLI TWO WAYS: Cook the flower heads for one meal. Serve with Brown Butter-Crumb Sauce (see Index). For a second meal, slice the stems very thin diagonally. Cook in salted water no longer than 5 minutes. Drain and serve with melted butter or sour cream.

BUTTERED CABBAGE: Cook 1 lb. shredded cabbage in ½ c. water, 3 tblsp. butter or margarine added, until water is absorbed, 5 to 7 minutes. Season with salt, pepper and 1 tsp. caraway seeds, lightly crushed.

CABBAGE CASSEROLE

Take it directly from oven to table

1 medium head cabbage, shredded
2 c. diced ham
1 can condensed cream of mushroom soup
½ c. milk
⅓ c. buttered bread crumbs

Steam cabbage in covered saucepan with small amount of water until tender-crisp. Drain if necessary.

Arrange cabbage and ham in alternate layers in greased 2 qt. casserole.

Blend soup and milk; pour over cabbage-ham mixture. Top with crumbs.

Bake in moderate oven (350°) 30 minutes. Makes 8 servings.

CREAMY CABBAGE

Cooks in less than 10 minutes

1 medium head cabbage
½ c. butter or margarine
½ c. light cream or evaporated milk
½ tsp. salt
¼ tsp. caraway seeds

Shred cabbage. Melt butter in skillet; add cabbage and cook, covered, 5 minutes.

Pour in cream; add salt and caraway seeds. Heat 3 or 4 minutes longer. Makes 6 servings.

SWEDISH CABBAGE: Cook 1 lb. cabbage, shredded, in salted water to cover 5 minutes. Drain and add 3 tblsp. butter, 1 tsp. lemon juice and 2 tsp. dill weed. Makes 6 servings.

CAULIFLOWER WITH SOUR CREAM: Quick cooking makes for superior flavor. Boil cauliflower florets in salted water about 10 minutes. Drain and add dairy sour cream with chopped chives.

PRONTO SAUCY CAULIFLOWER: Cook cauliflower florets in boiling salted water until barely tender, 8 to 10 minutes. Drain. Pour in enough heavy cream to cover bottom of saucepan.

Break sliced process American cheese over the top. Cover and let stand a few minutes or until cheese is melted.

CARROTS AND ONIONS ON TOAST

Cook double the usual batch of carrots —heat the left-over half like this

6 to 10 carrots (1 ½ to 2 lbs.)
1 (8 oz.) can whole cooked onions
⅓ c. milk
1 can condensed cream of celery soup
12 bread slices
Butter or margarine

Scrape carrots and cut in thin slices. Cook in 1" boiling salted water (½ tsp. salt to 1 c. water) 15 minutes.

Add onions; heat. Drain. Add milk and soup. Stir carefully; bring to boiling point. Season.

Toast bread; butter.

Heap carrots and onions on toast. Makes 6 servings.

HASTY CREAMED CARROTS

Creamed carrots the fastest way! Try them—they're delicious

6 to 10 carrots (1 ½ to 2 lbs.)
2 c. water
1 tsp. salt
½ c. dairy sour or sweet cream
½ c. chopped parsley or chives

Peel carrots; cut them into thin lengthwise slices, using vegetable peeler or slicer.

Bring water and salt to boil; add carrots; cover and cook 5 to 7 minutes, just until they are tender-crisp. Drain.

Slowly stir in cream and parsley. (Parsley snips quickly with kitchen scissors.) Makes 6 servings.

Variation: Season cooked, shaved carrots with butter and a pinch of dill weed (not seeds). Add a few drops of lemon juice to accent the flavor.

SKILLET CARROTS AND ONIONS

Key to superior flavor is the carrot-onion combination

2 to 3 tblsp. butter or margarine
4 c. sliced raw carrots (⅛" slices)
2 c. sliced onions
1 tsp. salt
¼ tsp. pepper

Melt butter in heavy skillet; add carrots and onions. Season with salt and pepper. Brown slowly on one side, then turn and brown other side. Do not cover. Makes 6 servings.

WHIPPED CARROTS AND POTATOES

Gay golden frame for green limas, peas or chopped broccoli

3 lbs. carrots, peeled and cut up (about 12 c.)
¾ tsp. salt
⅛ tsp. pepper
3 tblsp. light cream
½ pkg. instant mashed potatoes

Cook carrots in boiling salted water to cover, until soft enough to mash.

Drain and mash slightly; then whip in salt, pepper and cream.

Prepare potatoes according to package directions; whip into mashed carrots. Makes 8 servings.

more

Note: For an attractive serving, drop a ring of whipped carrots (or carrots and potatoes) on plate and fill with hot buttered peas or with buttered green lima beans (frozen, cooked as directed on package) with a few tiny pickled onions, drained, added.

Have a Head Start with Canned Baked Beans

Some of the great American dishes depend on long, slow cooking to maintain their fame. Boston Baked Beans is a classic example.

The New England woman who gave us her short-cut recipe for baking the brown beauties often serves them to company. Frequently a guest exclaims, "One reason we like to come to your house for bean suppers is that you bake beans the good, old-fashioned way." Clever hostess that she is, she keeps the secret—she doesn't want to dampen the enthusiasm of her guests.

She neither soaks the beans overnight nor cooks them slowly for eight hours. Here's how she does it.

BOSTON BAKED BEANS

Use this jet-age way to cut baking time from 8 to 3 hours

2 (1 lb. 11 oz.) jars New England-style baked beans
½ c. maple blended syrup, or maple syrup

Combine beans and syrup in 2 qt. bean pot or casserole.

Bake in slow oven (325°) 3 hours. Makes 8 servings.

Note: To cut the baking time in two, heat the beans, with syrup added, to the boiling point before pouring into the bean pot. If you have a freezer, double or triple this recipe; bake and freeze the extra supply of beans.

BEANS WITH DEVILED HAM

These beans have a subtle, spicy taste —extra fine with mustard pickles

2 (1 lb.) cans New England-style pork and beans
2 (4½ oz.) cans deviled ham
⅛ tsp. ground cloves

Place beans in saucepan over moderate heat. Blend ham and cloves thoroughly through beans. Heat about 10 minutes, stirring occasionally. Makes 6 to 8 servings.

DOUBLE-QUICK BEAN BAKE

Takes 15 minutes to fix them

1 (1 lb. 5 oz.) can pork and beans
1 tblsp. instant minced onion
¼ c. ketchup
2 drops Tabasco sauce
2 tblsp. brown sugar
½ tsp. salt
½ tsp. dry mustard

Combine all ingredients in saucepan. Bring to a boil and simmer 10 minutes. Makes 4 servings.

BAKED BEANS WITH PINEAPPLE

Pineapple and bean flavors make this dish distinctive and appetizing

2 (1 lb.) cans pork and beans
1 (8¾ oz.) can pineapple tidbits, drained

½ c. ketchup
½ c. brown sugar
1 tsp. dry mustard
2 bacon slices

Combine beans, pineapple, ketchup, brown sugar and mustard in saucepan. Simmer 30 minutes, stirring occasionally, to cook down liquid.

Pour into greased 1½ qt. casserole. Top with bacon. Bake in moderate oven (350°) 30 minutes. Makes 6 servings.

BAKED KIDNEY BEANS

Requires no attention while it bakes, gets plenty at mealtime

2 (1 lb.) cans red kidney beans
1 large onion, chopped fine
½ c. ketchup
3 tblsp. brown sugar
2 slices bacon

Combine beans, onion, ketchup and sugar in greased 2 qt. casserole. Top with bacon.

Bake in hot oven (400°) 1¼ hours. Makes 6 servings.

Note: Substitute 1 or 2 (⅕ oz.) packages instant minced onion for chopped onion and bake beans 1 hour.

IOWA CORN ON THE COB

An Iowa woman says, "Most good cooks in our neighborhood rush the corn from the garden, husk it; use a dry vegetable brush to handle the stubborn silk, and drop the ears into boiling water to cover. They cook it 8 minutes—never more than 10. But I get more praise from folks around the table when I cover the corn with cold water; bring it to a boil—then drain the steaming ears and serve them at once. No smart country cook around here adds salt to the water when cooking sweet corn. It toughens the kernels."

CORN DELICIOUS

Open three cans, add cream and heat

2 (12 oz.) cans whole kernel corn
1 (3½ oz.) can French-fried onions
¼ c. light cream

Heat corn; stir in onions and cream. Heat 2 minutes longer and serve immediately. (Onions become soggy if they wait.) Makes 6 to 8 servings.

CREAMY CHEESE-CORN BAKE

Fine choice for an oven meal

1 egg, beaten
1 (1 lb.) can cream-style corn
½ c. tiny cubes process American cheese

Combine egg, corn and cheese. Pour in greased 1 qt. casserole.

Bake in moderate oven (350°) until cheese is melted, about 30 minutes. Makes 5 servings.

ROASTED CORN

IN FOIL: Spread husked ear of corn with butter and wrap securely with foil. Roast over embers, 15 to 25 minutes, or in hot oven (400°) 15 to 30 minutes (time varies with size of ears). Turn ears several times while cooking.

BAKED LIMA BEANS

Good travelers to community meals—the smoky taste adds interest

3 (10 oz.) pkgs. frozen lima beans
6 bacon slices, cut in ½" pieces
½ c. chopped onion
⅔ c. molasses
¾ c. ketchup
½ c. water
2 tblsp. prepared mustard
¾ tsp. salt
¾ tsp. smoke salt
¼ tsp. pepper

Cook beans as directed on package until barely tender; drain.

Pan-fry bacon in skillet until partly cooked. Add onion and continue cooking until bacon is browned.

Mix together molasses, ketchup, water, mustard, salts and pepper in a 2 qt. casserole. Stir in beans, bacon and onion with bacon drippings.

Bake in moderate oven (350°) 1 hour. Makes 8 servings.

Note: The beans are quite sweet. Reduce amount of molasses if you want less sweetening. For a peppy note, add 1 tblsp. prepared horse-radish with the seasonings.

LIMA BEANS WITH CELERY

Drop-in bouillon cubes provide quick, intriguing seasoning

2 chicken bouillon cubes
1 (1 lb.) can green lima beans
1 c. sliced celery
2 tblsp. butter or margarine

Place bouillon cubes, liquid drained from lima beans and celery in saucepan. Cook, covered, until celery is almost tender. Stir once to help dissolve bouillon cubes.

Add limas and butter. Mix and heat. Makes 5 servings.

SPANISH LIMAS

Frozen limas and canned tomatoes combine to make this quick, hearty dish

1 medium onion, chopped
1 chopped green pepper
2 tblsp. butter or margarine
1 c. cooked or canned tomatoes
1 tsp. Worcestershire sauce
1 tsp. salt
¼ tsp. pepper
⅛ tsp. cayenne pepper
2 c. cooked frozen or canned lima beans
1 ½ c. grated process American cheese

Fry onion and pepper slowly in butter until golden. Add tomatoes; simmer 10 minutes. Add seasonings and well-drained beans.

Alternate layers of bean mixture and cheese in greased 1 qt. casserole.

Bake in moderate oven (350°) 30 minutes. Makes 6 servings.

WONDERFUL LIMA BEANS

A dish that waits patiently if family or guests are late to dinner

1 (10 oz.) pkg. frozen lima beans
2 tblsp. butter or margarine
1 tblsp. instant parsley flakes
1 tblsp. instant minced green onion, or 1 medium onion, chopped
½ tsp. sugar

1 tsp. lemon juice
⅛ tsp. pepper

Cook beans as directed on package; drain. Add remaining ingredients and cook over low heat until butter melts. Makes 4 servings.

OKRA AND TOMATOES

Choose firm tomatoes, small, tender okra for this quick-cooking dish

3 c. okra, cut in rounds
¼ c. butter or margarine
3 c. tomatoes, peeled and cut in wedges or chopped
¾ c. onion slices
2 tsp. salt
¼ tsp. pepper

Sauté okra in butter until tender.

Add remaining ingredients and simmer gently, covered, 5 minutes. (Don't overcook.) Makes 6 servings.

Variation: Use green tomatoes instead of ripe ones.

Onion Tips from a Smart Country Cook

SPEEDY ONION JUICE: Cut a slice from a peeled onion. Scrape cut-onion surface with a knife. Cut a second slice and repeat. When you have enough onion juice, place slices in a plastic bag, close tightly and refrigerate to use in stew, over the pot roast or in any dish you wish to season with onion. Good cooks know the flavor magic of adding a few drops of onion juice to fruit salads, cottage cheese, tomato juice and many other foods.

GREEN ONIONS ON TOAST: Trim and cook small green onions in a little salted water until tender, about 12 minutes. Drain and serve on buttered toast. Spoon over cheese sauce.

CURRIED ONIONS

Especially good with pork or chicken —canned onions speed the cooking

2 (1 lb.) cans onions, drained
1 can condensed cream of chicken soup
2 tblsp. mayonnaise
¼ tsp. curry powder
½ c. cracker crumbs
2 tblsp. butter or margarine, melted
2 tblsp. parsley flakes

Place onions in greased 1½ qt. casserole. Combine soup, mayonnaise and curry powder. Spoon over onions. Top with crumbs tossed in butter and parsley.

Bake in moderate oven (375°) until hot and bubbly, about 30 minutes. Makes 8 servings.

NEW PEAS IN CREAM

A FARM JOURNAL *master recipe*

4 c. peas, shelled
2 tsp. sugar
2 tsp. salt
Pea pods
1 small green onion with top, chopped
Water
2 tblsp. butter
½ tsp. pepper
1 c. light cream

Cook peas with sugar, salt, 5 or 6 pea pods, onion and enough water to cover for 10 to 15 minutes, or until just tender (water should almost evaporate). Add butter and hold over heat to melt. Add pepper and cream. Heat but do not cook. Makes 6 servings.

NEW PEAS, 12 WAYS

WITH MINT: Cook 2 or 3 fresh mint leaves with the peas.

WITH MINT JELLY: Omit sugar and add 3 to 4 tblsp. mint jelly to peas with butter. Hold over heat to melt. Add pepper and cream and heat to warm.

WITH PIMIENTO: Add ¼ c. chopped pimiento to peas just before adding cream.

WITH SOUR CREAM AND CHIVES: Add 3 tblsp. chives, chopped, to peas before buttering. Then add 1 c. dairy sour cream instead of light cream and heat to warm; do not cook.

WITH POTATOES: Cook 12 small new whole potatoes until just tender. Mix with peas before adding cream.

WITH MUSHROOMS: Sauté 1 c. canned sliced mushrooms in 1 tblsp. butter. Mix with peas before adding cream.

WITH ONIONS: Cook 1 c. small green onions, sliced (use tops, too), until just tender. Add to peas before buttering.

WITH CARROTS: Cook 1½ c. thinly sliced carrots until just tender. Add to peas before buttering.

WITH CELERY: Cook ¼ c. chopped celery in small amount of water until tender. Add to peas before buttering.

WITH BACON: Sprinkle ½ c. finely crumbled bacon over top of peas just before serving.

WITH HAM: Cut ham slices (boiled or baked) in thin strips 1″ in length. Mix with peas just before serving.

WITH LETTUCE LEAVES: Line saucepan with several leaves of leaf lettuce, wet from washing. In center place peas, salt, pepper, sugar, tops of small green onions and 3 or 4 tblsp. water. Cover and cook until tender. Discard lettuce; season peas with cream.

NEW-POTATO CASSEROLE

Quick dress-up for new potatoes

24 small new potatoes
2 cans condensed cream of chicken soup
1 c. grated process American cheese

Cook potatoes; peel. Place in greased 2 qt. casserole. Pour soup over potatoes; sprinkle with cheese.

Bake in hot oven (400°) about 15 minutes. Makes 8 servings.

POTATOES CHANTILLY

Puffed up and brown—fit for a king—you skip peeling and mashing of spuds

1 pkg. instant mashed potatoes
1 c. heavy cream
½ c. grated sharp cheese
Salt and pepper to taste

Prepare potatoes as directed on package; place in greased shallow baking dish.

Whip cream; fold in cheese. Season with salt, pepper. Spread over potatoes.

Bake in moderate oven (350°) until golden, about 20 minutes. Serve immediately. Makes 8 servings.

POTATO-CHEESE BALLS

Potatoes with a surprise—you can refrigerate them ready for baking

- ½ pkg. instant mashed potatoes
- 6 (½") cubes process American cheese
- 2 tblsp. butter or margarine
- ½ c. corn flake crumbs

Prepare potatoes as directed on package. Divide into 6 equal portions. Put a cheese cube in each portion of potatoes and form ball around it.

Melt butter in skillet. Roll potato balls in butter, then in crumbs. Bake in skillet or greased shallow pan in hot oven (400°) 15 minutes, or until browned. Makes 6 servings.

Note: You can get potato balls ready for baking and refrigerate them. Bake 5 minutes longer.

BAKED CREAMED POTATOES

Boil potatoes for two meals at a time. Make these the second day

- 1 c. dairy sour cream
- ½ c. milk
- 1 tblsp. instant minced onion
- 1 tsp. instant parsley flakes
- 1 tsp. salt
- ⅛ tsp. pepper
- 5 c. sliced cooked potatoes (5 or 6 medium potatoes)
- ½ c. grated Cheddar cheese

Mix together sour cream, milk, onion, parsley, salt and pepper. Place half the potatoes in a greased baking dish (10" × 6" × 1½"). Top with half the sauce. Repeat layers. Sprinkle cheese over the top.

Bake in moderate oven (350°) 20 to 25 minutes. Makes 6 servings.

HERB POTATO CHIPS

Snacks that are decidedly different

- 1 (7 oz.) pkg. potato chips
- ¼ c. grated Parmesan cheese
- Orégano

Spread potato chips in shallow baking pan. Sprinkle with cheese and dust lightly with orégano. Bake in moderate oven (350°) 5 minutes. Makes about 12 servings.

Note: Instead of orégano, you may use a touch of mixed salad herbs, thyme, dill or curry powder.

OVEN-ROASTED POTATOES

Convenient to fix for an oven meal—no watching needed as they cook

- ½ c. butter
- 6 or 8 medium potatoes, peeled
- ½ tsp. salt
- Dash pepper
- 1 tsp. paprika
- 2 tsp. chopped parsley

Place butter in a shallow pan (13" × 9" × 2"). Put in moderate oven (350°) until butter is melted.

Roll potatoes in butter. Sprinkle with salt and pepper. Cover pan tightly with foil. Return to oven and bake 1¼ hours.

Put potatoes in serving dish and pour over butter from baking pan. Sprinkle with paprika and parsley if desired. Makes 6 servings.

more

Note: If dinner is delayed, remove foil. Continue baking up to 30 minutes longer; the potatoes brown attractively.

BROILED POTATO SLICES

Takes 15 minutes to fix these spuds

3 medium potatoes
⅓ c. salad oil
½ tsp. salt
Paprika

Scrub potatoes, but do not peel. Cut into ¼″ crosswise slices. Dip slices in oil and place one-layer deep on broiler rack. Season with salt and dust with paprika.

Broil until potatoes are golden brown, about 7 minutes. Turn and continue broiling until brown. Serve hot. Makes 4 servings.

Note: The size of your broiling pan is the limiting factor in the quantity of potatoes you can fix this speedy way. If you have more than four people to feed, you may find Oven-fried Potato Slices (see next column) the solution.

CHEESE FRENCH FRIES

Everyday French fries become worthy of teaming with your finest steaks

2 (9 oz.) pkgs. frozen French-fried potatoes
1 tsp. onion salt
¼ tsp. paprika
⅓ c. grated Parmesan cheese

Place potatoes in shallow baking pan. Sprinkle with onion salt and paprika. Bake as directed on package.

Sprinkle with cheese, shaking pan to coat potatoes evenly. Makes 6 servings.

CHURCH-SUPPER POTATOES: A group of Minnesota church women use packaged instant mashed potatoes, making them as directed on package. They heap the fluffy potatoes in an electric roaster pan, lightly oiled, and keep them warm. They serve the potatoes from the roaster, or from chafing dishes and casseroles with candle warmers. By experience they found that people like their potatoes piping hot. The economy of using the packaged kind comes in avoiding the waste of left-overs. More potatoes may be fixed in a jiffy if the supply runs low—just enough to satisfy appetites.

OVEN-FRIED POTATO SLICES

No turning of potato slices, no watching while they bake and brown

⅔ c. salad oil
5 medium potatoes, scrubbed
Salt
Pepper

Pour ⅓ c. oil into each of two large shallow pans. Slice potatoes crosswise ¼″ thick. Turn slices to coat both sides in salad oil.

Arrange potato slices in pans, one layer deep.

Bake in very hot oven (450°) until potatoes are lightly browned, 20 to 25 minutes. Sprinkle with salt and pepper and serve hot. Makes 6 servings.

Variation: To make Giant French Fries, scrub 3 large baking potatoes, cut each in quarters lengthwise, then crosswise in center to make 8 pieces. Pour ⅓ c. salad oil in a shallow pan (13″ × 9″ × 2″). Add potatoes and toss to coat with oil. Bake in moderate oven (350°) until tender and brown, about 1 hour. Season with salt and pepper. Makes 6 servings.

DELICIOUS MASHED POTATOES

Serve potatoes piping hot

½ pkg. instant mashed potatoes
½ c. dairy sour cream
Salt

Prepare potatoes as directed on package, omitting butter. Stir in cream and heat until piping hot. Add additional salt if needed. Makes 4 servings.

POLISH POTATOES

Unusual and unusually good

18 small new potatoes
1 c. dairy sour cream
1 tblsp. chopped green onions or chives

Cook potatoes in jackets in salted water until tender. Serve unpeeled with sour cream, onion added. Makes 6 servings.

Variation: Add a little chopped peeled cucumber to the sour cream.

HASH-BROWN ONION POTATOES

You can fix these on short notice

8 c. cubed raw potatoes
¼ c. butter or margarine
1 (1 ½ oz.) pkg. onion-soup mix
1 c. water

Lightly brown potatoes in butter. Add onion-soup mix and water. Cover and simmer until potatoes are tender, about 10 minutes. Uncover and cook a few minutes until liquid is absorbed. Stir occasionally. Makes 8 servings.

SWISS POTATOES

When time is really short, reach for canned potatoes

1 (1 lb.) can whole white potatoes
2 tblsp. bacon drippings or shortening
1 small onion, chopped
½ tsp. salt
⅛ tsp. pepper

Drain potatoes and chop fine. Cook with onion in hot fat until browned and crisp, stirring occasionally with a broad spatula. Season with salt and pepper. Makes 4 servings.

TWO-STEP POTATOES

Boil and chill potatoes one day, assemble and bake at mealtime

12 medium red potatoes
1 tsp. salt
¼ tsp. pepper
½ tsp. onion or garlic salt
½ lb. mild Cheddar cheese, grated
1 c. heavy cream

Cook unpeeled potatoes in water until almost tender, but still firm. Cool, peel and grate, using wide grater (makes about 4½ c.).

Grease baking dish (9″ × 9″ × 1½″) with butter; cover bottom with half the potatoes. Sprinkle with half the seasonings; top with half the cheese. Repeat for top layer.

Pour cream over top. Bake in moderate oven (350°) until browned, about 1 hour. Makes 6 servings.

BUTTER-CRUMBED SPROUTS

To hasten cooking fresh sprouts, slit each one almost in two

2 slices bread
2 (10 oz.) pkgs. frozen Brussels sprouts (1 qt. cooked Brussels sprouts)
¼ c. butter or margarine
1 ¼ tsp. instant or fresh parsley
1 ½ tsp. instant minced green onion
½ tsp. salt
⅛ tsp. pepper
⅔ c. light cream
¼ c. grated Parmesan cheese

Set oven for 375°. Break bread into tiny pieces; spread in shallow pan. Place in oven to toast slightly while oven is heating.

Meanwhile cook sprouts as directed on package, 8 to 10 minutes.

Melt butter, add parsley, green onion, salt and pepper. Pour half of butter mixture into greased 1 qt. casserole. Add drained sprouts. Pour cream over. Top with bread crumbs; sprinkle with cheese. Drizzle on remaining butter mixture.

Bake in moderate oven (375°) 12 minutes. Makes 6 to 8 servings.

Note: Drain Brussels sprouts thoroughly for superior flavor.

SUMMER SQUASH WITH SOUR CREAM

Young squash is a natural convenience food—no peeling, no seeds big enough to need removing

2 lbs. squash, cut in 1″ strips
1 tsp. salt
⅓ c. chopped onions
2 tblsp. butter or margarine
1 c. dairy sour cream
4 tsp. flour
Paprika

Sprinkle squash with salt; let stand 1 hour to improve flavor; drain.

Cook squash and onions in butter over low heat. When squash is tender, add sour cream mixed with flour. Bring to a boil; remove from heat. Sprinkle with paprika. Makes 6 servings.

ORANGE SWEET POTATOES

Just a matter of combining cans

3 (1 lb. 2 oz.) cans whole sweet potatoes
1 (6 oz.) can frozen orange-juice concentrate
2 orange-juice cans water
½ c. sugar
1 tsp. salt
2 tblsp. cornstarch
¼ c. butter or margarine

Empty sweet potatoes into shallow pan. Combine orange juice, water, sugar and salt in saucepan. Bring to boil.

Mix cornstarch with a little cold water to make thin paste. Pour slowly into orange mixture, stirring constantly. Cook 2 or 3 minutes until thickened. Add butter. Pour over potatoes in pan.

Bake in moderate oven (350°) 30 minutes. Or make sauce in electric skillet; add potatoes and simmer over low heat. Makes 8 to 10 servings.

SAUERKRAUT AND TOMATOES

Tangy and colorful spring favorite

1 (1 lb. 11 oz.) can sauerkraut
¾ tsp. salt

½ tsp. caraway seeds
2 tsp. sugar
1 (1 lb.) can stewed tomatoes
1 bay leaf

Combine ingredients in saucepan; heat thoroughly, about 15 to 20 minutes. Good with Potato-stuffed Franks (see Index). Makes 6 servings.

SAUERKRAUT WITH APPLES

Red apples brighten this wonderful casserole—serve it with meat

1 c. chopped onion
¼ c. butter or margarine
1 (1 lb. 11 oz.) can sauerkraut
1½ c. apple slices
2 tblsp. brown sugar
¼ tsp. dry mustard

Sauté onion in butter until soft and clear, but not brown. Mix with sauerkraut.

Place alternate layers of sauerkraut and apples in greased 1½ qt. casserole; sprinkle with brown sugar and mustard.

Cover, bake in moderate oven (375°) 30 minutes. Good with sliced ham, pork chops and meat loaf. Makes 6 to 8 servings.

NEW ORLEANS SUCCOTASH

Ready-to-go tomatoes from a can provide just-right seasoning

2 (10 oz.) pkgs. frozen succotash
1 (1 lb.) can stewed tomatoes
2 tblsp. butter or margarine

Cook succotash as directed on package. Drain; add tomatoes and heat. Stir in butter. Serve hot. Makes 5 to 6 servings.

Note: You can cook a package each of frozen corn and baby butter beans and combine for this dish, but it will be more work. A quick garnish that Southerners like is a little extra butter dotted over the top of the succotash just before it goes to the table.

BROILED TOMATOES—TWO WAYS

Remember how Grandmother fixed sliced ripe tomatoes? She spread a coverlet of heavy cream over them, sprinkled on salt and pepper to season and broiled them just long enough (never more than 10 minutes) to make the cream bubble. Delicious!

Her granddaughter follows in her footsteps, but makes a few changes. She covers sliced tomatoes with equal parts of dairy sour cream and mayonnaise, mixed, with a faint suspicion of curry powder folded in, plus salt and pepper. She broils them the same way her grandmother did. You can bake the sliced tomatoes in a moderate oven (375°), but it takes twice as long.

Juicy, red tomatoes and cream are an answer to summer's challenge to the busy country cook.

A Smart Country Cook Suggests:

"When tomatoes are in season and plentiful, Hot Buttered Tomatoes are a favorite of my family and friends. To make them: Peel 2 lbs. (about 6 medium) ripe tomatoes and squeeze out the seeds and pulp around them. Cut the tomato flesh in pieces and add to a heavy skillet containing ¼ c. butter, melted. Season with salt, pepper, a touch of sugar and a dash of basil. Cover and cook 3 to 5 minutes to heat tomatoes." Makes 4 to 6 servings.

Variation: Omit basil and add ¼ to ½ tsp. chili powder for Mexican Skillet Tomatoes.

BAKED TOMATO HALVES

Faint herb seasoning is delightful

- 8 medium tomatoes
- 1 c. herb-seasoned bread-stuffing mix
- 2 tblsp. butter or margarine

Wash tomatoes; remove stem and flower ends. Cut in crosswise halves. Place in shallow baking pan.

Top each tomato half with 1 tblsp. bread-stuffing mix. Dot with butter. Bake in moderate oven (375°) until tender and top browns, about 20 minutes. Makes 8 servings.

BAKED WHOLE TOMATOES

They flatter many dishes—serve them on platter with scrambled eggs, fish, ham, chicken, meat loaves

- 6 medium tomatoes
- 1 tsp. salt
- ⅛ tsp. pepper
- ¾ c. salad dressing
- 3 tblsp. grated sharp process cheese

Cut stem ends from tomatoes. Cut thin slice from top of each. Place tomatoes in shallow pan; make a cross about ½" deep in top of each.

Sprinkle tomatoes with salt and pepper; spread with salad dressing and sprinkle with cheese.

Bake in moderate oven (375°) until tomato is thoroughly heated, about 20 minutes. Makes 6 servings.

FRIED GREEN TOMATOES

When leaves on the trees outside kitchen windows turn crimson and gold, the country cook hustles to the garden to get green tomatoes. Sharp-flavored and firm, the unripened vegetable-fruit is a seasonal countryside favorite. And no method of cooking it surpasses old-fashioned pan-frying.

Cut the unpeeled tomatoes in scant ½" slices, flour both sides of them and then sprinkle with salt, pepper, a touch of sugar and basil. Brown them slowly in butter or bacon fat. Lift the tender tomatoes to a warm platter and add a little light cream to the pan drippings. Pour the rich, flavorful sauce over the steaming tomatoes and hurry them to the table.

But you also can bake green tomatoes with delicious results. And you need pay no attention to them while they are in the oven.

BAKED GREEN TOMATOES

Best way to salvage tomatoes before frost—tuck them in oven to bake while you attend to other chores

- 8 medium green tomatoes
- 1 c. small bread cubes, toasted
- 1 ½ tsp. salt
- ⅛ tsp. pepper
- 3 tblsp. butter or margarine
- ⅓ c. grated Parmesan cheese

Cut tomatoes a little under ½" in thickness and arrange half of them in a single layer in greased baking dish. Scatter on half the bread cubes, salt and pepper; dot with half of the butter. Repeat, making a second layer. Sprinkle cheese on top.

Bake uncovered in moderate oven (350°) until tender, 45 to 50 minutes. Makes 6 servings.

BAKED TOMATO CASSEROLE

Good Virginia cooks serve this dish with black-eye peas—fine combination

1 (1 lb.) can tomatoes
1 tsp. salt
¼ tsp. pepper
⅓ c. sugar
½ c. butter or margarine
4 (2 oz.) medium sharp-cheese slices
3 slices dry bread or toast

Put half of tomatoes in greased, deep 1 qt. baking dish. Sprinkle with half of salt, pepper and sugar and dot with half of the butter. Top with half the cheese and half the bread, broken in pieces. Finish with remaining ingredients in same order.

Bake in moderate oven (350°) 30 minutes. Makes 3 or 4 servings.

Ever Freeze Tomatoes?

When tomatoes are dead ripe, try freezing them. Just peel them and cut or chop fine. Season with salt and pepper and freeze them to a mush in the refrigerator tray. Serve in chilled sherbet glasses garnished with blobs of mayonnaise for the first course or an accompaniment to meat or chicken.

CHERRY TOMATOES: They freeze successfully. When you take them from the freezer, drop them into warm water for five minutes. Add them to salads. If eaten within an hour they retain the tart, tingling taste almost equal to their summer flavor.

VEGETABLES IN FOIL

Tuck the silvery packages in the oven—forget about them for an hour

6 medium-size carrots
6 small whole onions
3 celery stalks
1 medium green pepper
Salt
6 tblsp. Basic Red Sauce (see Index)

Peel carrots and onions; clean celery. Remove seeds from green pepper. Cut carrots in quarters lengthwise, celery in diagonal strips and green pepper in lengthwise strips. Leave onions whole.

Place vegetables on 6 pieces of aluminum foil, dividing them evenly. Sprinkle salt over them and add 1 tblsp. Basic Red Sauce to each of the six groups. Close foil around vegetables, using drugstore wrap and folding ends. Do not wrap tightly.

Bake in hot oven (400°) 50 to 60 minutes or until vegetables are tender. Serve steaming hot in foil, opening tops of packages and folding edges back. Makes 6 servings.

SHORT-CUT ZUCCHINI

Don't bother to peel the zucchini

1 lb. small zucchini
¼ c. butter or margarine
¼ tsp. garlic salt
⅛ tsp. pepper
2 tblsp. water
2 tblsp. grated Parmesan cheese

Slice zucchini (do not peel). Melt butter in skillet; add zucchini and seasonings and water.

more

Cover tightly and simmer over low heat about 10 minutes. Sprinkle with cheese. Simmer an additional 5 minutes. Makes 3 servings.

Rice Plays the Vegetable Role

Rice is not a vegetable, but it often serves as one. It's an accompaniment to meats and poultry; it rates high with many excellent cooks.

BAKED TOMATO RICE

It bakes without attention

- 3 tblsp. butter or margarine
- 1 c. regular rice
- 1 small onion, finely chopped or grated
- 1 c. tomato juice
- 1 can condensed beef broth
- 2 tblsp. instant minced parsley

Melt butter in heavy skillet; add rice and cook, stirring, 3 minutes, or until rice is golden. Stir in remaining ingredients, cover tightly and bake in moderate oven (350°) 30 minutes.

Remove lid and toss rice lightly with a fork; cover and continue to bake until rice is tender and dry. Add salt if needed. Makes 6 servings.

QUICK TOMATO RICE

You fix it in less than 15 minutes

- 1 small onion, chopped
- 2 tblsp. butter or bacon drippings
- 1 ⅓ c. precooked rice
- 1 (15 oz.) can meatless spaghetti sauce
- ¼ c. water
- ¼ tsp. basil or chili powder
- ⅛ tsp. pepper

Cook the onion in butter in heavy skillet. Stir in the remaining ingredients. Heat to boiling; cover and simmer over very low heat until rice is tender and liquid is absorbed, 8 to 10 minutes. Makes 4 servings.

RED AND GREEN RICE

Looks like Christmas and tastes extra good. A buffet supper specialty

- 1 ⅓ c. precooked rice
- 1 tblsp. butter or margarine
- ¼ c. chopped parsley
- ¼ c. chopped canned pimiento

Prepare rice as directed on package. Toss with butter, parsley and pimiento. Serve at once. Makes 4 servings.

Portable Vegetables

Difficult to decide what to fix when it's your turn to take a vegetable dish to a potluck supper? If your answer is yes, the following recipes are for you. You'll be proud to set them on the table while your friends look on. And you'll like what people say when they eat. Of course, you can also use these recipes when fixing home meals.

SQUASH-PINEAPPLE CASSEROLE

This vegetable dish fits into oven meals

- 2 (12 oz.) pkgs. frozen squash, thawed, or 4 c. cooked, mashed squash
- 1 (8 ½ oz.) can crushed pineapple
- 2 tblsp. sugar
- ½ tsp. salt
- 2 tblsp. butter or margarine

Combine squash, pineapple, sugar and salt in a greased 1½ qt. casserole. Dot with butter. Bake in moderate oven (350°) 35 to 40 minutes. Makes 8 servings.

MIXED VEGETABLES MORNAY

You'll be proud to set these on the buffet—also of compliments they get

- 2 (10 oz.) pkgs. frozen mixed vegetables
- 3 tblsp. butter or margarine
- 3 tblsp. flour
- 1½ c. milk
- ½ tsp. salt
- ⅛ tsp. pepper
- ½ c. shredded sharp Cheddar cheese
- ½ c. grated Parmesan cheese
- 2 slices bread, torn in tiny pieces
- 2 tblsp. butter or margarine, melted

Cook vegetables as directed on package until barely tender.

Melt 3 tblsp. butter; blend in flour (do not brown). Add milk and cook over low heat, stirring constantly, until mixture thickens. Add seasonings and cheese, stirring until cheese melts.

Place drained vegetables in greased 1½ qt. shallow casserole. Cover with sauce. Toss bread in remaining butter and scatter on top.

Bake in very hot oven (450°) about 10 minutes, or until browned. Makes 6 to 8 servings.

Note: You can buy grated Parmesan cheese in cans, and shredded Cheddar cheese in packages.

STUFFED POTATOES WITH SOUR CREAM AND CHIVES

If you can run these potatoes in an oven to reheat before serving them at the potluck supper, they'll make a hit.

SPEEDY STUFFED POTATOES

Shape foil, silvery or gold, in ovals the size of shells of big baked potatoes (made by cutting potatoes in half). Fill foil with instant mashed potatoes prepared as directed on package. Heap up attractively; then make a depression in each "potato" with spoon. Just before serving, heat in hot oven; fill centers with sour cream and chopped chives (or green onions added). Serve at once.

CINNAMON-CANDIED SWEET POTATOES

Glistening candied sweets sugared and spiced just right

- 3 tblsp. butter or margarine
- ¼ c. brown sugar
- ½ tsp. cinnamon
- 1 (1 lb. 7 oz.) can sweet potatoes in syrup

Melt butter in skillet. Add brown sugar, cinnamon and ¼ c. syrup drained from sweet potatoes. Simmer a few minutes and add drained sweet potatoes. Cook over medium heat, stirring frequently, to coat potatoes with glaze. Makes 4 servings.

Soup-bowl Vegetables

CHICKEN-CORN SOUP

Inviting any time, but perfect on a blustery, cold day

- 1 can condensed cream of chicken soup
- 1 (1 lb.) can cream-style corn
- 3 c. milk
- 1 tsp. salt
- Chopped parsley

Combine soup, corn, milk and salt. Simmer 5 minutes. Sprinkle with parsley (or paprika). Makes 6 servings.

CORN CHOWDER

No potatoes to peel, no onions to chop —tomato soup adds extra flavor

- 4 bacon slices, chopped
- 2 tblsp. instant minced onion
- ½ (9 oz.) pkg. quick hash-brown potatoes
- 4½ c. water
- 1 tsp. salt
- ¼ tsp. pepper
- 1 can condensed tomato soup
- 1 (1 lb. 1 oz.) can whole-kernel corn
- 1 (6 oz.) can evaporated milk

Cook bacon in large saucepan until crisp. Pour off excess fat.

Add onion, potatoes, water and seasonings. Bring to a boil; simmer until potatoes are tender, 15 to 20 minutes.

Add soup and corn; simmer a few minutes. Stir in milk and heat. Makes 8 servings.

Variation: It takes longer to make this chowder with raw onions and potatoes. Cook bacon and 2 medium onions, chopped, until bacon is crisp; drain off excess fat; add 3 medium potatoes (3 c.), peeled and cubed, 3 c. water; add salt and cook until potatoes are tender. Add tomato soup and corn, simmer a few minutes, stir in the milk and heat.

SUCCOTASH CHOWDER

A full-meal soup—there's no old-fashioned, tedious simmering

- 2 (10 oz.) pkgs. frozen lima beans
- 2 cans condensed cream of celery soup
- 2 (12 oz.) cans Mexicorn
- 2 tsp. sugar
- 2 tsp. salt
- ½ tsp. celery salt
- ½ tsp. garlic salt
- 1 qt. milk

Cook beans as directed on package; add remaining ingredients. Heat thoroughly; do not boil. Makes 8 servings.

Hasty Creamed Carrots (top), Whipped Carrots and Potatoes, shaped into ring with spoon and filled with lima beans, and Skillet Carrots and Onions are samples of last-minute vegetable dishes in Chapter 6 (page 81).

Frozen Sherbet Salad (recipe page 100) will double for dessert. Layer of clear gelatin on sherbet layer chills fast and adds jewel-like color. Keep these speedy wonder salads in your freezer for unexpected guests.

CHAPTER 7

SALADS AND SALAD DRESSINGS

Who says farm men won't eat salads? The number of recipes country cooks sent us settles that question and indicates real progress in good nutrition and taste-changing. Hundreds of salad recipes came as favored short-cut dishes. These recipes divide into four general classes–vegetable, fruit, molded and main-dish salads.

Some busy women prefer salads they can make ahead; many of them are molded. Several of the shimmering molded salads are real beauties: in Sunshine Fruit Salad, grapefruit and orange segments and Tokay grapes gleam through clear, pale-yellow lemon gelatin.

Overnight Bean Salad is an example of a he-man ranch favorite. It is not congealed. It's hearty and attractive.

Country women also know how to fast-toss green salads. The secret of making Tossed Salad in a Hurry comes out in a tip from a smart short-cut cook. You'll find it in this chapter. Use her method and the greens will crackle under the fork and contrast pleasantly with the soft foods in the meal.

Of the vegetable salads, none surpasses chilled tomatoes in appeal. Sometimes they are almost unadorned. One admirable example is Tomato Salad Platter, contributed by a Pennsylvania cook.

Cream, an old friend in country kitchens, frequently adds rich flavor to salad dressings. Farm women always have baked with their own sour cream, but dairy sour cream is gaining favor. Not only in salads, but in all parts of the meal, as recipes in this cookbook show. In one salad dressing it teams with raspberry jam to glorify peach and other fruit salads–delicious!

Farm-favorite Salads

They brighten country meals

Good cooks know that molded salads with two layers of different colors are decorative on the table. Clever short-cut cooks are on the look-out for salads that make their own layers as they chill. A knowledge of fruits and foods that float and those that sink in gelatin mixtures helps achieve the layered effects.

Examples of fine floaters are: marshmallows, sliced bananas, grapefruit sections, canned mandarin oranges, raspberries, strawberry halves, broken nuts, fresh peaches and pears, and diced apples.

Among the dependable sinkers are: canned apricots, pineapple, peaches, pears, orange sections, grapes, prunes and plums.

The size of the pan or mold used affects the top layering. If it is deep, rather than shallow with large surface, the top has the best chance of becoming an over-all layer.

The following salads make their own two-tone effects.

FROZEN CRANBERRY SALAD

Takes about 15 minutes to get this salad in freezer. As mixture freezes, marshmallows come to the top

1 (1 lb.) can jellied cranberry sauce
1 (8 ¾ oz.) can crushed pineapple
1 c. miniature marshmallows
1 tblsp. lemon juice
1 c. heavy cream, whipped
¼ c. mayonnaise
¼ c. confectioners' sugar

Combine cranberry sauce, pineapple, marshmallows and lemon juice. Spread in bottom of ice-cube tray.

Combine whipped cream, mayonnaise and sugar. Spread over cranberry mixture. Freeze. Cut in squares and serve on lettuce. Makes 6 servings.

ORANGE-MARSHMALLOW SALAD

Marshmallow "snow caps" top the orange and yellow fruits

1 (3 oz.) pkg. orange-flavor gelatin
1 (3 oz.) pkg. lemon-flavor gelatin
2 c. boiling water
2 (11 oz.) cans mandarin oranges
1 (13 oz.) can pineapple tidbits
2 c. miniature marshmallows

Mix gelatins and dissolve in boiling water. Drain oranges and pineapple. Add cold water to orange and pineapple syrups to make 2 cups. Stir into gelatin mixture.

Add orange segments, pineapple and marshmallows. Pour into a shallow pan (9" × 9" × 2") and chill until firm. Makes 12 servings.

SPRING-FLING FRUIT SALAD

Apple juice gives pleasing flavor

1 (12 oz.) can apple juice
1 (3 oz.) pkg. lemon-flavor gelatin
1 (1 lb.) can pear halves, drained
2 medium bananas, sliced

Heat 1 c. apple juice to boiling. Dissolve gelatin in hot liquid. Add water to remaining juice to make 1 c. Add to gelatin mixture.

Arrange pear halves in bottom of loaf pan (9″ × 5″ × 3″). Add bananas to gelatin and pour over pears. Chill. Makes 6 servings.

Note: This makes a white-topped or layered salad with the bananas on top. You can chill salad more quickly in an 8″ square pan, but then the bananas will not completely cover the top.

RASPBERRY-APPLESAUCE SALAD

"My family raves over this salad," said the woman who shares the recipe

2 c. thick, smooth applesauce or 1 (1 lb. 1 oz.) can applesauce
1 (3 oz.) pkg. raspberry-flavor gelatin
1 tsp. grated orange rind
3 tblsp. orange juice
1 (7 oz.) bottle lemon-lime carbonated beverage

Heat applesauce to boiling. Dissolve gelatin in hot applesauce. Add remaining ingredients. Chill until firm. Makes 6 servings.

SPICY APPLESAUCE MOLD

A red beauty—salad to make ahead

¼ c. red cinnamon candies
1 (3 oz.) pkg. apple-flavor gelatin
1 c. boiling water
1 (1 lb. 1 oz.) can applesauce
1 tblsp. vinegar

Dissolve candies and gelatin in water; stir in applesauce and vinegar. Chill until set. Makes 8 servings.

APRICOT SALAD

A 4-fruit make-ahead treat

2 (12 oz.) cans apricot nectar (3 c.)
1 (6 oz.) pkg. or 2 (3 oz.) pkgs. lemon-flavor gelatin
¼ c. lemon juice
1 (8 ¾ oz.) can crushed pineapple
2 bananas, diced

Heat nectar to boiling. Add to gelatin and stir until dissolved. Add remaining ingredients. Chill until firm. Serve on lettuce. Makes 8 to 10 servings.

MOLDED CRANBERRY-RELISH SALAD

Why not have this on Thanksgiving? It's worthy of the honor

2 c. hot water
1 (6 oz.) pkg. or 2 (3 oz.) pkgs. lemon-flavor gelatin
1 ½ c. cold water
3 c. Cranberry Relish (see Index)
1 c. chopped walnuts
1 c. chopped celery

Pour boiling water over gelatin; stir to dissolve. Add cold water and Cranberry Relish.

Chill until mixture starts to thicken. Fold in walnuts and celery. Chill in a 2 qt. mold until set. Makes 6 to 8 servings.

NO-COOK PRUNE SALAD

Partly fill a jar with prunes and cover with boiling water or pineapple juice. Put lid on jar, cool and refrigerate 24 hours or several days. To make a tempting salad with the prunes, remove pits and stuff with walnuts or cashew nuts. Serve on greens with cream cheese. Soften the cheese by adding a little water or lemon, orange or pineapple juice, and beat smooth with a fork.

OVERNIGHT FRUIT SALAD

You can get this luscious salad ready to chill in 5 minutes

1 (1 lb. 13 oz.) can fruit cocktail, drained
2 c. miniature marshmallows
1 c. dairy sour cream
Lettuce
½ c. nuts, chopped coarsely

Combine the fruit cocktail, marshmallows and cream. Cover and chill overnight. Serve on crisp lettuce. Sprinkle with nuts just before serving. Makes 6 servings.

AUTUMN FRUIT SALAD

Fix this make-ahead salad when you want to splurge a little

2 (3 oz.) pkgs. lemon-flavor gelatin
2 c. hot water
1 ½ c. cold water
1 (8 oz.) can crushed pineapple
1 (1 lb.) can whole cranberry sauce, chilled
2 apples, cut in small pieces
1 c. diced celery (optional)

Dissolve gelatin in hot water. Add cold water and pineapple; chill.

When mixture starts to thicken, add cranberry sauce, apples and celery. Pour into pan (12″ × 7½″). Chill until firm. Serve on greens, topped with mayonnaise. Makes 8 to 10 servings.

FRUIT-SALAD WHEEL

Red, yellow and green 5-minute salad

1 (12 ¼ oz.) can jellied cherry sauce
1 (14 ½ oz.) can pineapple slices, drained
Lettuce
Mayonnaise or salad dressing

Cut cherry sauce in 4 slices. Arrange on pineapple slices.

Serve on lettuce with a spoonful of mayonnaise on top of each salad. Makes 4 servings.

SUNSHINE FRUIT SALAD

A beauty—fruit distributes evenly in clear, shimmery gelatin

1 (1 lb.) can grapefruit segments
1 (11 oz.) can mandarin oranges
1 (3 oz.) pkg. lemon-flavor gelatin
1 c. Tokay or green grapes, halved and seeded, or seedless green grapes

Drain grapefruit and oranges. Add water to fruit syrups to make 2 c. Heat 1 c. syrup mixture to boiling.

Dissolve gelatin in hot syrup. Add cold syrup mixture and the fruit.

Pour into pan (8″ × 8″ × 2″). Chill until set. Makes 9 servings.

GARNISH FOR FRUIT SALADS: Crush peanut brittle and sprinkle over salads.

FROZEN SHERBET SALAD

Two-decker, double-duty sparkler to serve for salad or salad dessert

1 (6 oz.) pkg. or 2 (3 oz.) pkgs. raspberry-flavor gelatin
2 c. hot water
1 pt. raspberry-flavor milk sherbet

1 (3 oz.) pkg. lime-flavor gelatin
1 c. hot water
1 c. cold fruit juice
1 (13½ oz.) can pineapple tidbits, drained

Dissolve raspberry gelatin in hot water. Add sherbet; stir until melted (may be necessary to heat slightly). Pour into 2 qt. mold; freeze.

The day you serve the salad, dissolve lime gelatin in hot water; add juice and tidbits. Pour over frozen layer; refrigerate (will set in about 30 minutes). Unmold on greens. Makes 8 to 12 servings.

Note: You can freeze the sherbet mixture in paper liners in muffin-pan cups. When frozen, empty into plastic bags and store in freezer. Serve as dessert with a fluff of whipped cream.

VARIATIONS

LIME LEMON-ORANGE: Combine lime gelatin and lemon sherbet; use orange gelatin for second layer, adding 1 c. fresh or 1 (11 oz.) can mandarin orange sections, drained.

LIME-LIME: Combine lime gelatin and lime sherbet; use lime gelatin for second layer, adding 1 c. fresh or 1 (1 lb.) can grapefruit sections, drained.

LEMON LEMON-CHERRY: Combine lemon gelatin and lemon sherbet; use cherry gelatin for second layer, adding 1 (1 lb. 1 oz.) jar dark, sweet cherries, drained.

ORANGE ORANGE-STRAWBERRY: Combine orange gelatin and orange sherbet; use strawberry-flavor gelatin for second layer, adding 1 (10½ oz.) pkg. frozen strawberries, thawed and drained.

GREEN GAGE PLUM SALAD

An unusual, tart-sweet salad to make in advance and chill

1 (1 lb. 4 oz.) can green gage plums
1 (3 oz.) pkg. lemon-flavor gelatin
Juice of 1 lemon
½ tsp. salt
¾ c. slivered toasted almonds
Crisp lettuce cups
Salad dressing

Drain juice from plums; add water to make 2 c. liquid. Heat to boiling, and pour over gelatin. Add lemon juice and salt; stir to dissolve. Cool until thickened.

Pour 2 tblsp. gelatin mixture into 6 baking cups or individual molds. Chill until firm.

Pit and chop plums. Fold with almonds into gelatin. Spoon over clear gelatin in molds. Chill until firm.

Serve in lettuce cups with dressing. Makes 6 servings.

MANDARIN ORANGE SALAD

It's best chilled a couple of hours. Serve on crackling-crisp lettuce

1 (11 oz.) can mandarin oranges
1 (13½ oz.) can pineapple tidbits, drained
1 c. miniature marshmallows
½ c. flaked or shredded coconut
⅓ c. maraschino cherries
1 c. dairy sour cream

Mix all the ingredients. Chill about 2 hours. Serve in lettuce cups. Pretty garnished with extra cherries. Makes 6 servings.

Note: Some cooks like to chill this salad overnight before serving it.

PINEAPPLE-CHEESE MOLD

Almost everyone takes second helpings

1 (3 oz.) pkg. lime-flavor gelatin
1 c. boiling water
1 c. evaporated milk
1 c. cottage cheese
1 (1 lb. 4½ oz.) can crushed pineapple, well drained
½ c. mayonnaise
¼ c. chopped celery
¼ c. chopped nuts (optional)

Dissolve gelatin in water. Stir in remaining ingredients and pour into 1½ qt. mold; chill until firm. Makes 8 servings.

CHERRY-PINEAPPLE SALAD

A salad that doubles for dessert

1 (3 oz.) pkg. cream cheese
1 tblsp. mayonnaise
1 (9 oz.) can sliced pineapple, drained
1 (8 to 9 oz.) can light sweet cherries, drained and pitted
Salad greens
Paprika

Have cream cheese at room temperature; blend in mayonnaise.

Arrange chilled pineapple and cherries on crisp greens. Top each with spoonful of cheese mixture and sprinkle with paprika. Makes 4 servings.

PINEAPPLE-CUCUMBER SALAD

Cream cheese flecked with cucumber bits tops pineapple rings

1 (3 oz.) pkg. cream cheese
1 (8½ oz.) can pineapple slices
½ c. finely chopped cucumber
⅛ tsp. salt
Lettuce cups
French dressing

Combine cheese with 1 tblsp. syrup drained from pineapple. Stir in cucumber and salt.

Place each of the 4 pineapple slices in a lettuce cup. Top with cream-cheese mixture. Serve with French dressing. Makes 4 servings.

WALDORF SALAD: Chill the apples before making the salad. Cold apples are essential to topnotch salads in which they star. And use the tender, top celery branches in the salad.

A Country Cook Suggests:

Make gelatin mixture in a pitcher (a quart measure is ideal). When it thickens slightly (to consistency of egg white), pour over the fruit in the container in which you want to chill it. Easy, fast, neat trick.

COTTAGE CHEESE FOR SALADS: Add celery or caraway seeds for a treat.

Salads from the Garden

OVERNIGHT BEAN SALAD

A surprisingly good make-ahead salad

1 (1 lb.) can French-cut green beans, drained
1 (1 lb.) can wax beans, drained

1 (1 lb.) can kidney beans, drained
½ c. chopped green pepper
½ c. chopped onion
½ c. salad oil
½ c. vinegar
¾ c. sugar
1 tsp. salt
½ tsp. pepper
Lettuce

Combine beans, green pepper and onion. Blend together remaining ingredients except lettuce. Pour over bean mixture.

Chill in refrigerator overnight or at least six hours. Serve in lettuce cups. Makes 8 to 10 servings.

Variations: Omit green pepper, salad oil, vinegar and sugar and add ½. c. sweet-pickle relish, 1 tsp. celery seeds and 1 c. mayonnaise. When green onions are in season, use them, sliced, instead of chopped onion.

CABBAGE SALAD BOWL

The humble cabbage salad steps out in attractive new dress

½ c. light raisins
¼ c. orange juice
1 medium head cabbage, shredded
1 carrot, shredded
2 tblsp. sugar
½ tsp. salt
¼ c. mayonnaise
2 tblsp. tarragon vinegar

Soak raisins in orange juice while preparing other ingredients.

Combine cabbage, carrot, sugar and salt in salad bowl. Blend mayonnaise and vinegar. Add to cabbage along with raisins and orange juice.

Toss lightly. Makes 8 servings.

Variation: If you have green grapes, add a few, seeded.

CAROLINA AUTUMN SALAD

Marvelous with ham, sausage or baked beans—colorful, too

1 c. chopped cabbage
1 c. chopped celery
1 large unpeeled red apple, diced
½ c. seedless raisins
¼ tsp. salt
¼ c. mayonnaise or salad dressing

Combine all ingredients. Serve in lettuce cups or on green cabbage leaves. Makes 4 servings.

COUNTRY-STYLE CUCUMBER SALAD: Peel cucumbers and slice thin. Cover with cold, salted water (1 tsp. salt to 1 c. water). Let stand 10 to 20 minutes; drain and pour over French dressing with celery seeds added (¾ tsp. to ½ c. French dressing). Snip parsley with scissors and scatter over the cucumbers for a cool-looking garnish.

CREOLE SALAD

Bright color contrasts make salad appealing on a hot day

3 tomatoes, peeled and sliced
Lettuce
4 crosswise slices green pepper
1 hard-cooked egg, sliced
1 tsp. salt
4 chopped green onions
Salad dressing

Place 3 tomato slices on each of 4 lettuce-lined salad plates. Top each with green-pepper ring and a slice of hard-cooked egg. Sprinkle with salt and green onions.

Serve with your favorite salad dressing. Makes 4 servings.

BEET-RELISH SALAD

Marvelous blending of vegetable flavors and textures

- 2 c. finely chopped, cooked or canned beets
- 1 c. finely chopped onion
- 2 c. finely shredded cabbage
- 1 tsp. seasoning salt
- ⅛ tsp. pepper
- ½ c. mayonnaise

Combine all ingredients and serve in green cabbage leaves. Makes 6 servings.

BACON-SPINACH SALAD

Use only young, tender spinach leaves

- 4 slices bacon
- 1 tblsp. dry mustard
- ¼ c. salad oil
- ¼ c. vinegar
- ½ tsp. onion salt
- 1 lb. spinach, washed and stems removed

Pan-broil bacon until crisp. Remove and save for later use.

Measure bacon drippings. Place 3 to 4 tblsp. in skillet. Stir in mustard, oil, vinegar and onion salt; heat to boiling. Add spinach leaves and toss to coat with dressing. Serve at once in salad bowl or vegetable dish, crumbling bacon over top. Makes 8 servings.

KIDNEY-BEAN–APPLE SALAD

Main-dish salad for lunch. Apple adds bright color, celery gives crispness

- 1 (1 lb.) can kidney beans, drained
- ¼ c. chopped onion
- ¼ c. chopped celery
- 1 unpeeled red apple, cored and diced
- ⅓ c. diced Cheddar cheese
- ½ tsp. salt
- ⅓ c. mayonnaise or salad dressing

Combine all ingredients. Serve on lettuce. Makes 4 servings.

COUNTRY SALAD BOWL

Summer's favorite—a colorful vegetable salad served with a delicious, protein-rich cheese dressing

- 5 large tomatoes, ripe but firm
- 2 cucumbers
- 1 green pepper
- 1 large sweet onion
- Salt
- Pepper
- ¼ c. French dressing
- Creamy Cheese Dressing (see Index)

Chill vegetables.

Slice unpeeled tomatoes. Peel cucumbers; score with tines of fork; slice. Slice pepper and onion in rings.

Arrange vegetables in bowl. Cover tightly and refrigerate.

When ready to serve, sprinkle with salt and pepper (freshly ground if you have it). Drizzle lightly with French dressing. Serve with Creamy Cheese Dressing, passed in separate bowl. Makes 6 to 8 servings.

CUCUMBER-EGG SALAD

Yellow, white and green salad that's perfect when fish is on the platter

- 1 large head lettuce
- 2 cucumbers, sliced
- 3 or 4 hard-cooked eggs, sliced

1 or 2 sweet peppers, cut in rings
⅓ c. French-type salad dressing
Parmesan cheese

Cut lettuce into 8 wedges; arrange in salad bowl.

Add cucumbers, eggs and peppers.

When ready to serve, add salad dressing. Sprinkle generously with cheese. Makes 6 to 8 servings.

GRAPEFRUIT-BEET SALAD: Team canned or fresh grapefruit sections with drained and diced pickled beets for a colorful relish salad. Add French or Italian dressing.

LETTUCE SLAW: Shred a head of icicle lettuce. Toss in a bowl with 3 chopped green onions or 6 chopped pimiento-stuffed olives and French or Italian salad dressing. Makes 6 servings.

LOUIS SALAD: Toss 2 c. cooked and chilled green beans with crisp lettuce and 1 c. cooked or canned chilled shrimp or crab meat. Serve with ½ c. mayonnaise blended with ¼ c. chili sauce, 1 tblsp. chopped green onion and 1 tblsp. lemon juice. This makes a whole meal in a bowl.

SAUERKRAUT SLAW

Set a big bowl of this chilled salad on the picnic table

1 (1 lb. 11 oz.) can sauerkraut
¾ c. shredded carrots
½ c. chopped stuffed olives or diced cucumber
2 tblsp. minced parsley
1 tblsp. chopped onion
2 tblsp. sugar
1 tsp. salt
½ tsp. dry mustard
1 tsp. celery seeds
2 tblsp. French dressing

Chill sauerkraut. Open can and drain. Combine kraut with remaining ingredients; mix well. Cover and chill. Serve on crisp salad greens or outer cabbage leaves. Makes 8 servings.

Men's Special: Top frankfurters or hamburgers in buns with this slaw.

Tips from a Country Cook

TOSSED SALAD IN A HURRY: Tear the washed greens in bite-size pieces. Place them in a garlic-rubbed bowl. Sliced cucumbers and green pepper may be added. Put bowl in a large plastic bag (size for freezing turkeys) and close tightly. Refrigerate several hours or until mealtime. At the last minute before serving, add dressing and toss. For a potluck supper, carry bowl of greens and bottled dressing. Toss to serve.

TOMATO-HERB SALAD

You're lucky if you have an herb garden—this salad is extra good

½ tsp. minced fresh basil
½ tsp. minced fresh marjoram
¼ c. French dressing
2 large tomatoes, peeled and sliced
Lettuce

Combine herbs and dressing. Place tomatoes on 6 lettuce-lined salad plates. Pour over dressing. Makes 6 servings.

Variation: Use fresh thyme, rosemary or savory for basil or marjoram.

TOMATO-SALAD PLATTER

A new way to serve sliced tomatoes

8 medium tomatoes, peeled and sliced or cut in quarters
1 (5/8 oz.) pkg. Italian salad-dressing mix

Arrange chilled tomatoes on platter or chop plate. Just before serving, sprinkle on salad-dressing mix. The juicy tomatoes make their own dressing. Makes 8 servings.

TOSSED SALAD

Something different, something good—a salad you partly make ahead

1 (8 oz.) can green beans, drained
1 (8 oz.) can cut asparagus, drained
2 tblsp. chopped green onion or chives
½ c. bottled blue-cheese French dressing
1 c. sliced cauliflower florets
1 qt. salad greens

Combine beans, asparagus, green onion and salad dressing. Chill 1 to 2 hours (or several hours) to blend flavors. Add cauliflower and greens. Toss lightly. Makes 6 to 8 servings.

MIXED VEGETABLE SALAD

A favorite with blue-cheese fans

1 head lettuce
2 c. raw cauliflower florets
2 large tomatoes, peeled and cut in wedges
½ large Bermuda onion, sliced and separated into rings
3 tblsp. crumbled blue cheese
⅔ c. bottled Italian salad dressing

Tear lettuce in bite-size pieces. Combine with cauliflower, tomato, onion rings and cheese. Add dressing and toss until blended. Makes 8 to 10 servings.

FIESTA VEGETABLE SALAD

Pretty on the buffet

Lettuce
4 tomatoes, peeled and sliced
1 sweet onion, thinly sliced
1½ c. cooked whole green beans, or 1 (1 lb. 1 oz.) can whole green beans
1 large cucumber, unpeeled, but sliced
French dressing

Line platter or chop plate with lettuce. Arrange tomatoes, onion, beans and cucumber on lettuce in separate sections. Serve with French dressing. Makes 6 servings.

LEFT-OVER EGG YOLKS: Poach the yolks in hot water until hard-cooked. Chill and slice or crumble over potato, lettuce and other vegetable salads.

Salads on the Hearty Side

Put dead-ripe tomatoes and snowy cottage cheese together this way and you have a tasty treat for weight-watchers. The salad is attractive and simple to fix, and satisfying.

TOMATO–COTTAGE-CHEESE SALAD

The herbs fleck the cheese with green

1 (12 oz.) carton cottage cheese, or about 1 ½ c.
1 tsp. mixed dry herbs
½ tsp. onion salt
3 medium to large tomatoes, peeled and sliced
Lettuce

Combine cottage cheese, herbs and onion salt. Arrange 3 tomato slices on lettuce for each salad. Top with mound of cottage cheese. Makes 6 servings.

CHICKEN-APPLE SALAD: Add 1½ c. diced cooked chicken or 2 (5 oz.) cans to your favorite Waldorf salad, made with 2 c. diced and cored but unpeeled apples. A good proportion of other ingredients to add is: 1 c. diced celery, 3 tblsp. mayonnaise or salad dressing, 1 tblsp. lemon juice and ¼ c. chopped pecans. Season with ½ tsp. salt. Serve on lettuce. Makes 4 servings.

CHICKEN SALAD: Just before serving your favorite chicken salad, fold in a sliced banana; or add cubes of jellied cranberries. In strawberry season, garnish chicken salad with a few berries.

HOT POTATO SALAD: Put ⅔ c. bottled Italian-style salad dressing in your electric skillet. Heat slowly. Add 5 c. cooked, diced potatoes, 3 tblsp. chopped onion and 7 slices crisp, crumbled bacon. Toss lightly and heat. Garnish with chopped parsley or green pepper. Makes 6 servings.

ONION MAC

A peppy platter partner for cold cuts

8 oz. elbow macaroni, cooked
2 c. dairy sour cream
1 c. chopped green onion
⅓ c. chopped pimiento
1 tsp. salt

Mix macaroni with remaining ingredients. Chill. Stir before serving.

Serve as appetizer or as a salad—good at a picnic with fried chicken. Makes 8 servings.

SAUSAGE-POTATO SALAD

Proof there's something new and appetizing in hot potato salads

1 (12 oz.) pkg. smoked sausages
1 c. dairy sour cream
2 tblsp. prepared mustard
1 tsp. salt
1 tsp. sugar
1 tsp. instant minced green onion
4 c. hot cooked potato cubes

Simmer little sausages in hot water as directed on package.

Combine cream, seasonings and green onion. Heat, but do not let boil. Pour over hot potatoes and toss.

Serve potato salad topped with hot sausages. Makes 4 to 5 servings.

RELISH SALAD: Drain 1 (1 lb.) can red kidney beans and 1 (1 lb. 4 oz.) can garbanzos. Pour into two glass jars. Add ½ c. bottled Italian dressing or garlic French dressing to each. Cover and chill overnight or several hours. Mix and serve on lettuce.

more

Variations: Substitute 1 (15 oz.) can black-eye peas, drained, for the garbanzos. Heat the beans and garbanzos or peas and serve as a vegetable. Or serve the beans, garbanzos or peas on a relish tray along with cottage cheese, spiced crab apples, and other relishes.

TUNA-TOMATO SALAD

Just the colorful, hearty mold to carry to a potluck supper

- 1 (1 lb.) can tomatoes
- 1 (3 oz.) pkg. strawberry-flavor gelatin
- 3 tblsp. vinegar
- 1 (7 oz.) can tuna, drained, flaked
- 1 tblsp. chopped onion
- 2 tblsp. chopped green pepper
- ½ c. chopped celery
- ½ tsp. salt

Heat tomatoes to boiling; add gelatin; stir to dissolve. Add remaining ingredients; spoon into 1 qt. mold. Chill until firm. Unmold and serve on greens. Makes 6 servings.

TURKEY SALAD SUPREME

Can't miss with this salad, but do serve it chilled until very cold

- 2 c. diced cooked turkey
- ½ c. French salad dressing
- 1 c. diced celery
- ½ tsp. salt
- ½ c. mayonnaise or salad dressing
- ½ c. heavy cream, whipped (optional)
- Lettuce

Combine turkey and French salad dressing; cover and chill several hours or overnight.

Add celery, salt, mayonnaise, and fold in whipped cream for a fluffy salad. Serve on crisp lettuce.

Variations: Add ½ c. coarsely chopped salted pecans or 1 c. seedless green grapes. Serve salad on chilled and drained canned pineapple slices. To extend the turkey, add an equal amount of diced cooked ham. Makes 4 servings.

Easy Salad Dressings

BLUE-CHEESE SALAD DRESSING

Takes just about 5 minutes to make this tasty Southern salad dressing

- 1 c. mayonnaise or salad dressing
- 1 c. buttermilk
- ¼ tsp. salt
- ¼ tsp. pepper
- 1 tsp. grated onion
- 2 oz. blue cheese

Combine mayonnaise, buttermilk, salt, pepper and onion. Crumble in half of cheese. Beat with rotary beater until well blended. Break remainder of cheese in larger pieces and stir in. Serve over lettuce wedges or tomato salad. Makes 2 cups.

CREAM DRESSING

Use on tender, young lettuce in the spring when the garden is coming in

- ½ c. light or heavy cream
- 2 tblsp. sugar
- 1 tblsp. vinegar

Mix ingredients; pour enough over lettuce to coat leaves. Makes ¾ cup.

Variation: Add 2 tsp. horse-radish.

CREAMY CHEESE DRESSING

1 c. cottage cheese
¼ lb. blue or Roquefort cheese
½ tsp. grated onion
½ tsp. Worcestershire sauce
½ c. dairy sour cream

Combine ingredients in blender; blend until smooth. Or force cottage and blue cheese through a sieve; add remaining ingredients; mix until smooth. (For thinner dressing, add a little sour cream, milk or thin cream.) Makes 1¼ cups.

DAISY'S SALAD DRESSING

Excellent choice for fruit salads

1 c. mayonnaise
½ c. sweet pickle juice
1 tsp. celery seeds

Combine all ingredients. Store in refrigerator until time to serve salad. Makes about 1½ cups.

FRUIT-SALAD DRESSING

Honeyed dressing especially good on citrus fruit. Keep some on hand

1 ½ tblsp. flour
1 ¼ tsp. paprika
1 tsp. salt
1 tsp. dry mustard
1 tsp. celery seeds
⅓ c. lemon juice
¾ c. strained honey
1 c. salad oil

Combine all ingredients except honey and oil; add to honey in top of double boiler. Cook over hot water, stirring occasionally, until thickened.

Cool; then, using a fork, gradually beat in oil. Keep refrigerated. To serve, drizzle over fruit. Makes about 2 cups.

FRUIT-JUICE FRENCH DRESSING

Brings out the best flavors in pears

1 (6 oz.) can frozen orange-grapefruit-juice concentrate, thawed
¾ tsp. salt
Dash of paprika
1 ½ c. salad oil

Combine juice concentrate and seasonings. Beat in oil, a small amount at a time. Makes 2 cups.

RED FRENCH DRESSING

Gives the right tang to greens—keep a jar of it on hand in refrigerator

½ c. vinegar
1 ½ c. salad oil
2 tsp. salt
⅛ tsp. pepper
1 tsp. dry mustard
⅓ c. chili sauce
1 tblsp. prepared horse-radish (optional)
1 tsp. paprika

Mix all the ingredients with a rotary beater or electric mixer or shake in a quart fruit jar with tight lid. Store in refrigerator. Makes about 2 cups.

VARIATIONS

LEMON: Use lemon juice instead of vinegar. Excellent on fruits.

GARLIC: Add 1 garlic clove, crushed.

OLIVE: To 1 c. Red French Dressing, add ⅓ c. finely chopped pimiento-stuffed olives. Good on lettuce.

more

BASIC FRENCH DRESSING: Omit chili sauce and add 2 tsp. sugar. To 1 c. Basic French Dressing add ½ c. honey and ½ tsp. celery seeds or finely chopped candied ginger for Honey French Dressing.

PEANUT SALAD DRESSING

Perfect on apple and banana salads

2 tblsp. chunk-style peanut butter
2 tblsp. honey
½ c. mayonnaise or salad dressing

Blend peanut butter and honey; stir in mayonnaise. Makes about ⅔ cup.

RANCH-HOUSE SALAD DRESSING

Adds color and zippy flavor to head lettuce and other greens

1 c. mayonnaise
¼ c. vinegar
¼ c. ketchup
¼ c. chili sauce
2 tblsp. finely chopped onion
¼ tsp. salt
¼ tsp. paprika

Combine all ingredients. Serve with vegetable salads. Makes 1¾ cups.

SHORT-CUT SALAD DRESSING

Resembles Thousand Island dressing—try it on lettuce wedges

½ c. mayonnaise
2 tblsp. Basic Red Sauce (see Index)
1 hard-cooked egg, finely chopped
Salt to taste

Combine all ingredients. Chill until ready to use. Makes about ¾ cup.

Sour-cream Dressings

They are quick to make and give salads delightful flavor. There is no end to the variations.

PINK-CLOUD DRESSING

Invented for golden canned peach halves—also good on other fruits

1 c. dairy sour cream
2 tblsp. red raspberry jam

Combine ingredients and spoon over fruit salads. Makes about 1 cup.

SOUR-CREAM DRESSING

Excellent for cabbage, tomato and cucumber salads

½ c. sour cream
1 tblsp. sugar
¼ tsp. salt
⅛ tsp. pepper
1 tblsp. lemon juice
1 tblsp. vinegar

Combine ingredients and pour over vegetables. Makes about ⅔ cup.

Variations

CHIVES: Add ½ c. dairy sour cream to ½ c. mayonnaise and fold in 2 tblsp. minced chives. Serve on sliced cucumbers or tomatoes, lettuce or mixed chopped vegetables.

CELERY: To ½ c. dairy sour cream add ½ tsp. celery seeds, ¼ c. minced onion, 1 tblsp. vinegar and ¾ tsp. salt. Use on vegetables.

CHAPTER 8

CAKES AND FROSTINGS

No wonder country cooks excel in cake-making: they bake so many of them. Busy women sent us more recipes for cakes than for any other dessert. Our pick of the farm-cake array appears in this chapter. You'll find about every kind you ever tasted or dreamed about. There are tender, delicate, moist layers and loaves, an angel food, high and handsome, and enough chocolate cakes to satisfy the most ardent chocolate devotees. There are also desserts that owe their inclusion in this collection to the use of cake as an ingredient. Several from scratch cake recipes are adjusted for high altitudes.

True, you will not find traditional, long-method cakes, but charming versions of them. For example, we present a new way to make wonderful cake with lard. Many top home bakers, when pressed for time, however, use packaged mixes, adding touches of talent to make the production their own. But they also make one-bowl and other from scratch cakes that are easy on the cook. And they are getting results–country cakes are recognized as the best in the world.

Even our short-cut wedding cake maintains the high standard of beauty. Yet we leave the time-consuming pastry tube in the drawer when the cook, scarce on time, decorates the most important cake in a woman's life. And Chocolate Mound Cake has a combination of flavors that tempts crowds at country cake walks. Or, as one rancher said, "I'd walk a mile just for a piece of it." Cherry Crown Cake, if you like chocolate-coated cherries, is the cake for you. Don't miss speedy Sweet Cream Cake with its old-fashioned, rich flavor.

You'll find recipes for frostings and toppings that glorify cakes, for country cooks know cake is no better than its frosting. Some of these bake along with the cake; others broil on the baked cake. All are quick. All are easy. Be sure to try the ones made with Basic Sugar Syrup, a new short route to superlative frostings.

Home-style Country Cakes

Winners in our popularity poll

Country cakes never were better tasting or more glamorous than they are today. Cooks have little time to fuss over decorations, but their quick tricks yield big dividends. Angel food cakes continue to hold their own. And it's a rare woman who does not have a few simple dress-ups for these tall, light cakes.

SURPRISE ANGEL FOOD CAKE

Chocolate rippled in white cake is pretty—just add cocoa mix

1 pkg. angel food cake mix
3 tblsp. instant cocoa mix

Prepare batter as directed on package. Pour one fourth of batter in a 10″ tube pan. Spread evenly to eliminate air pockets. Sprinkle half of cocoa mix over batter. Add another fourth of the batter; spread evenly with spatula. Sprinkle on remainder of cocoa mix. Top with remaining batter. Run a knife in batter in spiral fashion.

Bake as directed on package.

Note: For a festive dessert, frost the cake in white and sprinkle tiny chocolate decorating candies on frosting.

ANGEL FOOD À LA MODE: Brush angel food cake slices with melted butter and sprinkle lightly with brown sugar and flaked or shredded coconut. Run under broiler to melt sugar and brown coconut delicately. Top with vanilla ice cream and serve immediately.

BUSY COOK'S SHORTCAKES

One busy country woman prefers to bake angel food cake batter in individual servings. She cools the little cakes, freezes them and then stores them in the freezer in plastic bags. This enables her to take out as many servings as she needs without cutting a big cake.

ANGEL SHORTCAKES: Prepare batter from angel food cake mix as directed on package. Drop from ½-cup measure about 2″ apart on ungreased baking sheet. Bake in moderate oven (375°) until a light golden brown, 10 to 15 minutes. Remove from baking sheet immediately. Repeat until all the batter is used. Makes 18 to 20 shortcakes. Serve little cakes topped with ice cream and your favorite dessert sauce or partly thawed frozen strawberries, raspberries or sliced peaches.

FROZEN MINT-FROSTED CAKE LOAF

You can skip the freezing and serve dessert as soon as it's made, but it's nice to have on hand

1 pkg. angel food cake mix
1 qt. brick strawberry ice cream
1 c. heavy cream, whipped
3 tblsp. confectioners' sugar
¼ tsp. peppermint extract
4 to 6 drops green food color

Bake cake according to package directions in 2 loaf pans (10¼″ × 3⅝″ × 2⅝″). Cool.

Split 1 loaf into 3 lengthwise slices (freeze other loaf for use later).

Cut ice cream into 7 equal slices.

Cover bottom cake layer with 3½ slices ice cream; top with middle cake layer; cover with remaining ice cream; top with third cake layer.

Blend whipped cream, sugar, extract and food color; use to frost sides and top of cake.

Let cake set a few minutes after you frost it; freeze uncovered until firm. Remove from freezer; wrap and return to freezer. Will keep about 8 weeks. Makes 8 servings.

Variation: Substitute chocolate ice cream for the strawberry.

APPLE SPICE CAKE

Easy enough to make for the family, tasty enough to serve company

- 1 pkg. apple-spice-cake mix
- 1 c. heavy cream
- 2 tblsp. sugar
- ⅛ tsp. cinnamon
- ½ c. applesauce

Prepare cake mix as directed on package. Bake in greased pan (13″ × 9″ × 2″). Cool and cut in 12 to 15 individual servings.

Combine cream, sugar and cinnamon; whip until cream mounds slightly. Fold in applesauce. Spoon on cake.

LADY BALTIMORE CAKE

Simplified version of an elegant Dixie dessert—tastes wonderful

- 1 pkg. white-cake mix
- 1 pkg. white-frosting mix
- ¼ tsp. almond extract
- ¼ c. chopped dates
- ½ c. chopped seeded raisins
- 12 candied cherries, chopped
- ½ c. chopped pecans

Mix and bake cake as directed on package in two 8″ round or square layers. Cool.

Prepare frosting as directed on package, adding almond extract.

Combine ¾ c. frosting with fruits and nuts; spread between layers.

Frost top and side of cake with remaining frosting.

Variation: Substitute well-drained maraschino cherries for candied cherries. Use syrup from cherries as part of liquid in frosting to tint a delicate pink. Or, tint frosting with red food color.

LORD BALTIMORE CAKE

The Lady's companion—quick version of an old-time Dixie favorite

- 1 pkg. yellow-cake mix
- 1 pkg. white-frosting mix
- ¼ tsp. lemon or orange extract
- ¼ c. blanched chopped almonds
- ¼ c. chopped pecans
- ½ c. dry macaroon crumbs
- 12 candied cherries, chopped

Mix and bake cake as directed on package in two 8″ round layers. Cool.

Prepare frosting as directed on package, adding extract.

Toast nuts and crumbs in moderate oven (350°) 5 minutes.

Blend nuts, crumbs and cherries into 1 c. frosting; spread between layers.

Frost top and side of cake with remaining frosting. Decorate side of cake with strips of candied cherries and nuts.

BUTTERSCOTCH CRUNCH CAKE

Exciting new version of upside-down cake. It's good served hot or cold

- ⅓ c. butter or margarine
- ½ c. graham-cracker crumbs
- ¼ c. chopped nuts
- ½ c. butterscotch morsels
- ⅓ c. shortening
- 1 ⅓ c. sifted flour
- 1 c. sugar
- 2 tsp. baking powder
- ½ tsp. salt
- ⅔ c. milk
- 1 tsp. vanilla
- 1 egg

Melt butter in pan (9″ × 9″ × 2″). Sprinkle evenly with crumbs and nuts combined, then with morsels.

In a bowl, stir shortening to soften. Sift in flour, sugar, baking powder and salt. Add milk and vanilla; beat 2 minutes, medium speed on mixer. Add egg and beat 1 more minute.

Pour batter over crumb mixture and spread evenly. Bake in moderate oven (350°) 40 to 45 minutes.

Remove from oven and let stand 3 or 4 minutes. Then invert on plate and let stand a minute before removing pan. Cut in squares and serve warm with whipped cream. Or serve cold.

HIGH ALTITUDE ADJUSTMENT

For all altitudes above 3500 feet: Increase baking temperature to 375° and bake 35 to 40 minutes.

From 3500 to 6000 feet altitude: Use 1½ tsp. baking powder and ¾ c. milk.

Above 6000 feet altitude: Use 1¼ tsp. baking powder and 1 c. minus 2 tblsp. milk.

CHERRY CRUMB CAKE

You'll look a long time to find a dessert so easy, colorful and tasty

- 1 c. sugar
- 2 c. sifted flour
- 2 tsp. baking powder
- ½ tsp. salt
- ½ c. butter
- 1 egg
- 1 (1 lb. 6 oz.) can cherry-pie filling

Mix sugar and flour, sifted with baking powder and salt. Cut in the butter, add the egg and mix to make crumbs.

Place half of the crumb mixture in the bottom of a greased pan (13″ × 9″ × 2″). Pour over it, distributing evenly, the cherries. Top with remaining crumbs.

Bake in moderate oven (350°) 30 minutes. Serve with whipped cream, ice cream or plain.

Variations: Use peach, blueberry or other canned pie fillings instead of cherries. Add a touch of pumpkin-pie spice or cinnamon to the top crumbs.

HIGH ALTITUDE ADJUSTMENT

Above 3500 feet altitude: Increase baking temperature to 375° and bake 30 to 35 minutes or until delicately browned.

CRUMB CAKE

You save out enough flour, brown sugar and butter when mixing cake to bake on batter for a crunchy top

- 2 c. sifted flour
- 1 ½ c. brown sugar, firmly packed
- ½ c. butter or margarine
- 1 tsp. baking soda

1 tsp. salt
1 tsp. cinnamon
½ tsp. nutmeg
¼ tsp. ground cloves
¾ c. plus 2 tblsp. buttermilk or sour milk
2 eggs
½ c. chopped walnuts

Mix flour and brown sugar (free from lumps) with pastry blender. Then cut in butter until dry mixture is evenly coated. Remove ¾ c. of this mixture and reserve for later use.

Stir soda, salt, cinnamon, nutmeg and cloves into remaining mixture. Add ¾ c. buttermilk and beat 2 minutes on medium speed of mixer.

Add remaining buttermilk and eggs; beat 1 more minute. Pour batter into greased and floured pan (13″ × 9″ × 2″).

Add walnuts to the ¾ c. sugar mixture. Sprinkle evenly over the batter.

Bake in moderate oven (350°) 25 to 30 minutes.

HIGH ALTITUDE ADJUSTMENT

For all altitudes above 3500 feet: Increase baking temperature to 375° and bake 30 to 35 minutes. From 3500 to 5000 feet altitude: Use ingredients as listed in Crumb Cake recipe.

Above 5000 feet altitude: Use 1¼ c. brown sugar and 1 c. buttermilk.

UPSIDE-DOWN CHOCOLATE CAKE

The cake is from a mix; the chocolate-nut-marshmallow topping bakes under the batter to tempting richness

2 c. miniature marshmallows
1 c. brown sugar
½ c. cocoa
2 c. hot water
1 (1 lb. 3 oz.) pkg. devils food cake mix
1 c. chopped walnuts

Place marshmallows in bottom of greased pan (13″ × 9″ × 2″). Combine sugar, cocoa and hot water. Pour over marshmallows.

Spoon cake batter, made as directed on package, over marshmallow mixture. Top with walnuts.

Bake in moderate oven (350°) 45 to 50 minutes. Remove from oven. Turn out of pan. Cut in rectangles.

Note: Especially luscious topped with vanilla ice cream or whipped cream.

WHIZ CHOCOLATE CAKE

You whip up the batter in a saucepan

¼ c. shortening
2 (1 oz.) squares unsweetened chocolate
½ c. water
1 c. sugar
½ tsp. salt
1 tsp. vanilla
¼ c. buttermilk
1 c. sifted flour
½ tsp. baking powder
½ tsp. baking soda
1 egg

Heat shortening, chocolate and water together in a 1 qt. saucepan until they are melted. Remove from heat. Cool.

Stir in sugar, salt, vanilla and buttermilk. Beat in flour, baking powder and soda, which have been sifted together. Add egg and beat well.

more

Pour batter into greased pan (9″ × 9″ × 2″).

Bake in moderate oven (350°) 30 minutes. Remove from oven. Turn out of pan. Frost with Saucepan Chocolate Frosting (see Index) or as desired.

CRESTED DESSERT CAKE

Use a cake from the freezer or bakery for this hot-from-the-oven treat

- 1 (8″ or 9″) layer white or sponge cake
- ½ c. chunk-style peanut butter
- 1 c. apricot jam
- ½ c. flaked or shredded coconut

Turn cake bottom side up on baking sheet. Spread with peanut butter, then with jam. (Or mix peanut butter with jam before spreading–it goes on easier.) Sprinkle with coconut.

Place cake in cold oven, then turn on heat and set temperature control at 350°. Turn off heat in 5 minutes. Leave cake in oven while first part of dinner is eaten. Cut in wedges.

Variation: Use raisins, rinsed in warm water and wiped dry with paper towel, instead of coconut. Raisins puff up in oven. For a company touch, top cake with scoops of vanilla ice cream.

Country Cake Walks

Cake walks are popular in many country communities. They provide entertainment for a crowd and raise money for worthy causes. Here is the way to set the stage for a jolly evening.

Draw the face of a clock, as large as possible, on the floor. Write numbers representing the day's 12 hours near the outer rim of the circle. Draw a line on both sides of a number to the center, making triangles. Repeat until there are 12 triangles of equal size.

The master of ceremonies brings out a home-baked cake to tempt everyone with the prize someone will win. Twelve people walk at a time. They pay for the chance to try for the cake.

Each person stands at the outer edge of a triangle. Walking starts with the music and ends simultaneously with it. Then the master of ceremonies asks a child to draw one of the 12 numbers in a hat or basket. The person standing in the triangle with the number corresponding to the one drawn gets the festive cake.

The cakes of the evening are trophies worth capturing. The best cooks in the neighborhood vie with each other in decorating them. The idea is to produce a cake that is showy and glamorous–and delicious.

CHOCOLATE MOUND CAKE

A cake worth walking for

- 1 (1 lb. 3 oz.) pkg. devils food cake mix
- 1 recipe Coconut Topping (see Index)
- 1 (14 oz.) pkg. fluffy white-frosting mix
- Chocolate syrup

Prepare cake mix as directed on package. Bake in 2 (8″) layers.

Top each cooled layer with Coconut Topping and broil as directed in recipe.

Prepare frosting mix as directed on package. Put layers together with frosting and frost sides. Leave top unfrosted with coconut showing.

Dip tip of teaspoon in chocolate syrup and swirl lightly through frosting for decorative effect.

SWEET CREAM CAKE

Speedy to mix—no creaming. Cake is light, feathery and flavorful

2 ½ c. sifted flour
1 ¾ c. sugar
3 tsp. baking powder
½ tsp. salt
1 ⅓ c. heavy cream (30 to 35% butterfat)
⅓ c. milk
1 tsp. vanilla
3 eggs

Sift dry ingredients into mixing bowl. Add cream, milk and vanilla. Mix to dampen dry ingredients. Beat 1 minute at medium speed of electric mixer, or 150 vigorous strokes by hand.

Add eggs and mix one minute longer.

Pour into 2 paper-lined round cake pans (8″ × 1½″). Tap sharply on table top to remove air bubbles. Bake in moderate oven (350°) about 40 minutes.

Cake for High Altitudes

The recipe for Quick Cake was developed for use in altitudes of 4000 to 6000 feet. We give the changes to make if you live in altitudes of 3000 to 4000 feet and above 6000 feet. Frost the cake as you like. Chocolate and coconut frostings are two favorites.

QUICK CAKE

Not as rich as some cakes, but it's moist and flavorful
For altitudes 4000 to 6000 feet

2 c. sifted cake flour
1 ¼ tsp. baking powder
¾ tsp. salt
1 c. plus 2 tblsp. sugar
½ c. vegetable shortening, at room temperature
¾ c. milk
1 tsp. vanilla
2 eggs, unbeaten

Measure sifted flour into sifter; add baking powder, salt and sugar.

Stir shortening just to soften. Sift in dry ingredients. Add milk and vanilla; mix until flour is dampened. Beat 2 minutes at medium speed of electric mixer or 300 vigorous strokes by hand.

Add eggs. Beat 1 minute longer with mixer or 150 strokes by hand.

Pour batter into 2 greased layer pans (8″). Bake in a moderate oven (375°) 25 to 30 minutes.

Baking Variations: Bake 30 to 35 minutes in a greased pan (9″ × 9″ × 2″); 25 to 30 minutes in a greased pan (13″ × 9″ × 2″); and 20 to 25 minutes in 2½ dozen greased medium muffin-cup pans.

Ingredient Variations: Substitute butter or margarine for vegetable shortening. Use 1 c. minus 2 tblsp. milk and 1¼ c. sugar. Add ¾ c. of milk and vanilla to dry ingredients and the remaining milk with the eggs.

Altitude Variations: For altitudes of 3000 to 4000 feet, increase baking powder to 1¾ tsp. For altitudes above 6000 feet, decrease baking powder to 1 tsp. and sugar by 2 tblsp.

A reliable recipe for a 2-egg cake is at a premium in any busy woman's file. That's why we include one for this cake that gives excellent results in lower altitudes.

QUICK CAKE

For altitudes under 3000 feet

1 ¾ c. sifted cake flour
2 ¼ tsp. baking powder
½ tsp. salt
½ c. shortening
1 c. plus 2 tblsp. sugar
2 eggs, unbeaten
¾ c. milk
1 tsp. vanilla

Sift flour, baking powder and salt together. Cream shortening thoroughly. Add sugar gradually and cream together until light and fluffy. Add eggs, one at a time, beating well after each addition. Then add flour alternately with milk, beating after each addition until smooth. Stir in vanilla.

Pour batter into 2 greased layer pans (8″). Bake in moderate oven (375°) 25 to 30 minutes.

CHERRY CROWN CAKE

Give Sweet Cream and other layer cakes glamor with this gala cherry crown

2 baked chocolate-cake layers
2 tblsp. butter or margarine
¼ c. brown sugar, firmly packed
2 tblsp. heavy cream, or sour cream
16 maraschino cherries, drained and halved
1 recipe Glossy Fudge Frosting (see Index)

Place one chocolate-cake layer on baking sheet.

Melt butter, stir in brown sugar and cream and add cherries. Spread mixture on cake layer, spreading out to edges all around.

Place cake in broiler 6″ to 8″ from heat and broil until bubbly all over and golden brown, 2 to 3 minutes. Use this for the top layer of cake.

Put layers together and frost sides of cake with Glossy Fudge Frosting. Leave top of cake unfrosted with the cherries showing.

Modern Recipes Speed Up Fruit Cakes

No fruit-cake recipe published in FARM JOURNAL is more popular than Fruit Cake Delicious. It's not quite as sweet as many traditional cakes.

FRUIT CAKE DELICIOUS

Nuts are not chopped—you cut them when you slice cake

1 ½ c. sifted flour
1 ½ c. sugar
1 tsp. baking powder
1 tsp. salt
2 lbs. pitted dates (do not chop)
2 lbs. shelled walnuts
1 lb. shelled Brazil nuts
1 (8 oz.) bottle maraschino cherries, drained
5 large eggs, beaten
1 tsp. vanilla

In large bowl, sift together flour, sugar, baking powder and salt.

Add dates, nuts and cherries.

Combine eggs and vanilla. Mix into flour-nut mixture. (Easy way is to use your hands.)

Spoon into 3 greased loaf pans (8½″ × 4½″ × 2½″).

Bake in slow oven (325°) 1 hour. Cool thoroughly before slicing or freezing.

EASY-DOES-IT FRUIT CAKE

No cooking required—just mix ingredients and chill

- ¾ c. evaporated milk
- ½ c. frozen orange-juice concentrate, thawed
- 3 c. miniature marshmallows
- 1 ⅓ lbs. graham crackers, crushed into fine crumbs
- 1 tsp. cinnamon
- 1 tsp. ground cloves
- 1 tsp. allspice
- ½ tsp. salt
- 1 c. chopped dates
- 1 c. seedless raisins
- 1 c. chopped nuts
- 2 c. chopped mixed candied fruits

Combine evaporated milk, orange-juice concentrate and marshmallows. Let stand while you prepare other ingredients.

Combine cracker crumbs, spices and salt in large bowl. Add dates, raisins, nuts and candied fruits. Stir into orange-juice mixture until crumbs are moist.

Press mixture firmly into 2 waxed paper-lined loaf pans (9″ × 5″ × 3″). Store in refrigerator at least 2 days before serving. Slice thin. Makes 2 loaves.

Note: Cake, well wrapped, will keep several weeks in refrigerator.

FROZEN FRUIT CAKE

A famous FARM JOURNAL *recipe*

- 2 c. milk
- ½ c. sugar
- ¼ c. flour
- ¼ tsp. salt
- 2 eggs, beaten
- 1 tsp. vanilla
- 1 c. light raisins
- 2 c. vanilla wafers or macaroon crumbs
- ½ c. candied red cherries, halved
- ¼ c. candied mixed fruits
- 1 c. broken pecans
- 1 c. heavy cream, whipped

Scald milk in top of double boiler.

Mix together sugar, flour, salt, and add to milk all at once. Cook over hot water about 3 minutes until smooth and medium thick, stirring constantly.

Pour cooked mixture over beaten eggs and return to double boiler. Cook until thick, about 3 minutes, stirring constantly. Add vanilla. Cool.

Stir raisins, crumbs, and fruits and nuts into mixture.

Fold cream into mixture. Pour into 1½ qt. loaf pan, bottom greased and lined with waxed paper. Cool, wrap and freeze. Makes 8 servings.

Note: To decorate top of fruit cake, arrange a few whole nut meats and candied red and green cherries on waxed paper in bottom of mold before pouring in batter.

Gingerbread for Dessert

Spicy gingerbread wearing rich, fruity topknots is to autumn what strawberries and cream are to June. This molasses cake tempts at any season, but its tantalizing fragrance coming from the oven, once summer ends, signals everyone the trees soon will dress in brilliant colors.

You can use a packaged mix if you are in a hurry. But in case you want to bake, cool and freeze old-fashioned gingerbread when you have some free time, we give you an exceptionally good from scratch recipe.

GINGERBREAD DE LUXE

A FARM JOURNAL *5-star recipe—and this means it's extra good*

- 2 c. sifted flour
- ¾ tsp. salt
- 2 tsp. baking powder
- ¼ tsp. baking soda
- ¾ to 1 tsp. ginger
- ¾ tsp. cinnamon
- ⅛ tsp. cloves
- ½ c. shortening
- ⅔ c. sugar
- 2 medium eggs
- ⅔ c. molasses (light or dark)
- ¾ c. boiling water
- 1 c. heavy cream, whipped

Sift together flour, salt, baking powder, soda and spices.

Cream together shortening and sugar. Beat in eggs, one at a time.

Gradually add molasses, beating constantly (scrape beaters and sides).

Blend in flour, using low speed on mixer. Add water; mix until smooth.

Pour into well-greased and floured (8″ or 9″) square pan. Bake in moderate oven (350°) 35 to 45 minutes.

Serve warm, topped with whipped cream.

NUT-TOPPED GINGERBREAD

Frosting bakes with the cake

- 1 (14½ oz.) pkg. gingerbread mix
- ½ c. brown sugar, firmly packed
- 2 tblsp. flour
- 1½ tsp. cinnamon
- 2 tblsp. melted butter or margarine
- ⅔ c. chopped walnuts

Prepare gingerbread batter as directed on package. Pour into greased 9″ square pan.

Combine brown sugar, flour and cinnamon. Blend in butter and nuts. Sprinkle mixture over batter.

Bake in moderate oven (350°) 25 to 30 minutes. Cut in squares; serve hot.

Variation: Omit nut topping; sprinkle 1 c. flaked or shredded coconut on top of batter. Coconut toasts during the baking.

TROPICAL GINGERBREAD

You'll have calls for seconds

- 1 (14½ oz.) pkg. gingerbread mix
- 1¼ c. grated coconut (packaged)
- ¼ c. sifted confectioners' sugar
- ½ tsp. vanilla
- 1 c. heavy cream, whipped
- 2 large bananas

Prepare gingerbread batter as directed on package. Fold in coconut. Pour into greased 9″ square pan. Bake in moderate oven (350°) 25 to 30 minutes. Cut in squares.

Fold sugar and vanilla into whipped cream. Spoon on top of hot gingerbread. Decorate whipped cream with bananas, sliced. Serve at once.

Variations: Omit bananas. Fold 3 tblsp. instead of ¼ c. confectioners' sugar into whipped cream. Fold in 1 (9 oz.) can crushed pineapple, well drained (about ¾ c.), and ¼ c. chopped and drained maraschino cherries. Serve on warm gingerbread. Or top with ice cream or whipped cream; add spoonful of sparkling peach preserves to every serving for a garnish.

Country Lard Cakes

Requests from many farm women for superior lard-cake recipes encouraged our staff of home economists in Countryside Kitchens to experiment. Of the many cakes baked, the four following ones won top honors. They are made by the meringue method. That's the secret of their success. All are moist, tender and delicious with that old-fashioned flavor Grandmother's cakes had. Taste tests brought high scores for them.

You may say, "But a lard cake isn't short-cut." That depends on the cook's point of view and perhaps to some extent on how much lard she has in the freezer. Certainly they are not as simple to fix as cakes made with packaged mixes. But with an electric mixer, it is surprising what little work it is to whip up the batter of most of the conventional stand-by favorites. And no wonder, for the results obtained by one minute of beating with the mixer equals 150 vigorous hand strokes.

When you have lard on hand and try these recipes, we guarantee you will treasure them and use them again.

To cut down on the time required to produce a finished cake, you can use packaged frosting mixes. We also suggest speedy kinds.

CHOCOLATE LARD CAKE

Velvety, moist cake with tempting light-chocolate color

- 2 eggs, separated
- ½ c. sugar
- ⅓ c. lard
- 1 ¾ c. sifted cake flour
- 1 c. sugar
- ¾ tsp. baking soda
- 1 tsp. salt
- 1 c. plus 2 tblsp. buttermilk, or sour milk
- 2 (1 oz.) squares unsweetened chocolate, melted

Beat egg whites until frothy. Gradually beat in ½ c. sugar. Continue beating until very stiff and glossy.

In another bowl, stir lard to soften. Add sifted dry ingredients and ¾ c. buttermilk. Stir to moisten dry ingredients; then beat 1 minute, medium speed, on mixer. Scrape sides and bottom of bowl constantly.

Add remaining buttermilk, egg yolks and melted chocolate. Beat 1 minute, scraping bowl constantly.

Fold in egg whites.

Pour into 2 greased and floured 8″ round layer cake pans (or 13″ × 9″ × 2″ pan). Bake in moderate oven (350°) 30 to 35 minutes. Cool on rack 10 minutes. Remove from pans.

Brush crumbs from cake while warm to facilitate frosting. Frost with Glossy Fudge Frosting (see Index).

FEATHER SPICE LARD CAKE

Meltingly rich, tender cake

- 2 eggs, separated
- ½ c. sugar
- ⅓ c. lard
- 2 ¼ c. sifted cake flour
- 1 tsp. baking powder
- 1 tsp. salt
- ¾ tsp. baking soda
- ¾ tsp. cinnamon
- ¾ tsp. ground cloves
- 1 c. sugar (brown or white)
- 1 c. plus 2 tblsp. buttermilk, or sour milk

Beat egg whites until frothy. Gradually beat in ½ c. sugar. Continue beating until very stiff and glossy.

more

In another bowl, stir lard to soften. Add sifted dry ingredients and ¾ c. buttermilk. Beat 1 minute, medium speed on mixer. Scrape bottom and sides of bowl constantly.

Add remaining buttermilk and egg yolks. Beat 1 minute, scraping bowl constantly.

Fold in egg-white mixture.

Pour into 2 greased and floured 8″ round layer pans. Bake in moderate oven (350°) 30 to 35 minutes. Cool on rack 10 minutes; then remove from pans. Frost with Peanut Butter Frosting or Broiled Caramel Glaze (see Index).

Note: This cake may also be baked in a pan 13″ × 9″ × 2″.

Variation: To make Mocha Spice Cake, increase cinnamon to 1½ tsp., omit cloves and add 2 tsp. instant coffee.

ORANGE LARD CAKE

You'll use this recipe again and again

- 2 eggs, separated
- ½ c. sugar
- ⅓ c. lard
- 2¼ c. sifted cake flour
- 1 c. sugar
- 2½ tsp. baking powder
- 1 tsp. salt
- ¼ tsp. baking soda
- ¾ c. milk
- ⅓ c. orange juice, fresh or reconstituted frozen
- ¼ tsp. almond extract

Beat egg whites until frothy. Gradually beat in ½ c. sugar. Continue beating until very stiff and glossy.

In another bowl stir lard to soften. Add sifted dry ingredients and milk. Beat 1 minute, medium speed on mixer. Scrape bottom and sides of bowl constantly.

Add orange juice, egg yolks and almond extract. Beat one minute longer, scraping bowl constantly.

Fold in egg-white mixture.

Pour into 2 greased and floured round 9″ layer cake pans (or a 13″ × 9″ × 2″ pan). Bake in moderate oven (350°) 25 to 30 minutes for layers, 30 to 35 minutes for 13″ × 9″ × 2″ cake. Cool layers in pan on rack 10 minutes; then remove from pans. Frost with Fluffy Orange Frosting, Orange Butter Cream or Fruit Whip (see Index).

YELLOW LARD CAKE

A 2-egg cake with an old-time country taste made in a new way

- 2 eggs, separated
- ½ c. sugar
- ⅓ c. lard
- 2¼ c. sifted cake flour
- 1 c. sugar
- 3 tsp. baking powder
- 1 tsp. salt
- 1 c. plus 2 tblsp. milk
- 1½ tsp. vanilla

Beat egg whites until frothy. Gradually beat in ½ c. sugar. Continue beating until very stiff and glossy.

In another bowl stir lard to soften. Add sifted dry ingredients, ¾ c. milk and vanilla. Beat 1 minute, medium speed on mixer. Scrape sides and bottom of bowl constantly.

Add remaining milk and egg yolks.

Beat 1 minute, scraping bowl constantly.

Fold in egg whites.

Pour into 2 greased and floured 9″ round layer cake pans (or a 13″ × 9″ × 2″ pan). Bake in moderate oven (350°) 25 to 30 minutes for round layers (30 to 35 minutes for a 13″ × 9″ × 2″ cake). Cool layers on rack 10 minutes; then remove from pans.

Brush crumbs from cake while warm for ease in frosting. Frost with Peanut Butter Frosting, Pineapple Glaze or Caramel-Nut Glaze (see Index).

HUNGRY MAN'S LARD CAKE

A big cake to carry in pan to picnic or lunch in the field—made by Grandma's creaming method

- 1 ¼ c. lard
- 2 ½ c. sugar
- 6 eggs
- 5 ½ c. sifted flour
- 8 tsp. baking powder
- 2 tsp. salt
- 1 ½ c. milk
- 1 tblsp. vanilla

Cream lard 1 minute; add sugar; cream until light and fluffy.

Beat in eggs, one at a time, beating well after each addition.

Sift together dry ingredients. Add to creamed mixture alternately with milk and vanilla; beat until well mixed.

Pour into greased and floured pan (10″ × 14″).

Bake in moderate oven (375°) about 35 minutes. When cool, spread with caramel or chocolate-fudge frosting made from a packaged mix.

LEMON-COCONUT CAKE PIE

Busy-day pie from a bakery cake

- 1 (7 or 8 oz.) baker's loaf cake
- ½ c. flaked or shredded coconut
- 1 (3 ¼ or 4 oz.) pkg. lemon-flavor pudding and pie filling
- 2 eggs, separated

Cut cake into 12 or 14 slices. Line sides and bottom of a 9″ pie pan with them to make pie shell.

Sprinkle half of coconut over cake slices.

Prepare pudding according to package directions, using egg yolks. Pour immediately into pie shell.

Make meringue from the egg whites, using 6 tblsp. sugar or as directed on pudding package. Spread over filling; sprinkle with remaining coconut. Bake in moderate oven (350°) 12 minutes or until lightly browned. Cool and cut.

MERRY CHRISTMAS CAKE

Gala topping makes this cake a showpiece on the holiday buffet

- 1 (8″) square white cake layer
- 2 tblsp. soft butter or margarine
- ⅓ c. brown sugar, firmly packed
- 2 tblsp. heavy cream
- ⅓ c. chopped candied mixed fruits
- ⅔ c. broken nuts
- ⅓ c. coconut, flaked or shredded
- Candied cherries

Set cake on baking sheet. Cream together butter, sugar and cream. Add candied mixed fruits, nuts and coconut. Spread on cake. Dot with candied cherries.

Broil in preheated broiler until top bubbles and has a glazed appearance, 3 to 5 minutes. Serve warm.

more

Note: Make 2 (8") square cake layers from cake mix. Store in freezer. When company comes, add topping and broil.

ORANGE-RAISIN CAKE

Just the dessert to serve to 12 people with a minimum of effort

1 pkg. yellow-cake mix
Rind of 1 orange, grated
1 c. raisins
1 c. orange juice
Juice of 1 lemon
¾ c. brown sugar

Prepare cake batter as directed on package. Fold in orange rind and raisins. Bake in a greased 13" × 9" × 2" pan in moderate oven (350°) 30 minutes.

Remove cake from pan and, while warm, prick top with fork. Pour over it the orange and lemon juices mixed with the brown sugar. Serve topped with whipped cream, ice cream or plain.

Note: Omit raisins and orange rind when in a hurry.

Dress-ups for Cake Desserts

You'll find that glamorous cake desserts frequently consist of layers or loaves cut in horizontal halves and put together with luscious fillings. Sometimes it's difficult to cut tender cakes quickly without breaking them. Women who have freezers have a perfect solution to the problem. Freeze the cake before cutting it into crosswise halves. Frozen cake is not so tender.

MAPLE-JELLY CAKE

Glamorous dessert no more trouble to make than a frosted cake

1 pkg. sugar-maple-cake mix
½ c. red-currant jelly
1 ½ c. heavy cream

Prepare cake batter as directed on package. Bake in 2 (9") layer pans.

Split cake layers in half horizontally to make 4 layers.

Soften jelly with fork. Add cream and beat with electric mixer until fluffy and thick.

Spread about ⅔ c. cream mixture between each layer. Spread remaining cream over the top. (Decorate with small spoonfuls of jelly if desired.) Store in refrigerator until time to serve.

Note: For a deeper color, add 3 drops red food color to cream before whipping.

MOCHA DREAM CAKE

Make cake with a packaged mix or your favorite recipe

1 c. miniature marshmallows
4 tsp. instant coffee
2 c. heavy cream
2 (8" or 9") baked devils food cake layers

Add marshmallows and instant coffee to cream and stir to blend. Allow to stand at least 3 hours, or overnight, in refrigerator.

Cut each cake layer horizontally into 2 equal layers, making 4 layers.

Whip cream mixture until all marshmallows are dissolved and mixture stands in soft peaks. Spread between cake layers and on sides and top of them. Store in refrigerator until ready to serve.

Notes: A good way to cut unfrozen cake in even layers horizontally is to mark around it with a knife, cutting into the cake about ½″. Anchor a length of thread in the slit and gently pull it through the cake.

Make cake with packaged devils food cake mix or your favorite recipe for devils food cake.

TOPSY-TURVY CAKE

Let this dessert bake while everyone eats the main course

- 1 (1 lb. 8 oz.) jar apple-pie filling
- ½ tsp. cinnamon
- ¼ tsp. nutmeg
- ¼ tsp. ground ginger
- 1 tblsp. lemon juice
- 1 pkg. caramel-cake mix
- ½ c. chopped nuts

Mix apple filling, spices and lemon juice. Pour into greased pan (13″ × 9″ × 2″).

Prepare batter as directed on package; add nuts. Pour over filling. Bake in moderate oven (350°) 30 minutes. Cut in squares. Serve warm, upside-down, with whipped cream.

MINCEMEAT CAKE

Orange-cake mix and mincemeat flavors blend for superior flavor

- 2 tblsp. butter or margarine
- 1 c. sifted brown sugar, firmly packed
- 2 c. prepared mincemeat
- 1 (1 lb. 1 oz.) pkg. orange-cake mix
- 1 c. heavy cream, whipped

Put butter, sugar and mincemeat in 10½″ ring mold. Heat in moderate oven (375°) while making cake.

Prepare cake batter as directed on package and pour over hot mincemeat mixture in pan. Bake in moderate oven (375°) about 25 minutes or until cake is delicately brown and springs back to light touch.

Let stand a few minutes; turn out upside-down on chop plate. Or cool in pan, and just before serving, warm in slow oven (300°) 10 to 15 minutes. Place small dish of whipped cream in center.

AMBROSIA-CAKE DESSERT

Bake cake one day and chill or freeze —next day add filling and topping

- 1 (9 to 12 oz.) pkg. white- or yellow-cake mix
- 1 (3 ¼ oz.) pkg. coconut-cream pudding and pie filling
- 1 (3 oz.) pkg. orange-flavor gelatin
- 1 c. hot water
- ¾ c. cold water
- 3 large bananas

Prepare cake mix (loaf size) as directed on package. Bake in an 8″ or 9″ square pan. Chill or let stand several hours so tender cake may be easily handled.

Prepare pudding as directed on package; cool.

Dissolve gelatin in hot water; add cold water. Place bowl in iced water to chill.

To assemble: Split cake in half to make 2 layers (use sharp knife or a thread). Place bottom half of cake in pan in which it was baked; spread half the pudding over it. Place second layer on top; spread with remaining pudding.

more

Arrange layer of sliced bananas over pudding top. Spoon gelatin over bananas as soon as it reaches thick, syrupy stage. Chill until gelatin is firm.

Cut in 9 squares.

NUT-CRESTED CAKE

Rich nut topping bakes on the cake

- 3 tblsp. butter or margarine
- 2 tblsp. brown sugar
- ½ c. coarsely chopped nuts
- 1 (10 oz.) pkg. caramel-cake mix

Combine butter and brown sugar. Pat on sides and bottom of 9″ layer pan. Sprinkle nuts over butter mixture.

Prepare cake mix as directed on package. Pour into pan and bake in moderate oven (350°) 30 to 35 minutes. Serve warm or cold, plain or topped with vanilla ice cream.

Variation: Substitute peanuts for nuts and banana-cake mix for caramel-cake mix. (This is a small package of cake mix.)

BUSY WOMEN'S CUPCAKES: Make cupcakes as directed on package of yellow cake mix. Cool. Spread tops with orange marmalade and miniature marshmallows, 8 to 10 on each cake. Broil until marshmallows melt slightly and are golden brown. Extra delicious with hot tea.

DATE TEA CAKES

Dainty enough for a party

- 1 (10 oz.) pkg. white-cake mix
- ¾ c. (4 oz.) chopped dates
- ½ c. water
- ¼ c. chopped walnuts
- ½ c. heavy cream, whipped

Bake cake in muffin-cup pans as directed on package.

Place dates and water in small saucepan. Simmer until thickened, 3 to 5 minutes. Stir in nuts. Cool.

Split cooled cupcakes in horizontal halves with serrated knife. Spread bottom halves with date filling and top with other cupcake halves. Top with whipped cream. Store in refrigerator until ready to serve, briefly or several hours. Makes 12 cupcakes.

Variation: Substitute yellow-cake mix for the white one.

LITTLE PARTY CAKES

Cupcakes are easy to cut in halves because they are small. Cut cakes in halves, spread the bottom pieces with filling, add the cake tops, and then spoon on the hats of whipped cream.

The quick way to do the job is to complete each step before starting another.

FAST-FIX PETITS FOURS: Prepare batter with 1 (1 lb. 3 oz.) pkg. white-cake mix as directed on package. Pour into greased and floured jelly-roll pan (15½″ × 10½″ × 1″). Bake in moderate oven (350°) about 25 minutes. Cool and frost in pan. Use your favorite confectioners'-sugar frosting. Cut cake in small squares or diamonds and top each one with a tiny candy, using candies of different colors. Use candy corn for Halloween cakelets.

INFORMAL WEDDING CAKE

You needn't be a caterer to bake this gorgeous cake—it's mix-made

2 (1 lb. 2 oz. or 1 lb. 4 oz.) pkgs. white-cake mix
2 recipes Fluffy White Frosting (recipe follows)

Prepare 3-tier cake pan set (9″ × 1½″, 7¼″ × 1½″, and 5″ × 1½″) by lining bottoms with plain paper.

Prepare one package of cake mix as directed on package. Pour ½ c. batter into small pan, 1 c. batter into next-size pan and remaining batter into large pan. Spread batter evenly in pans. Tap pans sharply on table top to remove air pockets.

Bake small and medium layers in moderate oven (350°) about 20 minutes, the large layer, 30 minutes. Cool on rack 5 minutes and remove from pans. Brush crumbs from sides of cake while still warm.

Prepare batter from the second package of cake mix in the same manner.

Prepare one recipe of frosting. When layers are cool, put layers of same size together with frosting and coat the sides and tops with a thin layer of frosting to seal the crumbs. Stack layers on each other; hold in place with thin skewers. Let stand until set. Meanwhile, make Marshmallow Flowers.

Prepare another recipe of Fluffy White Frosting. Remove skewers from cake; frost entire cake, starting at bottom tier and working up. Apply thickly around bottom tier. Draw small spatula over frosting to smooth it. Then make ridges by pulling spatula in upward strokes all around. (If frosting seems to be crusting over quickly, do a small section at a time.) Pile frosting on bottom ledge and swirl around cake. Continue working up on the cake as directed for bottom tier. Pile and swirl frosting on top of cake.

Place miniature marshmallows in ridges in frosting as shown in picture, pressing firmly into frosting. Arrange Marshmallow Flowers on top of cake and around edge of plate for decoration. Makes 40 servings.

Note: Bake layers ahead; freeze.

MARSHMALLOW FLOWERS: Cut large marshmallows horizontally into 5 pieces, using kitchen scissors dipped in water. Attach these pieces as petals to a miniature marshmallow, used as a center. Dust fingers with confectioners' sugar if pieces stick to fingers. Dip finished flower in colored sugar crystals.

FLUFFY WHITE FROSTING

2 egg whites, unbeaten
1½ c. sugar
⅓ c. water
2 tsp. light corn syrup
Dash of salt
1 tsp. vanilla

Place all ingredients except vanilla in top of double boiler. Beat 1 minute with electric mixer or rotary beater.

Cook over boiling water, beating all the time, until mixture stands in stiff peaks—about 7 minutes.

Remove from heat. Transfer mixture to mixing bowl; add vanilla and beat until of good spreading consistency. Makes enough frosting for Informal Wedding Cake.

A Clever Cake Baker Says:

"Sometimes I frost party cakes with whipped cream and refrigerate them until time to serve. I often squirt a whipped topping from a pressure can on the frosted cake to make white roses. The effect brings out the compliments, and I add the decoration in a jiffy. It's much easier than using a pastry tube."

Special Frostings and Toppings

ALMOND GLAZE

Quick way to dress up sponge or angel food cake from the freezer or bakery

- 1/3 c. chopped or slivered unblanched almonds
- 2 tblsp. butter
- 1 c. apricot or peach jam
- 2 to 3 tblsp. water

Lightly brown almonds in butter over low heat. Add jam and water. Heat until jam melts. Drizzle over sponge or angel food cake.

BANANA FROSTING

Just the frosting for spice cakes and gingerbread—takes no cooking

- 1/2 c. mashed banana
- 1 tsp. lemon juice
- 1/4 c. butter
- 3 1/2 to 4 1/2 c. confectioners' sugar

Combine banana and lemon juice. Cream together butter and 1 c. confectioners' sugar. Beat in banana and enough confectioners' sugar to make mixture of spreading consistency. Makes enough for tops and sides of two 8" cake layers.

Note: If you have ripe bananas that will not keep long, mash them and freeze to use in this frosting.

BROILED CARAMEL GLAZE

The quickest way to put a 2-layer mix cake together with attractive results

- 1/4 c. butter
- 1/2 c. brown sugar, firmly packed
- 2 tblsp. heavy cream

Melt butter; stir in brown sugar and cream.

Place cake layers on baking sheet, one at a time. Spread each layer evenly with butter mixture, spreading out to edges.

Place cake in broiler 6" to 8" from heat, and broil until bubbly and golden brown, 2 to 3 minutes. Broil each layer separately.

When second layer is removed from broiler, place on cake plate immediately and place first layer on it. Layers will hold together, and glaze will have run down the side to give cake a finished, appetizing look. Makes enough glaze for 2 (8" or 9") layers.

VARIATIONS

CARAMEL-NUT GLAZE: Remove glazed top layer from broiler; sprinkle immediately with chopped nuts.

PINEAPPLE GLAZE: Spread top layer with glaze, dip well-drained pineapple tidbits in some of the glaze mixture and

A gorgeous Informal Wedding Cake to make at home (recipe page 127). Frosting is quickly and decoratively studded with miniature marshmallows. Flowers are cut from larger marshmallows, petals dipped in colored sugar.

Warm squares of spicy Gingerbread De Luxe (recipe page 120) topped with tart-sweet applesauce and vanilla ice cream, cinnamon dusted. Chapter 8 contains other gingerbread recipes and a variety of ideas for serving it.

arrange in sunburst effect on top of cake at least 1″ from edge all around. Broil like plain Caramel Glaze.

SOUR-CREAM–CARAMEL GLAZE: Use dairy sour cream for heavy cream.

COCONUT TOPPING

Broils on cake to a bubbling, golden brown in 2 or 3 minutes

1 egg white
⅓ c. sugar
1 ⅓ c. flaked or shredded coconut

Combine unbeaten egg white, sugar and coconut.

Place cake layers on baking sheets. Spread coconut mixture on them, using care to spread out to edges all around.

Place one layer at a time in broiler 6″ to 8″ from heat source and broil until bubbly and golden in color, about 2 to 3 minutes. Makes enough topping for 2 (8″) round layers.

Note: Broil each layer separately so you can watch easily, for the broiling is a fast process.

WHIPPED-CREAM COCOA FROSTING: Pour 1 c. heavy cream into bowl; stir in ⅓ c. cocoa mix. Chill thoroughly. Whip until light and fluffy. Spoon on slices of angel food or unfrosted white cake. Makes enough for 12 cake slices.

Note: You also can frost an angel food cake with Whipped-Cream Cocoa Frosting if you wish.

FRUIT WHIP

Different version of 7-minute frosting

2 egg whites
½ c. preserves, jam or marmalade
½ c. sugar
Dash of salt

Place all the ingredients in double boiler. Beat 1 minute with electric or rotary beater. Cook over boiling water, beating constantly, until mixture forms stiff peaks, 5 to 7 minutes. Remove from heat and beat until of spreading consistency. Makes enough frosting for tops and sides of 2 (8″ or 9″) cake layers.

Superior Frostings with Syrup

Sometimes it's a simple, quick trick that works magic in the kitchen. That's exactly what Basic Sugar Syrup does with frostings. Try our Glossy Fudge Frosting and Peanut Butter Frosting (see Index) and see if you don't agree.

Keep a jar of the syrup handy in the refrigerator. Also use it to sweeten beverages. And when you have an elegant cake that deserves an out-of-the-world frosting, or a plain one that needs a glamorous coverlet, put the syrup to work for you.

BASIC SUGAR SYRUP

2 c. sugar
1 c. water

Boil sugar and water together 1 minute. Pour into jar. Cool, cover and store in the refrigerator. Makes approximately 2 cups.

Note: Frostings made with Basic Sugar Syrup in higher altitudes (above 3500 feet) take longer and more beating than in lower altitudes to become thick enough to stay on the cake.

GLOSSY FUDGE FROSTING

Frosting has a fudge-like grain—the trick is the Basic Sugar Syrup

2 tblsp. butter or margarine
1 (6 oz.) pkg. semi-sweet chocolate pieces
⅓ c. Basic Sugar Syrup (see Index)

Melt butter over hot (not boiling) water. Remove from heat before the water boils.

Add chocolate pieces to butter over hot water and stir until melted, blended and thick.

Add Basic Sugar Syrup gradually, stirring after each addition until blended. Mixture will become glossy and smooth.

Remove from hot water and cool until of spreading consistency. Spread thinly over cake. Apply quickly by pouring a small amount at a time on top of cake; as it runs down on sides, spread with spatula. Frost top of cake last. Makes frosting for 2 (8″) layers, or 1 (13″ × 9″ × 2″) cake.

CHOCOLATE-BUTTERSCOTCH FROSTING

Chocolate plus butterscotch equals delicious taste—just try it

1 (6 oz.) pkg. butterscotch morsels
1 (1 oz.) square unsweetened chocolate
½ c. Basic Sugar Syrup (see Index)

Melt butterscotch morsels and chocolate over hot, not boiling, water. (Remove from heat just before boiling point is reached.)

Add Basic Sugar Syrup gradually to butterscotch-chocolate mixture, stirring until blended after each addition. (Mixture becomes glossy and smooth.)

Remove from hot water and cool until of spreading consistency. In warm weather, it may be necessary to set pan in iced water to cool quickly. Enough frosting for 2 (8″) cake layers or 1 (13″ × 9″ × 2″) cake.

CAKE TRIM: Make cake as directed on mix package. Frost with fluffy white frosting made from packaged mix. To decorate, pour a few drops of food color into saucer. Dip a piece of white sewing thread in color, keeping ends dry by holding one in each hand. Hold wet thread tight and press design on frosted cake. You can smear lines a little with a spatula if desired. Make a spoke design on round cake and squares or diamonds on a square or rectangular cake.

PEANUT BUTTER FROSTING

Surprise—an easy-does-it, fluffy frosting with rich peanut flavor, just sweet enough. Perfect on spice, chocolate and yellow cakes

¾ c. chunk-style peanut butter
¾ c. cold Basic Sugar Syrup (see Index)

Whip peanut butter with mixer (or wooden spoon). Add syrup gradually, beating all the time. Makes enough frosting for tops and sides of 2 (8″ or 9″) cake layers.

FLUFFY ORANGE FROSTING

Use this fruity frosting on plain cakes to make them glamorous

2 egg whites
1½ c. sugar
¼ c. frozen orange-juice concentrate, thawed
¼ c. water
Dash of salt

Place all ingredients in double boiler. Beat 1 minute with electric or rotary beater. Cook over boiling water, beating constantly until mixture forms stiff peaks, 7 to 8 minutes. Remove from heat and beat until of spreading consistency. Makes generous frosting for tops and sides of 2 (9″) cake layers.

Note: In high altitudes (above 3500 feet) cook frosting in a 2 qt. double boiler. Cook and beat it until frosting forms stiff peaks (about 3 to 4 minutes) when using an electric beater or mixer, longer (up to 14 minutes) with hand beater. The yield will be somewhat larger than in lower altitudes.

ORANGE BUTTER CREAM

Rich orange flavor complements many kinds of cake

½ c. butter
3 c. sifted confectioners' sugar
⅓ c. frozen orange-juice concentrate, thawed

Cream butter. Add sugar alternately with orange juice, creaming well after every addition until mixture is light and fluffy. Makes frosting for tops and sides of 2 (8″ or 9″) round layers.

SAUCEPAN CHOCOLATE FROSTING

Glossy, smooth and speedy

1 (1 oz.) square unsweetened chocolate
2 tblsp. butter or margarine
3 tblsp. light cream
½ tsp. vanilla
1 c. sifted confectioners' sugar

Place chocolate, butter and cream in saucepan; heat until chocolate and butter are melted. Add vanilla and confectioners' sugar and beat until mixture is of spreading consistency. Makes enough frosting for 2 (8″ or 9″) cake layers or for Saucepan Brownies (see Index).

A Country Cook Says:

When you make a confectioners'-sugar frosting for a cake, stir up more than you need. Store the extra amount in an air-tight container in refrigerator. Next time you take a cake baked in a 13″ × 9″ × 2″ pan from the oven, put a big spoonful of the cold frosting on it while hot. As frosting starts to melt, begin the spreading. Spread it over the entire cake. When the cake cools, it will wear a lovely, glossy glaze.

CHEESE-CHERRY CAKE TOPPING: Spread cream cheese, softened at room temperature, on squares of unfrosted chocolate cake. Spoon on canned cherry-pie filling. A simple, easy, pretty and extra-good dessert.

CHAPTER 9

PIES

Styles in desserts come and go, but flaky, tender-crusted pies are the favorite finale for many country dinners. That's because they rate as the farmer's pet dessert. Busy wives say pie must come to the table frequently to keep their husbands happy.

Changes are taking place in the country pie even though the men are unaware of it. As you look at the recipes in this chapter, sent by good cooks, you'll note that ice cream appears more frequently in the fillings. And often it *is* the filling! Luscious examples of easy-does-it holiday pies, adapted from traditional Thanksgiving and Christmas pies, are Frozen Pumpkin, nut-sprinkled, and Frozen Mincemeat, with its red-cherry topping.

Short-cut cooks are making more one-crust or open-faced pies, like the apricot and peach recipes in this chapter. Women say they are easier to make. Men who are waistline watchers say they have fewer calories, and then, as one wife told us, "They ask for a spoonful of ice cream on top of their servings."

How do women make pie when time is short? Many of them do the baking when they have free time, and freeze the dessert to reheat. Or they keep baked pie shells in the freezer or refrigerator to fill on the spur of the moment. And once you've tasted Black-Walnut Chocolate Pie, with sour cream on top, we think you'll want to keep a ready-to-go pie shell on hand at all times. Store it in the freezer.

The variety in pastry is great, especially in the crumb crusts that many cooks find a snap to fix. Look in this chapter for crust recipes made with crumbs, coconut, salad oil, lard and hydrogenated shortening. Choose the one you like or do as thousands of busy women do: use packaged pie-crust mix. And when a party is on your schedule bake Pink Pastry.

Best-ever Country Pies

They're here to stay

Fruit-filled Pies

QUICK APPLE PIE

You sprinkle on the top crust

5 to 6 tart cooking apples
1 c. sugar
1 tsp. cinnamon
⅛ tsp. salt
2 to 3 tblsp. water
2 tblsp. butter or margarine
½ pkg. prepared pie-crust mix
Sugar

Pare and core apples; dice or slice (need about 5 c.).

Mix sugar, cinnamon and salt; sprinkle over apples; toss lightly.

Put sugar-coated apples in 9″ pie pan; add water; dot with butter.

Sprinkle pie-crust mix over top of apples or cut chilled stick of mix into thin slices; cover apples. Sprinkle with sugar.

Bake in moderate oven (350°) 45 minutes or until apples are tender. Serve plain, with whipped cream or ice cream. Makes 6 servings.

APRICOT PIE À LA MODE

Omit ice cream for an everyday pie

1 (1 lb. 13 oz.) can apricot halves, drained
1 unbaked 9″ pie shell
1 tblsp. lemon juice
½ c. flour
¾ c. sugar
¼ tsp. cinnamon
¼ tsp. nutmeg
¼ c. butter or margarine
1 pt. vanilla ice cream

Spread apricots in pastry-lined pan. Sprinkle with lemon juice.

Combine flour, sugar and spices. Mix with butter until crumbly. Sprinkle over apricots.

Bake in hot oven (400°) 40 minutes. Serve warm or cold, topped with scoops of ice cream. Makes 6 servings.

CHERRY PIE AU GRATIN

Pie fresh from bakery to freezer, then to oven—an easy way to fix dessert

1½ c. grated or shredded sharp cheese
2 (7″) cherry pies

Sprinkle cheese over top of pies. Heat in moderate oven (350°) 10 minutes, or until cheese melts. Serve at once.

Variation: Your own apple or favorite berry pie also may be served this way.

CHERRY-BANANA PIE

Keep a baked pie shell in freezer so you can make this pie in 10 minutes

2 medium bananas
1 baked 9″ pie shell
1 (1 lb. 6 oz.) can cherry-pie filling
1 c. heavy cream
2 tblsp. sugar
⅓ c. chopped nuts

Slice bananas into bottom of pie shell. Top with cherry-pie filling.

more

Whip cream, add sugar and spread over cherry filling. Sprinkle nuts over.

Variation: Substitute flaked or shredded coconut for nuts.

HAWAIIAN PINEAPPLE PIE

Lush tropical flavors mingle in this elegant pie with cookie crust

1 pkg. refrigerator coconut-cookie dough
1 (3 oz.) pkg. vanilla pudding and pie filling
⅛ tsp. salt
½ c. water
1 (20 oz.) can crushed pineapple, drained
1 tblsp. butter or margarine
½ c. heavy cream, whipped
⅓ c. flaked or shredded coconut

Slice cookie dough in ¼" slices. Arrange slices in 9" pie pan, first lining bottom of pan, then sides. (Let side slices rest on bottom ones to make higher sides.) Bake in moderate oven (375°) until lightly browned, 9 to 12 minutes.

Meanwhile combine pudding mix and salt in saucepan. Blend in water. Add pineapple and cook over medium heat, stirring constantly, until mixture comes to a full boil. Stir in butter.

Pour hot filling into pie shell. Cool. Spread whipped cream over the top. Sprinkle with coconut.

OPEN-FACED PEACH PIE

A FARM JOURNAL *5-star recipe*

2 (1 lb.) cans peach halves, well drained
1 unbaked (9") pie shell
⅓ c. sugar
3 tblsp. cornstarch
¾ tsp. nutmeg
¼ tsp. salt
¾ c. heavy cream
¾ tsp. vanilla
Whipped cream

Arrange peach halves, cut side up, in pastry shell.

Combine sugar, cornstarch, ½ tsp. nutmeg, salt, cream and vanilla. Pour over peaches in shell; sprinkle with remaining nutmeg.

Bake in hot oven (400°) 30 minutes; reduce heat to moderate oven (350°) and bake 20 minutes. Serve with whipped cream.

Note: Extra good made with fresh peaches. Use ½ c. instead of ⅓ c. sugar.

STRAWBERRY BASKET

A luscious beauty resembling French pastry—make basket in advance

1 stick pie-crust mix
1 qt. fresh strawberries
1 (10 oz.) jar currant or apple jelly
Confectioners' sugar

Prepare pie-crust mix as directed on package. Roll and fit over a 9" square pan. Flute edges and prick pastry with a fork. Bake in hot oven (425°) about 13 minutes or until a light golden brown. Cool. Place on plate.

Arrange fresh strawberries (quantity varies slightly with size of berries) in straight rows in pastry basket.

Melt jelly over hot water; brush over berries and lightly on basket's rim. Dust rim with confectioners' sugar.

cream for the peach and frozen strawberries for the raspberries.

Luscious Ice-Cream Pies

FROZEN MINCEMEAT PIE

A pretty Merry Christmas dessert

1 qt. vanilla ice cream, slightly softened
1 ½ c. ready-to-use mincemeat
1 baked (9″) pie shell
¼ c. chopped nuts
Maraschino cherries, well drained

Beat together ice cream and mincemeat. Spread into pie shell. Sprinkle with nuts and maraschino cherries, cut in halves.

Freeze until solid, about 4 hours. If kept longer, place in plastic bag. Serve frozen.

NORTH POLE CHERRY PIE

One of the most popular FARM JOURNAL *pie recipes*

1 qt. vanilla ice cream
1 baked (9″) pie shell or crumb crust
1 (1 lb. 6 to 8 oz.) jar cherry-pie filling

Spread slightly softened ice cream in pie shell and freeze. (You may tint ice cream delicate green.)

An hour before serving, spread filling over top. Return to freezer. Serve quickly.

PEACHY ICE-CREAM PIE: Press 1 qt. peach ice cream in a baked (9″) crumb or coconut-pie shell. Freeze. Serve topped with frozen red raspberries, partly thawed, and whipped cream, unsweetened. Or substitute strawberry ice cream for the peach and frozen strawberries for the raspberries.

Pink Party Pie

This ice-cream pie has three charms that make it a winner—beauty, deliciousness, and you make it ahead and freeze. All you do at serving time is brown the meringue in a hot oven for five minutes.

ICE-CREAM PIE

A FARM JOURNAL *5-star recipe*

1 recipe Pink Pastry (see Index)
1 qt. strawberry ice cream
1 (10 oz.) pkg. frozen strawberries, thawed and drained
2 egg whites
¼ tsp. cream of tartar
¼ c. sugar
Few drops red food color

Line a 9″ pie pan with Pink Pastry. Flute edges and prick pastry. Bake in hot oven (425°) 8 to 10 minutes. Cool.

Pile softened ice cream into baked pie shell and spread; freeze overnight.

Heat oven to extremely hot (500°). Arrange strawberries on ice cream.

Make meringue with egg whites, cream of tartar and sugar. Tint a delicate pink. Spread meringue over pie, covering edges so ice cream will not melt.

Set pie on wooden bread board in oven and bake about 5 minutes, or until lightly browned. Serve immediately.

Variations: Put 2 c. fresh strawberries in baked pie shell, top with 1 pt. vanilla ice cream, 1 c. berries and meringue. Brown as directed. Use pie-crust mix to make pie shell as directed on package, adding 4 drops of red food color to the water.

FROZEN PUMPKIN PIE

Keep one to serve on short notice

1 qt. vanilla ice cream, slightly softened
1 c. canned pumpkin, or cooked, sieved pumpkin
⅓ c. sugar
½ tsp. salt
1 tsp. cinnamon
½ tsp. ginger
½ tsp. ground cloves
1 baked (9") pie shell
¼ c. chopped walnuts

Beat together ice cream, pumpkin, sugar, salt and spices with electric beater until well blended.

Pour into pie shell. Sprinkle with nuts. Freeze until firm. If pie is kept longer, store in a plastic bag. Serve frozen. Makes 6 servings.

Short-cut Farm Favorites

THREE QUICK PIES

QUICK APRICOT-CHIFFON PIE

Fluffy, pastel, fruit-flavored fillings in crisp pie shells

1 (3 oz.) pkg. lemon-chiffon-pie filling
½ c. boiling water
1 c. apricot nectar
⅛ tsp. almond extract
Red and yellow food color
⅓ c. sugar
1 baked (9") pie shell
Toasted coconut

Thoroughly dissolve filling in water. Beat in the nectar, almond extract and 3 drops each of the two food colors (makes orange hue). Add sugar and beat until mixture stands in peaks.

Pile filling into baked shell; swirl top. Chill until set. Garnish with coconut.

Variations: Thoroughly dissolve lemon-chiffon-pie filling in ½ c. boiling water, and proceed as follows:

QUICK LIME PIE: Beat in ¼ c. each frozen limeade concentrate and cold water; add 4 drops green food color. Add ⅓ c. sugar; beat until mixture stands in peaks. Spoon filling into pie shell; swirl top. Chill until set.

QUICK ORANGE PIE: Beat in juice from 1 orange plus cold water to make ½ c.; add 1 tsp. grated orange rind and 3 or 4 drops red food color. Add sugar; beat until peaks form. Spoon filling into pie shell; swirl top. Chill until set. Garnish with shredded rind from ½ orange.

BLACK-WALNUT CHOCOLATE PIE

A good cook says: "My mother's recipe —too good to forget"

½ c. butter or margarine
¾ c. sugar
1 (1 oz.) square unsweetened chocolate, melted and cooled
1 tsp. vanilla
2 eggs
1 baked (8") pie shell

½ c. dairy sour cream
⅓ c. black walnuts

Beat butter with electric mixer until creamy. Add sugar and beat until fluffy.

Beat in chocolate and vanilla. Add 1 egg; beat 3 minutes. Repeat with second egg. Spread in pie shell. Chill ½ hour. Spread sour cream over top and sprinkle with walnuts.

Note: Try slightly sweetened whipped cream instead of the sour cream.

BROWNIE PIE

Rich with full chocolate flavor. Small servings are adequate

1 stick pie-crust mix
1 (1 lb.) pkg. brownie mix
¼ c. chocolate syrup
¼ c. chopped nuts
Whipped cream

Prepare pie mix as directed on package. Line a 9″ pie pan with pastry.

Prepare brownie mix as directed on package for fudgy brownies. Spread mixture evenly in unbaked pie shell. Pour chocolate syrup evenly over the top. Sprinkle with nuts.

Bake in moderate oven (350°) 40 to 45 minutes. Serve warm topped with whipped cream. Makes 10 servings.

BUTTERMILK PIE WITH CORNMEAL PASTRY

Delicate, lemon-flavored custard pie—a treasured Tennessee recipe

3 eggs, separated
1 c. sugar
1 tblsp. butter
¼ c. flour
2 c. buttermilk
¼ tsp. grated lemon rind
2 tblsp. lemon juice
1 unbaked (9″) cornmeal pie shell
6 tblsp. sugar

Beat yolks, adding 1 c. of sugar gradually.

Cut butter into flour; add buttermilk, lemon rind and juice; fold in yolks.

Pour into pastry-lined pan (pie-shell recipe follows). Bake in hot oven (425°) 10 minutes; reduce heat to moderate (350°), and bake 20 to 25 minutes longer. Cool.

Beat egg whites until frothy; gradually add 6 tblsp. sugar; beat until stiff and glossy. Pile lightly over cooled filling. Bake in moderate oven (350°) 12 to 15 minutes.

CORNMEAL PIE SHELL: Sift together 1 c. sifted flour and ½ tsp. salt; stir in ½ c. cornmeal. Cut in ½ c. shortening until mixture resembles fine crumbs. Stir in ⅓ c. grated Cheddar cheese; sprinkle ¼ c. water over mixture gradually, mixing lightly with fork. Shape into ball; flatten on lightly floured surface. Roll to about ⅛″ thickness. Line 9″ pie pan; trim and flute edge. Fill and bake as directed.

OVERNIGHT CHERRY PIE

Scrumptious no-bake dessert

18 graham crackers, crushed
½ c. sugar
⅓ c. melted butter
1 c. heavy cream, whipped
2 c. miniature marshmallows
1 (1 lb. 6 oz.) can cherry-pie filling

more

Combine graham-cracker crumbs, sugar and melted butter. Reserve 2 tblsp. mixture. Press remainder into 9″ pie pan. Chill. (Chills quickly in freezer.)

Combine whipped cream and marshmallows. Spread half of mixture in bottom of crumb-lined pie pan. Top with cherry-pie filling. Cover with remaining whipped-cream mixture. Sprinkle with reserved crumbs. Chill overnight.

Note: You can buy graham-cracker crumbs in handy (13½ oz.) bags—enough to make 3 pie crusts.

CHOCOLATE-AND-CREAM PIE

Another make-ahead dessert

- 1 c. milk
- ½ lb. marshmallows (30 to 32)
- ⅛ tsp. salt
- 1 tsp. vanilla
- 1 c. heavy cream
- 2 (1 oz.) squares unsweetened chocolate, grated
- ½ c. chopped walnuts or pecans
- 1 baked (9″) pie shell
- ¼ c. flaked or shredded coconut

Heat milk in double boiler. Add marshmallows; dissolve. Chill until partly congealed. Add salt and vanilla.

Whip cream until stiff. Fold cream, grated chocolate and nuts into marshmallow mixture.

Pour into pie shell. Sprinkle top with coconut. Chill until serving time.

CHOCOLATE-BAR PIE

Garnish top with daisies, using almonds for the petals

- 20 marshmallows
- 4 (⅞ oz.) chocolate-almond bars
- 1 (1 oz.) square unsweetened chocolate
- ⅔ c. milk
- 1 c. heavy cream, whipped
- 1 baked (8″) pie shell

Combine marshmallows, chocolate bars, chocolate and milk in top of double boiler. Heat over hot, not boiling, water until melted. Cool.

Fold in whipped cream. Pour into pie shell. Chill 2 hours.

CHOCOLATE-LIME REFRIGERATOR PIE

Chocolate-brown and luscious green pie that requires no baking

- 1¼ c. chocolate-cookie crumbs
- ⅓ c. melted butter
- 1 (15 oz.) can sweetened condensed milk
- ½ c. lime juice
- 1 tsp. grated lime rind (optional)
- 1 c. heavy cream, whipped

Combine cookie crumbs and butter. Reserve 2 tblsp. crumb mixture. Press remaining crumb mixture on sides and bottom of greased 8″ pie pan. Chill. (You can chill it quickly in freezer.)

Combine condensed milk, lime juice and lime rind. Stir until mixture thickens. Fold in half the whipped cream. Pour into pan lined with cookie crumbs.

Spread remaining whipped cream over the top. Sprinkle with 2 tblsp. cookie-crumb mixture. Chill.

DAMSON-PLUM WHIPPED CREAM PIE

Speedy version of the sweet-tart pie that rates high in the Old Dominion

1 pkg. pie-crust mix
¾ c. damson-plum preserves
1 pkg. dessert-topping mix
½ tsp. vanilla
⅛ tsp. almond extract
1 tblsp. confectioners' sugar
Nutmeg

Mix, bake and cool 8″ pie shell as directed on package.

Spread preserves over bottom of pie shell.

Prepare topping as directed on package, adding flavorings and sugar before whipping. Spread over preserves. Sprinkle very lightly with nutmeg. Chill before serving.

Variation: To make Damson Custard Pie, prepare a package of instant vanilla-pudding mix as directed on package. Pour over preserves. When set, add topping.

CRANBERRY-CHIFFON PIE

Pink of perfection—packaged filling and bottled juice make it hasty

1 c. cranberry-juice cocktail
1 (3 oz.) pkg. lemon-chiffon-pie filling
⅓ c. sugar
1 (9″) graham-cracker pie shell

Chill ½ c. cranberry juice.

Heat remaining juice to boiling; stir into filling mix. Add chilled juice; beat until foamy with mixer at highest speed.

Add sugar; beat until mixture stands in peaks—1 to 3 minutes. Spoon into pie shell. Chill until set (about 2 hours). Serve plain or with whipped cream.

CRANBERRY-MINCEMEAT PIE

Something new in a traditional winter pie—spring it on company

3 c. ready-to-use mincemeat
1 c. Cranberry Relish (see Index)
1 unbaked (9″) pie shell

Combine mincemeat and relish; pour into pie shell.

Bake in hot oven (400°) 35 minutes.

REFRIGERATOR PUMPKIN PIE

Spicy filling requires no cooking

1 (15 oz.) can sweetened condensed milk
⅓ c. lemon juice
1 (1 lb. 13 oz.) can pumpkin
3½ tsp. pumpkin-pie spice
½ tsp. salt
1 baked (9″) pie shell
½ c. heavy cream, whipped
2 tblsp. chopped nuts

Combine condensed milk and lemon juice; stir until mixture thickens. Stir in pumpkin, spice and salt. Lightly spoon into pie shell.

Chill in refrigerator until firm, about 4 hours. Spread whipped cream over the top. Sprinkle with nuts. Makes 6 servings.

Variation: Top with Whipped Maple Topping instead of whipped cream. Drizzle 2 tblsp. maple or maple-blended syrup on ½ c. heavy cream, whipped. Carefully fold in the syrup.

DATE-NUT PIE

Crisp crust luscious with dates and nuts is perfect background for ice cream

12 soda crackers, crushed
½ c. chopped walnuts
12 dates, chopped
3 egg whites
½ tsp. baking powder
¾ c. sugar
½ tsp. vanilla
1 pt. vanilla ice cream

Combine crackers, nuts and dates. Beat egg whites until frothy; add baking powder. Continue beating, adding sugar gradually, until mixture forms stiff peaks. Beat in vanilla.

Fold cracker mixture into egg whites. Spoon into greased 9" pie pan.

Bake in slow oven (325°) 25 to 30 minutes. Fill with spoonfuls of vanilla ice cream just before serving.

EASY PECAN PIE

A gourmet dish to set proudly before guests. Be ready to share the recipe with women who taste it

20 round buttery crackers, crushed
1 c. chopped pecans
1 c. sugar
3 egg whites
1 tsp. vanilla
½ c. heavy cream, whipped
½ c. flaked or shredded coconut

Combine crackers, pecans and ½ c. sugar.

Beat egg whites until stiff; beat in remaining sugar and vanilla. Fold into cracker mixture.

Spread in greased 9" pie pan and bake in slow oven (325°) 30 minutes. Cool.

Top with whipped cream and sprinkle with coconut.

DANISH RASPBERRY PIE

The pie filling will double for dessert. Swirl whipped cream on top

1 c. cold water
1 pkg. Danish-dessert mix, currant-raspberry flavor
1 (10 oz.) pkg. frozen raspberries
1 baked (8") pie shell
1 c. heavy cream

Add water to Danish-dessert mix. Bring to boil and boil 1 minute, stirring constantly. Add raspberries; cool. Pour into cooled pie shell; refrigerate several hours. Garnish with whipped cream.

A Country Cook Says:

"Immediately after I bake a frozen-fruit or berry pie, I carefully pour 1 tsp. light corn syrup into three steam vents in the upper crust. The hot fruit blends the syrup and juice and explains why everyone asks, 'How do you bake such juicy fruit pies?' "

Tender, Flaky Pastry

Many a superior country cook looks to the pie crust she makes to win laurels for her wherever she serves this great dessert—at home or at church suppers. Some cooks rely on packaged pie-crust mixes to give them the same good results every time. Other women treasure pet recipes. We give their favorites using lard, hydrogenated fats and oil.

And we include a Coconut Crust and several Crumb Crusts.

COCONUT PIE CRUST

Party pie—use ice cream, cream or chiffon filling in crisp, golden crust

1 ⅓ c. flaked coconut
2 tblsp. butter, melted
2 tblsp. sugar
¼ c. graham-cracker crumbs

Combine coconut and butter; mix well. Add sugar and graham-cracker crumbs; mix and press firmly into bottom and on sides of an 8″ pie pan. Bake in moderate oven (375°) 10 to 12 minutes, or until golden brown. Makes 1 (8″) pie shell.

Variation: Substitute chocolate-wafer (cookie) crumbs for graham-cracker crumbs.

Crumb Pie Crusts

Some short-order cooks find crumb crusts help them to make pies in a jiffy. These crusts for open-faced pies are simple to make and introduce great variety in desserts because so many different kinds of crumbs can be used.

The universal favorites are graham crackers, vanilla and chocolate wafers, gingersnaps, corn flakes, zweibach and rusks. Almost any dry cereal or bread crumbs may be used. Corn flake, vanilla-wafer and graham-cracker crumbs are excellent for a lemon-meringue pie. Spiced crusts are especially tasty for pumpkin-, chocolate- and mocha-pie fillings. Here is a basic recipe with variations.

CRUMB CRUSTS

1 ⅔ c. very finely crushed crumbs
½ c. butter or margarine, melted
2 to 4 tblsp. sugar, or to taste

Mix crumbs, butter and sugar. Spread in a greased 9″ pie pan and press firmly against the bottom and sides of the pan, molding with an 8″ or 9″ pie pan.

Bake 8 minutes in moderate oven (375°). Cool and fill.

VARIATIONS

CHOCOLATE-CRUMB CRUST: Add 2 (1 oz.) squares unsweetened chocolate, melted, to corn flake, vanilla-wafer or graham-cracker crumb mixture.

COCONUT-CRUMB CRUST: Reduce crumbs to 1⅓ c. and add ⅓ c. flaked coconut.

ORANGE-CRUMB CRUST: To basic crumb-crust mixture, add 2 tblsp. grated orange rind.

NUT-CRUMB CRUST: Reduce crumbs to 1¼ c. and add ½ c. finely chopped nuts.

SPICED-CRUMB CRUST: Mix 1 tsp. cinnamon or ½ tsp. ginger with crumbs.

HOT-WATER PASTRY

Many champion pie bakers favor this method of making pastry

⅓ c. boiling water
⅔ c. shortening
2 c. sifted flour
¾ tsp. salt

Pour water over shortening; beat with spoon until creamy. Cool. Sift flour and salt into the shortening mixture; mix with a fork.

Wrap the soft dough in waxed paper and chill before rolling. Makes enough for 1 (8″) two-crust pie.

PASTRY FOR ONE-CRUST PIE

A farm favorite—country cooks say it's "short" or tender-crisp

1 c. sifted flour
½ tsp. salt
⅓ c. lard
2 tblsp. water

Mix sifted flour and salt; cut in lard with pastry blender. Sprinkle on the water and mix with a fork until all the flour is moistened. Gather the dough together and press firmly into a ball. Makes enough pastry for 1 (8″ or 9″) one-crust pie.

Variation: Substitute ⅓ c. plus 1 tblsp. hydrogenated fat for the lard.

PASTRY FOR 9″ TWO-CRUST PIE: Double recipe for Pastry for One-crust Pie.

PASTRY FOR 8″ TWO-CRUST PIE: Use 1½ c. flour, ⅔ tsp. salt, ½ c. lard (or ½ c. plus 1 tblsp. hydrogenated shortening) and ¼ c. water.

PINK PASTRY: Add 3 or 4 drops red food color to water when making Pastry for One-crust Pie.

OIL PASTRY

A quick and easy pastry—no shortening to cut into flour

½ c. salad oil
5 tblsp. iced water
2 c. sifted flour
1 tsp. salt

Beat oil and water until mixture is thick and creamy. Sift flour and salt into bowl and pour over the oil-water mixture to completely cover flour. Mix with a fork to form a ball. Makes enough pastry for 1 (8″ or 9″) two-crust pie.

FREEZING PIE SHELLS: Freeze pie shells baked or unbaked, as you like. They will keep satisfactorily 6 months. Freeze unbaked pastry in circles with a double fold of sheet-wrapping material, or one layer of foil or saran between. To use, remove pastry circle from freezer and fit into pans as soon as the dough can be manipulated. Quick-freeze baked shells in pie pans; remove and stack (to save space) with crumbled sheet-wrapping material between. Then package.

CHAPTER 10

OTHER DESSERTS

While cakes and pies are associated with country kitchens, there is great variety in other farm-favorite desserts. You might call this chapter a hit-and-miss collection of delicious ways to end meals. One short-cut cook sent recipes with this comment: "Here are the desserts I make to pamper myself (they take little time) and to pamper my family (they taste so good)."

Ice cream is a regular in country meals. It has become a staple, since the freezer makes it possible to store half-gallons and gallons. Busy women glamorize it in many ways, as this chapter shows. Make-ahead cooks use it as an ingredient in many dishes, like the frozen pies in the previous chapter. It rivals whipped cream for topping desserts.

Puddings, both from scratch and packaged mixes, have an honored place on farm tables. And there are fruity concoctions of infinite variety, often put together in a few minutes, like Jiffy Ambrosia. And the last-minute cooks delight in making gelatin desserts, adding frozen fruit or berries to speed up the congealing. Creative cooks do interesting things with canned pie fillings, not just for pie, but as an ingredient in other desserts. One example is Clover-Leaf Cherry Torte. It's party food. Three slices of refrigerator cookie dough make the clover leaves and cherry-pie filling its crimson topping. And Raspberry Crunch is a true delight.

You will note that familiar foods play new roles. Stacks of pancakes hot off the griddle make luscious shortcakes when topped with whipped cream and juicy berries and peaches. Waffles, baked and frozen, are quickly topped with a mixture of butter, coconut and brown sugar, and broiled. And a new peach cobbler, touched with cinnamon, still has that good, old-fashioned taste. Cinnamon rolls do the spicing and provide the crust.

But recipes are what count—we predict you'll find one in this chapter that you won't want to wait until tomorrow to fix.

Luscious Country Desserts

They're quick and sweet

Flavor-rich with Fruits

JIFFY AMBROSIA

A 60-second dessert—good served with fruit cake, sliced thin

1 (1 lb. 13 oz.) can fruit cocktail
1 (3½ oz.) can coconut, flaked or shredded
1 large banana, sliced
1 (6 oz.) can frozen orange-juice concentrate, thawed
8 maraschino cherries (optional)

Combine fruit cocktail, half of the coconut, banana and orange juice. Garnish mixture with remaining coconut and top each serving with a cherry. Makes 8 servings.

APPLE-ORANGE DESSERT

You can fix it just before a meal and let chill until dessert time

1 (16 to 17 oz.) can applesauce
1 c. miniature marshmallows
1 c. orange sections, fresh or canned

Combine ingredients, spoon into dessert glasses and chill a few minutes or an hour. Makes 5 servings.

Note: Crisp cookies make an excellent teammate.

HONEYED APPLESAUCE: Pour applesauce into a shallow heat-proof dish and spread thin layer of dairy sour cream over the top. Sprinkle lightly with mace or cinnamon and drizzle with honey. Run in broiler until top bubbles, about 4 minutes.

TRICKS WITH APPLESAUCE

While tart-sweet applesauce needs no dress-up, quick changes add welcome variety. Here are 3 ways to give 1 qt. applesauce, about 6 servings, a new taste. Other apple favorites follow. Add:

1 c. fresh raspberries or drained, partly thawed frozen raspberries and 1 c. flaked coconut. (Save some of the coconut to garnish tops.)

2 c. fresh strawberries, sliced, or frozen strawberries partly thawed and drained, and 1½ c. miniature marshmallows.

½ c. coarsely crushed peppermint-stick candy and 2 c. lightly toasted white- or yellow-cake crumbs. Mix well and let chill while you get the remainder of the meal and eat the main course.

GINGER-APPLE FLUFF

Spicy and delicious—a dessert you can whip up just before dinner

1 c. gingersnap crumbs
½ c. heavy cream, whipped
1 (1 lb.) can applesauce
Maraschino cherries

Reserve 2 tblsp. crumbs. Fold remaining crumbs and cream into applesauce. Spoon into sherbet or other dessert glasses. Sprinkle tops with the remaining crumbs. Top each serving with a cherry. Chill. Makes 6 servings.

VIRGINIA APPLE PUDDING

You mix and bake it in the same dish

½ c. butter or margarine
1 c. sugar
1 c. sifted flour
2 tsp. baking powder
¼ tsp. salt
¼ tsp. cinnamon
1 c. milk
2 c. cooked or canned apple slices

Melt butter in 2 qt. casserole.

Combine next 6 ingredients to make batter; pour on butter. Drain apples; pile in center of batter.

Bake in moderate oven (375°) until batter covers fruit and crust browns, 30 to 40 minutes. Makes 4 to 6 servings.

QUICK BANANA PUDDING

Children's special

1 (3 ¼ oz.) pkg. vanilla-pudding mix
27 vanilla wafers
2 large bananas, sliced

Prepare pudding mix as directed on package. Cool.

Line the bottom of a pan (9" × 5" × 3") with 12 cookies. Top with 1 banana, sliced. Spread half the pudding on top. Top with remaining cookies, then with 1 banana, sliced, and remaining pudding. Chill. Makes 8 servings.

BLUEBERRY DESSERT ROLL

Outside crust is brown and crisp; the inside is luscious and juicy

2 c. biscuit mix
⅔ c. milk
1 c. fresh blueberries or frozen blueberries, thawed
½ c. brown sugar
2 tblsp. butter or margarine, melted

Combine biscuit mix and milk as directed on package. Roll into rectangle ½" thick.

Sprinkle blueberries and brown sugar over dough, leaving 1" dough uncovered around edges. Roll like jelly roll. Seal lengthwise seam of dough tightly by pressing with fingers. Seal ends well and fold under.

Place roll, seam side down, in greased loaf pan (9" × 5" × 3"). With scissors make 4 small openings in top to permit escape of steam. Brush with melted butter.

Bake in hot oven (400°) 30 minutes. Slice with sharp knife and serve roll-ups with cream. Makes 6 servings.

Note: You may sprinkle 1 tblsp. lemon juice over berries.

LEMON-PEAR VELVET

Brown-yellow-and-white fruit dessert that's hard to resist

1 (3 ¼ or 4 oz.) pkg. lemon-pudding mix
1 c. heavy cream, whipped
1 (1 lb. 14 oz.) can pear halves
Tiny chocolate decorating candies

Prepare pudding mix as directed on package; chill. Stir until smooth and fold in whipped cream.

Spoon pudding into dessert glasses and top with drained, chilled pear halves. Sprinkle with candies. Makes 6 to 8 servings.

Variation: Instead of pear halves, use canned apricot or peach halves.

MINTED GRAPEFRUIT

Allow 5 minutes to make this—let it chill while you get remainder of meal

2 (1 lb.) cans grapefruit
⅓ c. small peppermint-flavored candy mints (pillow type)

Combine ingredients. Chill. Makes 6 servings.

Variation: Add 1 orange, peeled and sectioned, for a touch of color and interesting flavor.

FROZEN LEMON TORTE

Make in morning to serve for supper or to guests later in evening

1 c. finely crushed gingersnaps
2 tblsp. sugar
3 tblsp. butter or margarine
2 egg yolks
1 (15 oz.) can sweetened condensed milk
½ c. lemon juice
1 tblsp. grated lemon rind
2 egg whites, stiffly beaten

Combine cookie crumbs, sugar and butter. Reserve 3 tblsp. of mixture. Press remainder in bottom of buttered refrigerator tray. Chill in freezer section while you make filling.

Beat egg yolks well; stir in sweetened condensed milk. Add lemon juice and rind and stir until thick. Fold egg whites into mixture.

Pour into crumb-lined tray. Top with remaining crumbs. Freeze at least 4 to 6 hours. Makes 6 servings.

PEAR SHORTCAKES, ELEGANT AND QUICK: Set a drained canned pear half on a large sugar cookie. You can use cookies from bakery or package. Sprinkle with sliced Brazil nuts or chopped pistachio nuts and serve with Chocolate Sauce (see Index). Add a drop or two of peppermint extract to the sauce.

MINCEMEAT BROWN BETTY

Finish cooking it while first part of dinner is eaten—it's good hot

2 c. coarse dry bread crumbs
4 apples, sliced in eighths
1 c. prepared mincemeat
½ c. sugar
¼ tsp. cinnamon
¼ tsp. salt
3 tblsp. lemon juice (1 lemon)
¼ c. water
2 tblsp. butter or margarine

Put ⅓ of crumbs into bottom of buttered 1½ to 2 qt. casserole; cover with half of apples and half of mincemeat.

Mix sugar, cinnamon and salt together; sprinkle half over mincemeat.

Add layer of crumbs; then one of apples and mincemeat; sprinkle with remaining sugar mixture.

Top with remaining crumbs; pour lemon juice and water over all; dot with butter.

Cover; bake in moderate oven (350°) 20 minutes; uncover; bake 15 minutes longer. Serve hot or cold with plain or whipped cream. Makes 5 servings.

FROSTED PINEAPPLE

Lemon sherbet tops this dessert jewel

1 (1 lb. 4 oz.) can pineapple tidbits
1 c. flaked or shredded coconut

1 pt. lemon sherbet
1 c. blueberries (optional)

Place chilled pineapple in 6 dessert dishes. Sprinkle on ¾ c. coconut. Top with sherbet and scatter on remaining coconut. Garnish with blueberries. Makes 6 servings.

HONEYED BAKED PEARS

Serve with cream poured over or topped with scoops of vanilla ice cream

8 pear halves, peeled and cored
¼ c. lemon juice
½ c. honey
1 tblsp. butter
½ tsp. cinnamon

Arrange pears in a shallow, greased 1½ qt. casserole. Combine lemon juice and honey. Dot with butter and sprinkle with cinnamon.

Bake, covered, in moderate oven (350°) until pears are tender, 25 to 30 minutes. Serve warm or chilled. Makes 4 servings.

Variation: Substitute peeled and pitted peaches for pears.

BROILED PEACHES

Orange juice gives the peaches a fresh-from-the-orchard taste

2 (1 lb.) cans peach halves (about 12)
1 (6 oz.) can frozen orange-juice concentrate
2 tblsp. red-raspberry preserves
1 c. shredded coconut

Arrange peach halves in baking dish; fill each with 1 tblsp. thawed concentrate and ½ tsp. preserves; sprinkle with coconut.

Bake in hot oven (425°) 10 minutes, until coconut browns. Serve warm. Makes 6 servings.

PEACHES IN LEMON SAUCE

Frozen lemonade quickly does something wonderful to canned peaches

1 (1 lb. 4 oz.) can peach halves or slices
1 egg
2 tblsp. lemonade concentrate
½ c. syrup (from peaches)
1 tblsp. sugar
Dash of salt
1 (3 oz.) pkg. cream cheese

Drain syrup from fruit. Spoon fruit into individual dessert dishes.

Beat egg in top of double boiler. Add lemonade concentrate (don't add water), syrup, sugar and salt. Beat well.

Place over boiling water; cook until thick and smooth, stirring occasionally, about 6 to 8 minutes.

Add cream cheese. Beat with a rotary beater until smooth. Serve warm or cool over peach halves. Gingersnap cookies are good accompaniment, although any desired crisp cookie may be served. Makes 6 servings.

PINEAPPLE SUPREME

Perfect ending for fish dinner

1 (13½ oz.) can frozen pineapple, thawed and drained
½ c. dairy sour cream
2 tsp. sugar
Nutmeg

Put pineapple in sherbet or other dessert glasses. Mix sour cream with sugar and pour over pineapple. Dust with nutmeg. Makes two servings.

more

Variation: Substitute 1 (1 lb. 4 oz.) can pineapple chunks for frozen pineapple. Put drained fruit in 4 dessert dishes. Top with sour cream, omitting sugar. Dust with nutmeg. Makes 4 servings.

PEACH ISLANDS

Almost no work at all to make this luscious dessert with a golden top

1 (3 ¼ oz.) pkg. coconut-cream-pudding mix
1 c. heavy cream, whipped
1 (1 lb. 14 oz.) can peach halves

Prepare pudding mix as directed on package. Chill. Stir until smooth. Fold in whipped cream.

Put custard pudding in dessert dishes; top with drained, chilled peach half, rounded side up. Makes 6 servings.

MAPLED PEACHES—UNUSUAL COMBINATION: Simmer together ½ c. syrup drained from canned peach halves (1 lb. can) with 2 tblsp. brown sugar and ¼ tsp. maple flavoring. Add the drained peach halves and serve warm or cool topped with vanilla ice cream. Makes 6 servings.

Variations: Substitute canned pears for the peaches. Add a few drops of maple flavoring to your favorite fruit cup for elusive flavor.

QUICK PLUM PUDDING

A spicy, moist pudding

1 (1 lb. 1 oz.) can purple plums
Water
½ tsp. salt
1 (14 oz.) pkg. gingerbread mix
1 c. light raisins
½ c. chopped walnuts

Drain plums. Reserve ½ c. juice for sauce. To remaining juice, add water to make amount of liquid specified in package directions for making gingerbread.

Pit plums and cut in small pieces. Add salt, plums and required liquid to gingerbread mix. Mix as directed on package. Stir in raisins and nuts.

Pour into 10 greased and floured 4 oz. custard cups set on a baking sheet. Bake in moderate oven (375°) 25 to 30 minutes. Allow to stand a few minutes after removing from oven. Then remove from cups and pour Plum Sauce (recipe follows) over each. Makes 10 servings.

PLUM SAUCE

Boil ½ c. plum juice and ¼ c. Basic Sugar Syrup (see Index) together 5 minutes.

Variation: Serve warm plum puddings with Hard Sauce (see Index).

Frosty-cold Melons plus Sherbet

Give a busy country cook a hot day, ripe melons chilling in the refrigerator and sherbet in the freezer—she knows what to do. Here are samples of the kinds of desserts she serves.

CANTALOUPE: Cut cantaloupes in half, remove seeds and fill centers with lemon sherbet. Or cut cantaloupes in thick rings and drop a scoop of lime sherbet in center. It's sherbet framed with melon. Especially effective if the melon flesh is orange-colored. Lay a cluster of chilled seedless green grapes on each plate for a gala note.

HONEYDEW: Cut honeydew melons in quarters and place a scoop of raspberry sherbet on each.

WATERMELON: Arrange triangles of watermelon, petal fashion, on individual glass or other plates. Use scoops of orange, pineapple or lime sherbet for centers. Garnish with mint sprigs.

BAKED PRUNE WHIP

Quick-to-make version of a favorite—no cooking or sieving of prunes

- 1 (7 or 7½ oz.) can or jar junior baby prunes
- ½ c. sugar
- 1 tblsp. lemon juice
- 3 egg whites
- ⅛ tsp. salt

Combine prunes, sugar and lemon juice. Beat egg whites with salt until stiff. Fold into prune mixture. Spoon into a greased 1½ qt. casserole.

Bake in slow oven (325°) until firm, 25 to 30 minutes. Makes 6 servings. Serve with Custard Sauce (see Index).

RASPBERRY-LEMON FLUFF

A last-minute, low-calorie dessert—so fluffy and smooth, people think it contains whipped cream

- ⅔ c. hot water
- 2 envelopes unflavored gelatin
- ½ c. sugar
- 1 (6 oz.) can frozen raspberry-lemon-punch concentrate
- 2½ c. crushed ice

Put hot water and gelatin into blender. Cover and blend on high speed 40 seconds. Add sugar; cover and blend 2 seconds. Add frozen concentrate and ice. Cover and blend 30 seconds or until dessert begins to thicken.

Let stand a minute or two or until thick and fluffy. Serve in dessert glasses. Makes 6 servings.

Variation: Substitute other frozen punch concentrates or fruit juices for the raspberry-lemon punch.

STRAWBERRIES WITH SOUR CREAM: Serve ripe berries in dessert dishes and top with dairy sour cream. Sprinkle liberally with brown sugar. Or pass the sour cream and brown sugar in bowls. Allow 1 c. each brown sugar and sour cream to 1 qt. berries.

WHIPPED JELLIED STRAWBERRIES

Red dessert with frothy top especially pleases the children. Frozen berries hasten the chilling

- 1 (3 oz.) pkg. strawberry-flavor gelatin
- 1¼ c. boiling water
- 1 (10 oz.) pkg. frozen strawberries

Dissolve gelatin in water. Add unthawed berries and stir gently until they separate. Beat with rotary beater 1 minute.

Pour into sherbet or other dessert glasses and chill until firm. Makes 6 servings.

more

JELLIED STRAWBERRIES: For a molded dessert to make just before you serve dinner which will be ready 20 minutes later, use only 1 c. boiling water in recipe for Whipped Jellied Strawberries. Omit the beating. You may top the individual servings with dairy sour cream, whipped cream or scoops of vanilla ice cream.

Made with Ice Cream: Festive Ways to Serve Ice Cream

Busy hostesses have adopted help-yourself desserts. They're so easy to serve. And they flatter guests. People like to make their own choices.

Here are three easy ways country women serve ice cream to please—and to win compliments for the cook.

MAKE-YOUR-OWN SUNDAE: Serve vanilla ice cream. On a tray, pass small pitchers of two or more sauces and one of maple syrup, a small bowl of chopped nuts and strawberry preserves —or whatever toppings your fancy dictates. Let everyone dress up his ice cream the way he likes it.

ICE CREAM AND SHERBET BOUQUET: Place scoops of different kinds of ice cream and sherbet in a big bowl and set in the freezer. This may be done a day in advance. Serve at the table. Let everyone pick the kind he likes. The multicolored ice creams, like vanilla, strawberry and chocolate, and sherbets, like orange and raspberry, are festive.

PARTY ICE-CREAM CONES: Put scoops of two kinds of ice cream, like vanilla and chocolate, in a bowl. Set in freezer. Do this a day in advance if convenient. Serve with a platter of cones and let everyone have his pick of ice cream. Several kinds of ice cream may be served. Nice dessert for a backyard supper.

BANANA SUNDAE: Split small bananas in lengthwise halves. Arrange a banana half, cut side down, on each serving plate. Put a scoop of vanilla ice cream inside banana curve. Serve with frozen strawberries, partly thawed, spooned on top. Instead of strawberries, you can use your favorite caramel sauce or frozen sliced peaches.

Team Ice Cream with Cake

From the days when ice cream and cake festivals on the church lawn were important summer social occasions, the double dessert has won top honors. There are countless ways to serve these two dessert favorites together. Here are a few of them.

FAMILY SUNDAE: Top squares or diamonds of unfrosted cake with scoops of ice cream. Pour on your favorite sundae sauce. Try black-walnut cake, made from a mix, with vanilla ice cream and chocolate sauce.

COMPANY SUNDAE: Line a 9″ layer pan with 3 or 4 strips of waxed paper. Let ends of paper extend above edge of pan. Pack 1 pt. slightly softened ice cream in pan, making a smooth layer. Set in freezer. To serve, lift ice cream from pan and place between 2 (9″) layers of cool or frozen cake. Frost cake with whipped cream and return to freezer until time to serve. (Cake may be frosted a day or two before serving.) Pour partly thawed frozen strawberries, raspberries or sliced peaches over cake at serving time; let fruit juice trickle over sides of cake. Serve at the table. Makes 15 servings.

FROSTED CAKE: Spread 1 pt. vanilla ice cream over a layer of unfrosted cake. Top with chopped nuts, or chopped and drained maraschino cherries or berry preserves. Serve at once.

PARFAIT: Alternate layers of small cake cubes, ice cream and drained, partly thawed frozen or sliced fresh berries or peaches in parfait glasses. Top with spoonful of ice cream. A good way to extend a little cake.

SANDWICHES: Cut oblongs of unfrosted cake the same size as slices of brick ice cream. Split cool cake and put together with ice cream. Serve with dessert sauce or topping. (See Chapter 13, section on dessert sauces and toppings.)

Dessert on Short Notice

When friends telephone to say they're stopping by, hospitable farm women like to say, "Do stay for lunch." And when there's an acceptance, thoughts often center on selecting a hasty-tasty dessert. Here's what one smart cook did on such an occasion.

"I took an angel-food cake from the freezer and quickly coated it with a thin orange confectioners' sugar frosting," she says. "Of course, you can buy an angel-food cake from the bakery if you have time to send for one or can go yourself. But the icing will give it a homemade look.

"I set a pint each of vanilla ice cream and lemon sherbet on the kitchen counter to soften slightly. Then I dumped the ice cream on the platter, added the sherbet and stirred it through the ice cream. I put the mixture back in the freezer until serving time."

And how did the hostess' quick action work out? She says, "My company raved over the homemade ice cream and asked how I could bake an angel-food cake and glaze it with frosting on such short notice."

ROYAL-PURPLE SUNDAE

It will be the talk of the table, yet uses only three ingredients

1 qt. vanilla ice cream
1 (6 oz.) can frozen grape-juice concentrate, thawed
Pumpkin-pie spice

Place a scoop of ice cream in each sherbet or other dessert glass. Top each with 2 tblsp. grape juice and dust lightly with spice. Makes 6 servings.

Note: For a green and purple summer dessert, garnish each serving with a ring-around-the-edge of small, seedless green grapes.

ICE-CREAM COOKIE PIE

Cookie crust holds a sundae

1 roll toasted coconut refrigerator cookies
1 qt. strawberry ice cream
Ice-cream topping

Slice cookie dough ⅛" thick, using about ¾ roll to make crust. Line side of ungreased 8" or 9" pie pan with slices, overlapping slightly to make scalloped edge. Line bottom with more slices.

Bake in moderate oven (375°) about 9 minutes, or until lightly browned. Cool.

Fill with ice-cream scoops or balls, drizzle with peach or strawberry topping and serve at once. Or freeze ice cream in the baked crust and add topping at serving time. Makes 6 servings.

Variations: Substitute sugar or butterscotch-nut refrigerator cookie roll for toasted coconut cookies, and vanilla ice cream for strawberry ice cream. Use chocolate topping for Sugar Cookie Pie, and butterscotch topping for Butterscotch-Nut Cookie Pie.

Pie-pan Ice-cream Desserts

The Kansas woman who created these desserts in her country kitchen called them ice-cream pies. The ice cream makes the pie shell—you need no pastry. First you freeze the shell. Then you add the fillings and return "pies" to the freezer. It's a scrumptious dessert to have on hand for quick use.

ICE-CREAM "PIE" SHELL: Line an 8" pie pan with 1 pt. vanilla ice cream. Or use ice cream of any flavor you desire. For a more generous "crust," use 1½ pts. ice cream. Cut it in 1½" slices; lay on bottom of pan to cover. Cut remaining slices in half; arrange around pan to make rim. Fill spaces with ice cream where needed. With tip of spoon smooth "crust." Freeze until firm before adding filling.

CRANBERRY-NUT "PIE"

Grind frozen cranberries—they're less juicy, easier to work with

- 2 c. fresh or frozen cranberries
- 1 c. sugar
- 1 c. heavy cream, whipped
- ½ c. chopped nuts
- 1 (8") frozen vanilla ice-cream "pie" shell

Put cranberries through food chopper, using fine blade. Add sugar; let stand overnight.

Whip cream. Mix cranberries and nuts. Fold into whipped cream. Pour into ice-cream shell. Freeze. Makes 6 servings.

CHOCOLATE-PEPPERMINT PIE

Chocolate-pudding mix speeds up filling

- 1 tblsp. cocoa
- ½ c. sugar
- 1 (4 oz.) pkg. chocolate-pudding mix
- 1 tsp. vanilla
- 2 c. heavy cream, whipped
- 2 (8") frozen peppermint-stick ice-cream shells

Combine cocoa and sugar. Add to pudding mix and prepare as directed on package. Cool; fold in vanilla.

Fold cream into chocolate mixture. Pour into 2 peppermint-stick ice-cream shells. Freeze. Makes 2 (8") pies.

CHOCOLATE ICE-CREAM SANDWICHES

Especially pretty made with pink-peppermint ice cream

Chocolate graham crackers

Vanilla or peppermint ice cream

Spread cracker with ice cream and top with another cracker to make as many sandwiches as you need.

Serve at once if you like the crackers crisp. Or freeze and serve them when the occasion arises. Then crackers will be soft and moist like cake.

Short-cut Desserts with Pie Fillings

Give canned pie fillings a chance in your kitchen. Don't always bake these ready-to-use fruits between pastry crusts. They are versatile.

One farm woman spoons the bright red-cherry filling, chilled, on thick slices of angel food cake and tops the servings with fluffs of whipped cream. She heats raisin-pie filling and takes it to the table as an accompaniment to baked ham and ham loaf. Sometimes she crowns simple cakes and puddings with berry and peach fillings.

Cherry-pie filling walks away with honors as the favorite among farm women who shared their best short-cut recipes with us.

Here are some of the much praised desserts they make with colorful fruit fillings from the cupboard.

CLOVER-LEAF CHERRY TORTES

Fancy to look at, but easy to fix

1 roll refrigerator sugar cookies
1 (1 lb. 6 oz.) can cherry-pie filling
¼ tsp. almond extract
½ c. heavy cream, whipped

Slice cookie dough ⅛" thick. Arrange three slices with edges slightly overlapping, clover-leaf style, on ungreased baking sheet. Repeat, using all cookie slices.

Bake in moderate oven (375°) until golden brown, 7 to 9 minutes. Cool 1 minute before removing from baking sheet.

Fold extract into cherry-pie filling.

To serve, put cookie clover leaf on dessert plate. Top with 3 tblsp. cherry-pie filling, then with another clover leaf, and 1 tblsp. cherry-pie filling. Garnish each torte with whipped cream or vanilla ice cream. Makes 6 to 7 servings.

CHERRY-PUDDING DESSERT

So simple and so delicious

1 (3 ¼ oz.) pkg. vanilla-pudding and pie-filling mix
2 c. milk
1 (1 lb. 4 oz.) can cherry-pie filling

Prepare pudding mix with milk as directed on package. Chill.

To serve, place cherries in 6 dessert dishes. Top with pudding.

CHERRY-PEACH DUMPLINGS

Cook and serve this at the table if you have an electric skillet

½ c. water
2 tblsp. lemon juice
½ tsp. cinnamon
⅛ tsp. ground cloves
1 (1 lb. 8 oz.) jar cherry-pie filling
1 (1 lb.) can peach halves, drained
Milk
1 egg, beaten
1 ½ c. biscuit mix

Stir water, lemon juice, cinnamon and cloves into pie filling in 10" skillet. Add peaches; bring to boil.

more

Add milk to egg to make ½ c.; stir into biscuit mix to form soft dough.

Drop dough by tablespoonfuls on top of boiling fruit. Cook over low heat 10 minutes; cover skillet and cook 10 minutes more. Serve warm (spooning fruit over dumplings), with cream. Makes 6 servings.

RASPBERRY CRUNCH

A juicy pudding-type baked dessert

- 1 (1 lb.) can raspberry-pie filling
- ½ c. brown sugar
- ½ c. flour
- ½ c. quick-cooking oats
- ⅓ c. butter or margarine

Place pie filling in greased 8" square pan.

Combine brown sugar, flour and oats. Cut in butter. Sprinkle on top of raspberries.

Bake in moderate oven (350°) 40 to 45 minutes. Serve hot or cold in dessert bowls with cream. Makes 6 servings.

Variation: Substitute other canned-fruit or berry-pie fillings for the raspberry filling.

Farmhouse Favorites

BROWNIE PUDDING

Chocolate with nuts—named for the mix from which it is made

- 1 (1 lb.) pkg. brownie mix
- 1 or 2 eggs
- ½ c. chopped nuts
- ¾ c. brown sugar
- ¼ c. cocoa
- 1 ¾ c. hot water

Mix batter according to directions for cake-like brownies, adding eggs and nuts as directed. Pour into greased pan (9" × 9" × 1½").

Mix together brown sugar and cocoa. Sprinkle over top of batter. Gently pour hot water over sugar mixture. (When baked, this topping makes a small amount of chocolate sauce in bottom of pan.)

Bake in moderate oven (350°) 45 to 55 minutes until cake layer tests done. Serve warm or cold. Spoon into serving dishes. Serve with light cream or whipped cream. Makes 6 to 9 servings.

BUTTERSCOTCH DESSERT WAFFLES

Good to serve with coffee for evening refreshments—or for dessert any time

- ¼ c. butter or margarine
- ½ c. brown sugar
- ½ c. flaked or shredded coconut
- 6 full-size frozen-waffle sections
- Vanilla ice cream

Combine butter, sugar and coconut. Spread on waffles and broil until delicately browned. Top with ice cream. Makes 6 servings.

Note: If you bake waffles and freeze them, the amount of topping is correct. The frozen waffles you buy usually are smaller. You'll need 12 of them.

CHRISTMAS CRANBERRY ICE

Cheerful cranberry-red color makes it a holiday natural—superior!

- 1 qt. cranberries
- 4 c. water

2 c. sugar
¼ c. lemon juice
½ c. orange juice

Cook cranberries in 2 c. water 8 to 10 minutes, or until skins are broken. Rub through fine sieve for smooth pulp.

Stir in remaining ingredients. Pour into refrigerator trays or loaf pan. Freeze until firm, 2 or 3 hours (stir 2 or 3 times). Makes 8 servings.

Note: Serve the pretty red ice in sherbet glasses as an accompaniment for turkey, chicken or other meat. Or decorate fruit salads with spoonfuls of it. And although the colorful ice is on the tart side, try it for dessert with coconut cake or cookies.

CRANBERRY SHERBET

Blended cranberry and orange flavors highlight this cooling dessert

1 (1 lb.) can jellied cranberry sauce
¼ c. sugar
2 tsp. grated orange rind
⅓ c. orange juice
1 c. heavy cream, whipped

Mash cranberry sauce with fork; add sugar, orange rind and juice. Freeze in refrigerator tray until almost firm.

Beat with electric mixer or rotary beater until smooth; fold in whipped cream. Return to tray and freeze until firm. Makes 6 servings.

CARAMEL-CANDY CUSTARD

Make it ahead and chill or serve warm

3 c. milk
3 eggs
2 tblsp. sugar
½ tsp. salt
1 tsp. vanilla
6 tblsp. Quick Caramel Sauce (recipe follows)

Scald milk. Beat eggs slightly and add sugar, salt and vanilla. Gradually add hot milk to eggs, stirring constantly.

Put 1 tblsp. caramel sauce into each of 6 custard cups. Carefully pour in the milk and egg mixture and place cups in pan containing hot water. Bake in moderate oven (350°) 30 to 35 minutes, or until mixture does not adhere to knife. Loosen edges of custard and turn out so the caramel sauce will run down over custards.

QUICK CARAMEL SAUCE

You make this velvety sauce without the tedious caramelizing of sugar

½ lb. (about 28) caramel candies
½ c. hot water

Place caramels and water in top of double boiler. Heat, stirring frequently, until caramels melt and make a smooth sauce. Makes 1 cup.

Note: Serve Quick Caramel Sauce, warm or cold, on vanilla ice cream.

SOUTHERN SOFT CUSTARD

Make it in 8 minutes—serve plain or on sliced bananas or peaches

2½ c. evaporated milk
2½ c. cold water
1 (3¾ oz.) pkg. instant vanilla-pudding mix

Combine milk and water in mixing

bowl. Add mix; beat gently with rotary beater 1 minute, or until blended. Let set 5 minutes.

Serve immediately in dessert dishes, or pour into jar or pitcher, cover and refrigerate. Makes 5 cups.

Variation: For sweeter custard, add ½ c. sugar and 1 tsp. vanilla before mixing.

COCONUT-CREAM PUDDING

Pudding mix and frozen rhubarb join forces to help the cook make time

- 2 (3 ¾ oz.) pkgs. instant coconut-cream-pudding mix
- 3 c. milk
- 1 c. light cream
- 4 tsp. grated orange rind

Combine all ingredients in bowl.

Beat until well blended, about 1 minute. Pour into bowl or pan; let stand about 5 minutes.

Spoon into serving dishes. Garnish with orange sections or Rosy Rhubarb Sauce (recipe follows).

ROSY RHUBARB SAUCE

Put following ingredients in saucepan: 1 (1 lb.) pkg. quick-frozen rhubarb or 1 lb. fresh rhubarb, cut in 1″ pieces, ¼ c. light corn syrup, and dash of salt. Bring to slow boil; cook 5 minutes or until pieces are tender. Cool; chill. Spoon over coconut-cream pudding. Makes about 2 cups.

ROCKY-ROAD CHOCOLATE PUDDING: Make pudding from 1 pkg. regular chocolate-pudding mix as directed on package. Cool about 10 minutes. Fold in 1 c. miniature marshmallows and serve, or chill before serving. Or substitute butterscotch-pudding mix for chocolate-pudding mix.

COCONUT TORTE

Serve this on special occasions to get rave notices for the cook

- 1 recipe Butter Pecan Crisps cookie dough (see Index)
- 1 (3 ¾ oz.) pkg. instant coconut-cream-pudding mix
- ½ c. heavy cream, whipped
- Toasted coconut (optional)

Prepare cookie dough. Spread a thin layer of dough in a greased pan (8″ × 8″ × 2″). (Remainder of dough may be baked as cookies. Makes 1½ dozen.) Bake in moderate oven (350°) 15 to 20 minutes, until lightly browned.

Prepare pudding mix as directed on package. Pour over cooled cookie crust. Chill in refrigerator.

Sweeten whipped cream to taste; spread evenly over chilled pudding. Sprinkle with toasted coconut for garnish. Chill until time to serve. Makes 9 servings.

Note: Toasted coconut adds an attractive, crisp topping. To fix it: spread flaked or shredded coconut thinly on baking pan; bake in moderate oven (350°) 8 to 12 minutes, or until browned. Shake pan or stir coconut to toast evenly.

COFFEE-BUTTERSCOTCH CREAM

Gourmet-type dessert

- 1 (4 oz.) pkg. butterscotch-pudding mix and pie filling
- ⅓ c. sugar
- 1 tblsp. instant coffee
- 1 ½ c. milk

2 egg yolks, slightly beaten
½ c. heavy cream, whipped

Combine pudding mix, sugar, coffee and milk in saucepan. Cook and stir over medium heat until mixture begins to thicken. Pour a little of hot mixture into egg yolks and stir quickly to blend. Pour eggs into remaining pudding mixture and continue cooking until mixture comes to a full boil.

Cool and chill.

At serving time, fold whipped cream into pudding. Spoon into dessert glasses. Makes 6 servings.

Note: For a pretty trim, save out a little of the whipped cream and use to garnish pudding tops. For a touch of glamour, scatter on a sprinkling of tiny chocolate decorating candies.

DATE-BAR DESSERTS: Make bars with date-bar mix as directed on package. When cool, cut into 9 bars. Top with vanilla ice cream, whipped cream or Hard Sauce (see Index).

GREEN AND GOLD DESSERT

Shimmery green gelatin holds golden peaches—fix gelatin ahead

2 (3 oz.) pkgs. lime-flavor gelatin
1 ¾ c. boiling water
¾ c. cold water
2 (10 oz.) pkgs. frozen sliced peaches
2 c. cold milk
1 c. light cream
½ tsp. vanilla
1 (3 ¾ oz.) pkg. instant vanilla-pudding mix

Dissolve gelatin in boiling water; add cold water. Pour into pan, making layer about 1″ thick. Chill.

To serve, cut chilled gelatin in 1″ cubes with sharp knife. Run spatula under cubes to loosen; lift with spatula.

Alternate spoonfuls of gelatin cubes and partially thawed peaches in individual dessert dishes.

To make sauce, combine milk, cream and vanilla in bowl. Add pudding mix; beat slowly with rotary beater until thoroughly mixed—about 1 minute. Pour over dessert. Makes 6 servings.

Variations: Substitute canned for frozen peaches, or use sliced bananas. Use gelatin of different flavors.

ORANGE-BANANA TAPIOCA

Old-fashioned pudding with a wonderful new-fashioned taste

¼ c. quick-cooking tapioca
3 tblsp. sugar
Dash of salt
1 (6 oz.) can frozen orange juice
1 ½ c. water
2 medium bananas

Combine tapioca, sugar and salt. Blend in thawed orange juice and water. Let stand 5 minutes. Bring to a boil over medium heat, stirring frequently.

Pour into individual serving dishes and serve warm or chilled with garnish of sliced bananas. Makes 4 to 6 servings.

Note: For a change, top dessert servings with whipped cream or coconut, flaked or shredded, or serve with light cream.

PINEAPPLE-MARSHMALLOW PARFAIT

A rewarding 2-step dessert

1 (1 lb. 4 ½ oz.) can crushed pineapple
1 ½ c. miniature marshmallows
1 c. heavy cream, whipped
½ c. chopped nuts
⅓ c. grated or flaked coconut
Maraschino cherries

Combine undrained pineapple and marshmallows. Refrigerate overnight, or at least 6 hours.

At serving time, fold in whipped cream, nuts and coconut. Serve in parfait glasses or dessert dishes. Garnish with cherries. Makes 6 to 8 servings.

PEACH FLIP-OVER

Foil holds peaches in place when you invert dessert on serving plate

1 (1 lb. 14 oz.) can sliced peaches, well drained
2 c. biscuit mix
2 tblsp. sugar
½ tsp. cinnamon
⅔ c. milk

Line 8″ square pan with foil; allow foil to extend over edge of pan. Spread peach slices on foil.

Combine biscuit mix, sugar and cinnamon. Add all the milk at once and stir with fork to make soft dough. Beat vigorously 20 strokes.

Turn out on surface floured with biscuit mix. Knead 8 or 10 times. Place dough between 2 sheets of waxed paper and pat to an 8″ square.

Place dough over peaches. Bake in very hot oven (450°) 15 to 18 minutes. Turn out on serving plate; remove foil while warm. Serve topped with whipped cream or ice cream. Makes 6 servings.

PUMPKIN PUDDING À LA MODE

Summer pumpkin special—no cooking, but plenty of good eating

1 c. canned pumpkin
¼ tsp. salt
¼ tsp. cloves
½ tsp. cinnamon
1 tblsp. molasses
1 ½ c. milk
1 (3 ¾ oz.) pkg. instant vanilla pudding
½ c. heavy cream, whipped

Combine pumpkin, salt, spices and molasses. Blend in milk. Add pudding; beat slowly until thick, about 1 minute.

Fold in whipped cream. Spoon into dessert dishes; chill. To serve, top with nut ice cream. Makes 6 to 8 servings.

CINNAMON-PEACH COBBLER

You don't have to go to the bother of making the topping from scratch

⅓ c. sugar
1 tblsp. cornstarch
⅔ c. water
6 fresh peaches, peeled and sliced
1 (9.5 oz.) pkg. refrigerator cinnamon rolls
Cream

Combine sugar and cornstarch in saucepan. Add water and bring to boil, stirring constantly. Add peaches and heat to boiling point. Pour into a 2 qt. casserole.

Lay cinnamon rolls on peaches, cinnamon side up. Bake in hot oven

(400°) until rolls are browned, 25 to 30 minutes. Spread frosting from package over top of rolls. Serve warm with cream. Makes 6 servings.

FROSTED SHORTCAKES

Dessert to get ready the night before

30 graham crackers
¾ c. raspberry jam
1 c. heavy cream, whipped
1 tblsp. sugar

Stack graham crackers 5 high with jam spread between. Frost top and sides of each stack with cream with sugar added.

Chill 6 hours or overnight. Makes 6 servings.

DESSERT SANDWICHES

No whipped cream? Take packaged dessert topping from cupboard shelf to make these coffee go-withs

½ c. cold milk
1 (2 oz.) pkg. dessert-topping mix
½ tsp. vanilla
Red or green food color
⅛ tsp. peppermint extract
1 (8 ¼ oz.) pkg. chocolate wafers

Combine milk with dessert topping and vanilla. Whip as directed on package. Tint a delicate pink or green with a few drops of food color. Add flavoring.

Frost crisp chocolate wafers with mixture. Top with chocolate wafers, sandwich style. Freeze several hours or days. Makes 15 (2¼") sandwiches.

OFF-THE-GRIDDLE SHORTCAKES

Wonderful dessert to climax a light meal of soup and salad

2 eggs
1 c. milk
2 ⅓ c. biscuit mix
2 tblsp. sugar
¼ c. salad oil
Strawberries, or other fruit
Heavy cream, whipped

Beat eggs until soft peaks form; blend in milk; add mix and sugar; stir until just blended; fold in oil.

Bake on preheated griddle, using ¼ c. batter for each. Stack; fill and top with fruit and cream. Makes 1 dozen (4") light, fluffy cakes.

JIFFY TOPPINGS: Just-thawed frozen strawberries and peaches in their own syrup; warm crushed pineapple; pineapple tidbits, blueberries or cherries stirred into dairy sour cream; whipped cream cheese with preserves blended in. For sauce- or syrup-topped pancakes, pass bowls of chopped nuts and flaked coconut, to add flavor and texture.

A Country Cook Suggests:

Before putting pudding into dessert dishes, arrange a surprise in the bottom —chocolate pieces, sliced bananas, any kind of berries or other fruits. An easy trick for me that brings pleasure to my family. They say, "We never know what to expect."

10-*Minute Desserts*

The secret to these time-saving desserts is to keep the makings on hand in cupboard and freezer. Cooks vary in speed of working, but the average time spent on each dish in our Countryside Kitchens was 10 minutes. And all the desserts passed taste tests with high honors.

COMPANY TORTE: Cut angel-food cake (from your freezer) in 3 crosswise layers; put together and frost with Fruited Cream, made this way: combine 1 (1 lb. 4 oz.) can crushed pineapple with 1 (4 oz.) pkg. instant vanilla pudding. Fold into 2 c. heavy cream, whipped. Garnish top with canned mandarin-orange sections or coconut. Serve at once, or chill.

HONEY-NUT SUNDAE: Combine ¼ c. peanut butter with ¾ c. warm honey. Serve over vanilla ice cream.

HOT JELLY CAKE: Spread sides and top of white or yellow cake from freezer with jelly; sprinkle with flaked coconut and broil until jelly bubbles and coconut browns lightly. Serve hot.

APRICOT TREAT: Top orange sherbet with cooked, sweetened dried apricots (chopped), or fill drained canned apricot halves with orange sherbet.

FRUIT FLUFF: With rotary beater, blend 1 (4 oz.) pkg. instant lemon pudding with 1 c. apricot nectar and 1 c. dairy sour cream. Serve in dessert glasses.

BROILED APPLES: Broil canned pie-sliced apples 5 minutes; pour on thin butterscotch sauce, sprinkling top with flaked coconut. Broil a few minutes longer to toast coconut.

MAPLE-CREAM WAFFLE TOPPING: Slowly add 1 c. maple-blended syrup to 1 c. heavy cream, whipped. Fold to blend. Serve in pitcher with waffles made from packaged mix or with waffles from the freezer heated at the table in an electric toaster.

Pretty Ice-Cream Pie with party-pink crust (recipe page 135) to make ahead and freeze. Run it in the oven at serving time for five minutes to tinge meringue with gold. This dessert wins compliments every time.

Raisin Griddle Cookies (recipe page 167), full of raisins, are unforgettable. Today's busy cooks freeze the cutout dough stacked like hamburger patties to bake when needed. Excellent with coffee or ice cream.

CHAPTER 11

COOKIES

"Come on in . . . and have a cup of coffee. I'll bake some cookies." This invitation often greets neighbors in the country who stop by for a minute. And while drop-in guests and hostess chat, the kitchen fills with the mingled scents of cookies baking and coffee brewing. Even the busiest of women take time to bake cookies, but they find the time in different parts of the day—often when they are getting a meal.

Many short-cut cooks will tell you that, besides the range itself, no appliance helps more with their baking than the freezer. It helps them "move time around" and replaces the cookie jar in thousands of country homes. Busy women, when they have free minutes, make cookies and freeze them ready-to-bake or ready-to-eat. Farm homemakers take advantage of low freezer temperatures to keep baked cookies fresh for weeks. Not infrequently a hostess passes an assortment of warm cookies that browned together on the same baking sheet—to amazed and appreciative guests.

Not all the recipes in this collection are brand new. When an old-fashioned one fits into today's streamlined living, it should be treasured. For a superb example, Raisin Griddle Cookies. But Grandma had to stir them up at the last minute. Now you freeze the circles of dough like hamburger patties to bring out when needed and bake on a griddle.

There's one cookie, Date-Marshmallow Balls, that skips the oven. And thin wafers made from pie crust are just right to serve with ice cream and many other desserts. Offer them to your friends with tea or coffee if you are willing to write down the recipes for your guests. They're bound to ask for them.

Most of the recipes that follow are for drop, bar and ball cookies or those that you cut quickly with a knife. And there are all kinds—thin, plump, crisp, moist, filled and sugar-sprinkled—cookies loaded with raisins, nuts, mincemeat, chocolate, coconut and other goodies. Why wouldn't the neighbors make it a point to stop by?

Cookies in Variety

The best from country kitchens

Tempting Bar Cookies

FROM-SCRATCH BROWNIES

If you are the kind of cook who likes to stir up brownies from scratch, you will never find a quicker recipe than the one that follows. Nor will you ever taste a more delicious brownie.

SAUCEPAN BROWNIES

Taste testers vote: excellent, outstanding–our highest rating

½ c. butter or margarine
2 (1 oz.) squares unsweetened chocolate
1 c. sugar
½ c. sifted flour
1 tsp. baking powder
1 tsp. vanilla
½ c. chopped walnuts
2 eggs

Melt butter and chocolate together in saucepan. Remove from heat and stir in sugar, flour, baking powder, vanilla and nuts. Add eggs and beat thoroughly.

Spread in a greased pan (9″ × 9″ × 2″). Bake in moderate oven (350°) 30 minutes. Dust with confectioners' sugar if desired.

Cut in 18 bars to serve as cookies or in 9 squares to serve as dessert topped with vanilla ice cream. Chocolate fans may wish to pour a chocolate dessert sauce over the ice cream.

Brownies—Many a Kind

The smart cook finds a package of brownie mix a challenge. So many different flavorings may be added for a tasty, personal touch. Here are a few favorites of farm women. In all of them the batter is prepared as directed on the mix package, but with these additions to the batter:

CHERRY BROWNIES: Add ¼ c. chopped and well-drained maraschino cherries.

DATE BROWNIES: Add 1 c. chopped dates instead of nuts. Roll baked brownies, cut in squares, in confectioners' sugar.

MOCHA BROWNIES: Add 1½ tblsp. powdered instant coffee, stirring it into dry mix.

DOUBLE FUDGE BROWNIES: Add ½ c. semi-sweet chocolate pieces. Cool brownies before cutting.

PEANUT BROWNIES: Omit nuts and add 3 tblsp. chunk-style peanut butter.

FROSTED BROWNIES: Frost brownies when cool, and before cutting in squares, with white or chocolate frosting made from packaged mix.

BROWNIES WITH NUTS

CASHEW BROWNIES: Make fudgy brownies as directed on package of brownie mix, only omit nuts from batter. Before baking, sprinkle batter with ¼ c. (¼ lb.) chopped salted cashew nuts.

Variation: Instead of cashew nuts, use chopped nuts from package of assorted salted nuts.

CHOCOLATE PEANUT BARS

Blending of flavors makes these easy-to-bake cookies distinctive

½ c. soft butter or margarine
½ c. peanut butter
1 c. brown sugar, firmly packed
⅓ c. light corn syrup
6 c. toasted rice cereal
1 (6 oz.) pkg. semi-sweet chocolate pieces

Cream butter and peanut butter together. Add brown sugar and cream well. Stir in syrup.

Add cereal and chocolate pieces. Mix until cereal is coated with butter mixture.

Pack mixture into a greased pan (13″ × 9″ × 2″).

Bake in hot oven (400°) 12 to 15 minutes. Makes 4 dozen (1½″) bars.

HONEY COOKIE BARS

You mix all the ingredients for these chewy cookies in one bowl

⅔ c. sifted flour
½ tsp. baking powder
¼ tsp. salt
½ c. sugar
½ c. honey
½ c. shortening
1 egg
½ c. shredded coconut
½ c. shredded-wheat cereal, crumbled
1 c. quick-cooking rolled oats
1 tsp. vanilla

Sift flour, baking powder and salt into mixing bowl. Add remaining ingredients and beat thoroughly. Spread mixture in greased pan (9″ × 9″ × 2″).

Bake in moderate oven (350°) until lightly browned, 30 to 35 minutes. Cut in squares. Makes 3 dozen (1½″) bars.

MINCEMEAT BARS

Very easy to make. Cookies are moist with a little crunchiness on top

1 (11.4 oz.) pkg. butterscotch refrigerator cookies
½ c. mincemeat
¼ c. brown sugar, firmly packed

Crumble ⅔ roll of cookie dough into a pan (8″ × 8″ × 2″). Pat down evenly to cover bottom of pan. Spread with mincemeat.

Crumble remaining dough into bowl and mix well with brown sugar. Sprinkle this mixture evenly over mincemeat.

Bake in moderate oven (350°) 30 to 35 minutes. Makes 32 (1″ × 2″) bars.

RAISIN-NUT BARS

Soft cookies—extra good (made with a cake mix)

1 (10 oz.) pkg. applesauce-cake mix
⅓ c. chopped raisins
¼ c. chopped nuts
Confectioners' sugar

Prepare cake mix as directed on package. Stir in raisins and nuts. Spread in a pan (13″ × 9″ × 2″), well greased and floured on bottom only.

more

Bake in moderate oven (375°) 20 to 25 minutes.

Sift confectioners' sugar over top. Cut into bars. Makes 32 (2″ × 1″) bars.

Just-Right Drop Cookies

CRUNCHY CHOCOLATE-CHIP COOKIES

Corn flakes—a fast way to give cookies a crunchy jacket

- 1 pkg. chocolate-chip cookie mix
- ⅓ c. corn flake crumbs

Prepare cookie dough as directed on package. Drop teaspoonfuls into corn flake crumbs. Roll into balls.

Bake on greased baking sheet in moderate oven (375°) 13 to 15 minutes. Makes 2½ dozen.

COCONUT-NUTMEG COOKIES

Wonderful taste companions—lemon, coconut and nutmeg

- 1 (1 lb. 3 oz.) pkg. yellow- or white-cake mix
- 1 c. flaked coconut
- ½ c. soft butter or margarine
- 1 tsp. nutmeg
- 1 egg
- 2 tblsp. cold water

Combine all ingredients and mix until well blended.

Drop teaspoonfuls of mixture on lightly greased baking sheet. Bake in moderate oven (350°) 12 to 15 minutes, until lightly browned. Transfer to cooling rack. Makes 3½ dozen (2¼″) cookies.

BUTTER-PECAN CRISPS

Double-duty recipe. Use it to make cookies or luscious Coconut Torte

- 1 (14 oz.) pkg. butter-pecan-cake mix
- ¼ c. brown sugar, firmly packed
- ¼ c. soft butter
- 1 egg
- 1 tblsp. cold water

Combine all ingredients and mix until well blended.

Drop by teaspoonfuls on lightly greased baking sheet. Bake in moderate oven (350°) 12 to 15 minutes, until lightly browned. Let stand a few minutes before removing from baking sheet to cooling rack. Makes 3 dozen (2½″) cookies.

HALF-AND-HALF MACAROONS

They'll be the talk of the party!

- 1 (13 oz.) pkg. white coconut-macaroon mix
- ¼ c. chopped maraschino cherries
- ¼ tsp. almond extract
- 1 (13 oz.) pkg. chocolate coconut-macaroon mix

Prepare white macaroon dough according to package directions for cherry macaroons, adding cherries and almond extract.

In separate bowl prepare chocolate macaroon dough by package directions.

With end of teaspoon, scoop up dab of chocolate dough to half fill spoon. Fill rest of spoon with cherry macaroon dough. Push off spoon onto paper-covered baking sheet; bake according to package directions. Makes about 4 dozen.

OATMEAL-GUMDROP COOKIES

No creaming—save time by cutting gumdrops with scissors dipped in water

- 2 eggs
- ⅔ c. salad oil
- ¾ c. sugar
- ¼ c. molasses
- 1 ½ c. sifted flour
- 2 tsp. baking powder
- ½ tsp. salt
- 1 ¼ c. quick-cooking rolled oats
- ½ c. gumdrops, cut in small pieces

Beat eggs with fork until blended. Stir in oil. Blend in sugar until mixture thickens. Stir in molasses.

Sift together flour, baking powder and salt; add to egg mixture with rolled oats and gumdrops. Stir until well blended.

Drop by teaspoonfuls about 2″ apart on greased baking sheet. Stamp each cookie flat with bottom of drinking glass, dipped in oil and then in sugar. Continue dipping in sugar for each cookie.

Bake in hot oven (400°) 8 to 10 minutes. Remove immediately from baking sheet. Makes about 3½ dozen (3″) cookies.

Note: Rinse baking sheet with hot water while still warm for easy washing.

Countryside Kitchen Specials

DATE-MARSHMALLOW BALLS

Skip-the-oven cookies, sweet and rich like candy

- 1 ½ c. chopped dates
- 1 ¼ c. chopped nuts
- 2 c. miniature marshmallows
- 3 ½ c. graham-cracker crumbs
- 1 (6 ½ oz.) pkg. fluffy white-frosting mix

Combine dates, 1 c. nuts, marshmallows and 2½ c. graham-cracker crumbs. Mix thoroughly.

Prepare frosting mix as directed on package. Add to the date mixture and mix until completely moistened.

Combine ¼ c. nuts and 1 c. graham-cracker crumbs in small bowl.

Form date mixture into 1½″ balls. Roll in graham-cracker crumbs and nuts. Store in covered container at least 12 hours to mellow. Makes 36 balls.

ORANGE-COCONUT CRISPS

Drop dough from spoon, pour shortening from bottle, orange juice from can

- 2 eggs
- ⅔ c. salad oil
- 1 c. sugar
- ¼ c. frozen orange-juice concentrate, thawed
- 2 ½ c. sifted flour
- 2 tsp. baking powder
- ½ tsp. salt
- 1 c. grated coconut

Beat eggs with fork until well blended. Stir in oil. Blend in sugar until mixture thickens. Stir in orange juice.

Sift together flour, baking powder and salt; add with coconut to egg mixture. Stir until well blended.

Drop by teaspoonfuls about 2" apart on ungreased baking sheet. Stamp each cookie flat with bottom of drinking glass dipped in sugar. (Lightly oil glass, then dip in sugar. Continue dipping in sugar for each cookie.)

Bake in hot oven (400°) 8 to 10 minutes. Remove immediately from baking sheet. Makes 3 dozen (3") cookies.

Note: Balls of cookie dough, rolled in sugar, may be packaged and frozen for future use. To bake: remove as many balls as desired from package, place on baking sheet and let stand about 30 minutes at room temperature. Bake as directed.

MEXICAN CHOCOLATE CRINKLES

Dough is easy to handle. Cookies flatten during baking—have a professional look that's pleasing

- ¾ c. soft shortening
- 1 c. sugar
- 1 egg
- ¼ c. light corn syrup
- 2 (1 oz.) squares unsweetened chocolate, melted
- 1 ¾ c. sifted flour
- 2 tsp. baking soda
- ¼ tsp. salt
- 1 tsp. cinnamon
- ¼ c. sugar (for dipping)

Cream together shortening, sugar and egg. Stir in syrup and melted chocolate.

Sift flour, soda, salt and cinnamon into creamed mixture and stir to make stiff dough.

Shape dough into balls about the size of walnuts and roll in sugar.

Place on ungreased baking sheet about 3" apart. Bake in moderate oven (350°) 15 minutes. Cookies will flatten and crinkle. Let stand a few minutes before removing to wire racks. Makes 3 dozen (3") cookies.

Old-fashioned Cookies

OVEN-BAKED SCONES

A first cousin of old-fashioned sugar cookies and so quick

- 2 c. sifted flour
- 1 tsp. salt
- 3 tsp. baking powder
- ½ c. sugar
- ½ c. shortening
- 1 egg, beaten
- ⅓ c. milk
- ¾ c. raisins

Sift flour with salt, baking powder and sugar. Cut in shortening until mixture resembles meal.

Combine egg and milk. Add with raisins to flour mixture; stir just enough to mix well.

Turn out on floured board. Knead lightly. Divide into thirds. Roll each piece into a 6" circle. Cut each circle into 4 wedges.

Place on greased baking sheet. Brush tops with milk and sprinkle with sugar.

Bake in hot oven (425°) 12 to 15 minutes. Serve warm. Makes 1 dozen.

SPEEDY SCOTCH SHORTBREAD

10 minutes to bake, 10 minutes to cool —call the clan

1 c. butter or margarine
½ c. sugar
2 c. sifted flour

Cream butter thoroughly. Add sugar gradually. Beat in the flour a little at a time.

Divide dough in half and place each half on a greased baking sheet. Pat in 8″ circles; flute edges. Prick surface with fork.

Bake in hot oven (450°) 8 to 10 minutes, or until golden brown. Remove from oven and cool on baking sheet 10 minutes. Cut each circle in 8 wedges. Makes 16 servings.

Griddle Cookies—Back in Style

Grandmother used to bake cookies on the griddle to avoid heating the oven in midsummer. Children stopping in her kitchen, hopeful of a handout, remember how good the warm cookies were with glasses of cold lemonade or bowls of ice cream. No childhood eating experience could be more memorable. So it's good news that the cookies again are coming off griddles to please people of all ages.

Give freezers the thanks. Today's cooks roll and cut the dough and stack the circles with foil between like hamburger patties. As they are wrapped in packages and frozen, it's easy to bring the desired number out. Bake them in your electric skillet—at the table, if that's convenient.

RAISIN GRIDDLE COOKIES

Keep packages of dough in your freezer to bake on short notice

3½ c. sifted flour
1 c. sugar
1½ tsp. baking powder
1 tsp. salt
½ tsp. baking soda
1 tsp. nutmeg
1 c. shortening
1 egg
½ c. milk
1¼ c. raisins

Sift dry ingredients together into bowl. Cut in shortening until mixture is mealy.

Beat egg, add milk and blend. Add egg mixture and raisins to flour mixture. Stir until all the ingredients are moistened and dough holds together.

Roll on lightly floured board to ¼″ thickness. Cut with 2″ round cookie cutter.

Heat griddle until a few drops of water dance on it. (Do not overheat griddle.) Oil griddle lightly and place cookies on it. As the bottoms brown, the tops become puffy. Then turn and brown on other side. Serve warm. Makes about 4 dozen cookies.

Variation: To make Lemon Griddle Cookies, omit raisins and add 1 tsp. grated lemon rind.

Freezing Short-cut: Pack unbaked cookies in freezer containers with pieces of foil between them; freeze. Then a few cookies may be removed from the freezer any time you want warm cookies. Let them thaw at room temperature 15 to 20 minutes. Bake on griddle as directed.

Wafers Made with Pie Crust

SESAME-SEED WAFERS

Crisp cookies with brown edges—not overly sweet

2 sticks pie-crust mix
3 tblsp. sesame seeds
1 egg
¾ c. sugar
½ tsp. vanilla

Crumble pie-crust mix into bowl. Add sesame seeds.

Beat egg in another bowl; add sugar and vanilla. Mix well.

Add egg mixture to pie crust mixture; stir with fork until well blended (dough will be soft).

Turn dough out on waxed paper and form a roll 1½" in diameter between layers of the paper. Chill dough thoroughly.

Slice dough thin and place on ungreased baking sheet. Bake in hot oven (400°) 8 to 10 minutes. Makes 4 dozen cookies.

Note: Roll of cookie dough may be frozen for future use. When ready to bake, allow dough to stand at room temperature 15 to 20 minutes before slicing.

MOCHA WAFERS

A crisp cookie with delicate flavor

2 sticks pie-crust mix
1 egg
¾ c. sugar
2 tblsp. instant coffee
1 tsp. baking powder
¼ tsp. almond extract

Crumble pie-crust mix into bowl.

Beat egg in another bowl; add remaining ingredients and mix well.

Add egg mixture to pie crust; stir with a fork until well blended. (Dough will be soft.)

Turn dough out on waxed paper. Form a roll 1½" in diameter between layers of waxed paper. Chill dough thoroughly.

Slice thin and place on ungreased baking sheet. Bake in hot oven (400°) 8 to 10 minutes. Makes 4 dozen cookies.

Variation: To make Black-Walnut Wafers, omit instant coffee and almond extract; add ½ c. finely chopped black walnuts to crumbled pie crust before adding egg and sugar.

Note: Roll of dough may be frozen. Follow directions for freezing and baking of Sesame Seed Wafers.

Freezing Cookies: Frozen baked cookies will keep a year if packaged properly; unbaked ones about 6 months. Most frozen unbaked cookies need to be partly thawed before baking.

CHAPTER 12

BREADS

Breads, hot and fragrant from the oven, occupy the spotlight in many hurry-up meals. And the best recipes for many choice ones, direct from country kitchens, appear in this chapter. The variety is wide and tempting, for no one knows better than country cooks that a hot or unusual bread makes a slim meal more substantial and interesting.

Many of the breads are baked, partly baked or are ready to bake before they reach the farm—loaf bread, brown-and-serve rolls, and refrigerator rolls and biscuits, for example. Imaginative cooks quickly add their own dress-ups to make fascinating loaves, like crusty, New-Way French Bread, and numerous spiced and fruited coffee go-withs.

Women with no minutes to spare in cooking keep "packages of time" like biscuit, muffin, pancake, roll and pizza mixes in their cupboards. From them they fast-fix all kinds of pancakes, waffles, muffins, rolls and coffee breads. And homemakers devoted to the yeasty taste and aroma, who like to bake loaf bread, settle for batter breads. They take about half as long to make as conventional bread.

You'll look a long time before you can find a coffee cake that tastes as good as Orange Sugar Bread. Yet the ranch woman who sent us this recipe says she fixes and bakes the glamorous ring in 20 minutes. Pancake Waffles are pancakes baked in the waffle iron right at the table if you wish. Add a topknot of Apricot Fluff to melt on them and you have a great, hasty dessert.

Many country cooks depend on hot breads for that delightful homemade touch and to create the impression the meal was planned with real thought. One reader says, "I often do a little selling—it pays off. When I pass the bread, I warn everyone to watch out because it's hot. I start the butter so it will melt on the bread. The way you present short-cut food is almost as important as its taste!"

Country Kitchen Breads

They're hot, fragrant and extra-good

Push-button Biscuit Specials

BISCUIT STICKIES

Keep ready-to-bake biscuits in refrigerator to bake in a jiffy

⅓ c. butter or margarine
½ c. dark corn syrup
¼ c. chopped nuts
1 pkg. refrigerator biscuits

Divide butter evenly in bottoms of 10 muffin-pan cups. Set in oven just long enough to melt butter.

Remove from oven; pour corn syrup and nuts in each cup.

Cut biscuits into thirds; roll each in syrup mixture. Put three pieces in each cup. Bake in preheated hot oven (400°) about 15 minutes. Makes 10 biscuits.

ONION-BUTTERMILK BISCUITS

Better fix two packages of biscuits

2 tblsp. butter or margarine, melted
2 tblsp. instant minced onion
1 pkg. refrigerator buttermilk biscuits

Combine butter and onion.

Flatten biscuits on ungreased baking sheet with bottom of floured custard cup. Leave rim that cup makes.

Fill biscuit centers with butter-onion mixture. Bake in hot oven (425°) 10 minutes, or until biscuits are baked and onions are a light golden brown. Makes 10 biscuits.

SUMMER SKILLET BISCUITS

Bake one package of biscuits while you put dinner on the table, the second batch while you eat

2 pkgs. refrigerator biscuits
1 tsp. butter or margarine

Preheat electric skillet to 375°. Grease skillet lightly with half of butter.

Break biscuits from 1 package apart; place in skillet with space between.

Cover and cook 3 minutes; turn and cover. Bake another 3 minutes. Serve at once.

Repeat with second package of biscuits. Makes 20 biscuits.

CORN-KERNEL BISCUITS

Try these topped with creamed chicken

3 c. biscuit mix
2 tsp. sugar
½ tsp. salt
2 tblsp. chopped onion
2 tblsp. chopped parsley
1 c. drained canned corn
1 egg, beaten
½ c. milk
2 tblsp. salad oil
Milk for tops

Combine biscuit mix, sugar, salt, onion, parsley and corn.

Mix egg with milk and oil; add all at once to flour mixture. Stir with fork into a soft dough; beat about 30 seconds (dough should be stiff and a bit sticky).

Dust board with flour; roll dough around in flour. Knead about 10 times to smooth dough. Roll out ½″ thick.

Cut with 3″ floured biscuit cutter. Brush tops with milk. Bake on ungreased baking sheet in very hot oven (450°) 12 to 15 minutes. Makes 1 dozen.

POTATO-CORNMEAL BISCUITS

Brown-crusted biscuits from a mix—they're surprisingly different

3 c. biscuit mix
½ c. cornmeal
1 tsp. baking powder
½ tsp. salt
1 tblsp. sugar
1 c. warm mashed potatoes
1 egg, beaten
1 tblsp. salad oil
½ c. milk
Milk for tops

Combine biscuit mix, cornmeal, baking powder, salt and sugar in mixing bowl.

Blend potatoes, egg, oil and milk until smooth. Add to dry ingredients; blend until completely mixed.

Knead half a minute on floured board to smooth dough. Roll out ½″ thick.

Cut with 3″ floured biscuit cutter. Place on ungreased baking sheet; brush with milk. Bake in very hot oven (450°) 12 to 15 minutes, or until done. Makes 15 biscuits.

Note: Place biscuits close together on baking sheet if you like soft sides, 1″ apart if you like crusty biscuits.

Use instant mashed potatoes when in a hurry.

HASTY-TASTY BISCUIT TRICKS

SAGE BISCUITS: Add ¼ tsp. sage to the dry ingredients for biscuits (2 c. flour or biscuit mix) and bake as usual. Wonderful with chicken or pork.

ONION BISCUITS: When you have leftover canned French-fried onions, chop them fine and add ½ c. of them to biscuits (2 c. flour or biscuit mix). Excellent with beef or lamb.

WAFFLED BISCUITS: Place canned refrigerator biscuits on hot waffle iron. Bake until light golden brown. The grid flattens the biscuits. They are crunchy-crisp outside, light within.

STRAWBERRY BISCUITS: Place 1 tblsp. strawberry preserves in bottom of each greased muffin-cup pan. Top with refrigerator biscuits and bake as directed on package. Turn out of pan at once.

CHEESE ROLLS

Serve these quickies piping hot

⅔ c. Cheddar-cheese spread
2 tblsp. butter
1 pkg. refrigerator butterflake rolls

Soften cheese spread and butter at room temperature; combine and mix thoroughly.

more

Spread cheese mixture on rolls, pulling sections to separate a little so some of cheese will melt between them.

Bake in moderate oven (375°) 15 minutes. Makes 12 rolls.

Variations: Add ½ to ¾ tsp. caraway seeds to the cheese-butter mixture. Or fix ready-to-bake brown-and-serve rolls this way.

FRUITED FANTAN ROLLS

A snap to fix with packaged rolls and frozen relish

- 3 tblsp. Cranberry Relish, thawed and drained (see Index)
- 3 tblsp. butter or margarine
- 1 pkg. refrigerator butterflake rolls

Combine Cranberry Relish with butter. Spread mixture between one slit in each roll.

Set rolls in large muffin-pan cups; bake in moderate oven (350°) 15 minutes. Makes 12 rolls.

DILL BISCUITS: Break package of refrigerator biscuits apart. Dip in butter and then sprinkle with poppy seeds and dried dill. Place on greased baking sheet; bake in hot oven (400°) about 10 minutes.

Beautiful Coffee Cakes

It takes a few minutes to get these fruited biscuit coffee cakes ready to bake, but once you have made them, repeat performances are quicker.

Take your choice of the coiled coffee go-with with its cheerful strawberry-red and coconut topping, or the fancy-looking Swedish-style ring with a tempting cherry-apple mixture at its heart. Both are wonderfully delicious.

BASIC COFFEE CAKE

A quick route to appetizing biscuit coffee cakes of many kinds

- 2 c. biscuit mix
- 2 tblsp. sugar
- 1 egg
- ¾ c. milk

Blend biscuit mix, sugar, egg and milk; beat vigorously 3 minutes or 75 strokes. Use one of the following three recipes. You'll want to work out other variations.

APRICOT SWIRL COFFEE CAKE

Apricot jam swirls its gold through batter to marbleize it

- 1 c. apricot jam
- 1½ tblsp. orange juice
- ½ tsp. grated orange rind
- 1 Basic Coffee Cake recipe (see Index)

Combine apricot jam, orange juice and rind.

Spread two thirds of Basic Coffee Cake batter in a 9" round pan.

Alternate spoonful of apricot-jam mixture and remaining batter on top. Run a knife through batter in spiral fashion to give a marbled appearance.

Bake in hot oven (400°) until golden brown, about 25 minutes. Serve warm. Makes 8 servings.

Variation: Substitute pineapple jam for apricot jam.

SPICY APPLE COFFEE CAKE

Cinnamon and apples make this a wonderful coffee go-with

1 Basic Coffee Cake recipe (see Index)
2 medium apples, peeled, cored and sliced (1 1/3 c. chopped)
1/2 c. sugar
1 1/2 tsp. cinnamon
2 tblsp. biscuit mix
2 tblsp. soft butter or margarine

Spread batter in greased 9″ round pan. Sprinkle apples over top. Top with sugar, cinnamon, biscuit mix and butter, mixed together.

Bake in hot oven (400°) 25 to 30 minutes. Serve warm. Makes 8 servings.

STREUSEL COFFEE CAKE

Takes only seconds to sprinkle on topping. It makes a crunchy crust

1 Basic Coffee Cake recipe (see Index)
1/2 c. brown sugar
1/2 c. chopped nuts
2 tblsp. biscuit mix
2 tblsp. butter or margarine, melted
1 tsp. cinnamon

Spread Basic Coffee Cake batter in greased round layer-cake pan (9″). Top with remaining ingredients, mixed.

Bake in hot oven (400°) 25 to 30 minutes. Serve warm. Makes 8 servings.

APRICOT COFFEE CAKE

Takes 5 minutes to get it ready to bake

3 c. biscuit mix
3 tblsp. sugar
2 eggs
1 c. milk
1 c. apricot jam
1/3 c. flaked or shredded coconut

Combine biscuit mix, sugar, eggs and milk. Beat 30 seconds. Spread in a greased pan (13″ × 9″ × 2″).

Drop jam by spoonfuls over top. Spread lightly to cover batter. Sprinkle with coconut.

Bake in hot oven (400°) until lightly browned, 25 to 30 minutes. Makes 12 servings.

STRAWBERRY-COCONUT SWIRL

Serve with coffee at a party or for dessert in a family meal

3 c. biscuit mix
1/4 c. sugar
Milk
1 egg, beaten
2 tblsp. melted butter
2/3 c. strawberry preserves
1 c. flaked coconut

Blend biscuit mix and sugar; add enough milk to egg to make 1 c.; add to sugar mixture. Stir with fork into soft dough; beat vigorously 20 strokes until stiff and slightly sticky.

Knead on a well-floured board half a minute. Roll into 7″ × 18″ rectangle. Spread with butter, then preserves (leave about 1″ uncovered on long side for sealing). Sprinkle with coconut; moisten edge.

Roll like jelly roll; let rest a minute on sealed side, then turn seam to top. Cut roll in half lengthwise.

Cut about 5″ from one strip; form loosely into small circle (keep cut surfaces up in forming ring). Use spatula to lift to center of baking sheet. Coil remainder of strip loosely in circle around it. Make outer circle from second strip; seal end. Ring will be about 8″ in diameter.

Bake in moderate oven (375°) 30 to 40 minutes, or until top is lightly browned and roll is baked through. Serve warm. Makes 8 to 10 servings.

APPLE-CHERRY RING

Fancy-looking enough for any coffee party—the mix is the short cut

- 2 ⅔ c. biscuit mix
- ½ c. sugar
- 3 tblsp. soft butter or margarine
- 2 c. finely chopped, peeled apples
- 1 tsp. lemon juice
- 3 tblsp. flour
- ½ c. cherry preserves

Prepare biscuit dough as directed on mix package, adding 2 tblsp. sugar to the dry mix.

Turn out on floured board. Knead about half a minute. Roll into rectangle (9″ × 18″). Spread with butter.

Combine apples, lemon juice, remaining sugar and 3 tblsp. flour. Spoon over dough.

Roll like a jelly roll; seal edge. Form into circle; join ends; seal. Transfer to greased baking sheet.

With kitchen shears or sharp knife, cut into 1″ slices (cut about halfway down into roll). Give each slice a half-turn, flattening roll into a pinwheel. Brush top with milk.

Bake in hot oven (400°) 30 to 40 minutes, or until done. Remove from oven and immediately spoon preserves in the open spaces. Serve warm. Makes 8 servings.

DATE-STREUSEL COFFEE CAKE

A foolproof, easy-does-it recipe

- 3 tblsp. sugar
- 2 tblsp. salad oil or melted shortening
- 1 egg
- ¾ c. milk
- 2 c. biscuit mix
- 1 (14 oz.) pkg. date-bar mix

Blend together sugar, oil, egg and milk. Stir in biscuit mix until it is thoroughly moistened.

Make date filling and crumb mixture from date-bar-mix package.

Spread ⅔ of biscuit dough in greased 9″ round or square baking dish. Cover with date-filling mixture; sprinkle about ⅓ of crumb mixture over date filling. Add remaining coffeecake dough, spreading as evenly as possible over crumbs. Sprinkle remaining crumb mixture on top.

Bake in moderate oven (375°) 25 to 30 minutes, or until crumbs are lightly browned. Cool slightly before serving. Makes 8 to 10 servings.

ORANGE SUGAR BREAD

Quick and delicious way to glamorize refrigerator biscuits

2 pkgs. refrigerator biscuits
¼ c. butter, melted
1 c. sugar
2 tsp. grated orange rind

Separate biscuits. Roll in butter, then in mixture of sugar and orange rind. Stand upright in well-greased 1½ qt. ring mold.

Bake in very hot oven (450°) 12 to 15 minutes. Turn out on plate. Makes 20 biscuits.

HOT ONION BREAD

The flavorful sour cream onion-bread squares dress up a simple meal of left-overs—complement party meals

2 medium onions, peeled
3 tblsp. butter or margarine
2 c. biscuit mix
⅔ c. milk
1 egg
1 c. dairy sour cream
½ tsp. salt
1 tsp. poppy seeds

Slice onions thinly and separate into rings. Cook gently in butter until soft, 10 to 15 minutes. (Do not brown.)

Meanwhile combine biscuit mix and milk as directed on package. Spread into a greased pan (8″ × 8″ × 2″). Top with onions.

Beat egg with sour cream and salt; spoon over onions. Sprinkle with poppy seeds.

Bake in moderate oven (375°) 30 minutes or until topping is set. Serve hot; makes 8 servings.

QUICK CRUMB COFFEE CAKE

From package to table in less than a half-hour. Serve it hot

2 pkgs. refrigerator biscuits
½ c. sugar
2 tblsp. brown sugar
1 tsp. cinnamon
¼ c. finely chopped nuts
2 tblsp. butter or margarine, melted

Flatten biscuits. Place 10 biscuits in a greased 9″ layer pan; press biscuit edges together so they cover the bottom of the pan.

Combine remaining ingredients. Spread over biscuits. Place remaining flattened biscuits on top to cover filling.

Bake in very hot oven (450°) until browned, about 15 minutes. Remove from pan.

Cool 5 minutes. Spread top with glaze. Makes 6 servings.

Glaze

Combine ¾ c. sifted confectioners' sugar, ½ tsp. vanilla and 3 to 4 tsp. water.

CARAMEL COFFEE CAKE

A whirl of coffee cake—shiny-topped and caramel-flavored

1 can refrigerator caramel nut rolls
2 tblsp. butter, melted

Cut dough into 8 slices. Unwind each slice and loosely twist into a coil, starting at center of greased 8″ round layer pan. Drizzle with butter; sprinkle topping from can over dough.

Bake in moderate oven (375°) until golden brown, 20 to 25 minutes. Cool 2 minutes before cutting. Serve warm. Makes 6 servings.

CRANBERRY COFFEE CAKE

Ready-to-bake biscuits and frozen relish are short-cut ingredients

3 tblsp. butter or margarine, melted
⅓ c. honey
¾ c. Cranberry Relish, partially thawed (see Index)
2 pkgs. refrigerator biscuits

Melt butter in tube pan (8″ or 9″). Add honey and relish; mix well.

Arrange biscuits on end around outer edge of pan. Bake in hot oven (425°) 10 minutes; reduce heat to 400° and bake about 20 to 25 minutes, until browned on top and inner edges. Let cake set 5 minutes before turning upside-down on serving plate. Serve hot. Makes 8 to 10 servings.

Made with Brown-and-Serve Rolls

Many busy women keep brown-and-serve rolls on hand. They add their own touches and heat them at mealtime or when serving coffee. You can get some of their specialties ready to heat and piping hot out of the oven in less than 20 minutes.

MAPLE-NUT STICKIES

Always a hit at a coffee party—only 10 minutes to bake

1 tblsp. butter or margarine
½ c. maple blended syrup
½ c. chopped nuts
12 brown-and-serve rolls

Place ¼ tsp. butter, 2 tsp. syrup and a sprinkling of chopped nuts in each muffin-pan cup.

Place a roll, top side down, over mixture in muffin-pan cup.

Bake in hot oven (400°) about 10 minutes. Serve warm. Makes 12 rolls.

CRUNCHY ORANGE ROLLS

A real treat at any meal—perfect with coffee

12 brown-and-serve rolls
1 tblsp. butter or margarine, melted
2 tblsp. grated orange rind
1 c. sugar
Orange juice

Brush rolls with butter. Combine orange rind, sugar and enough orange juice to moisten. Turn rolls in mixture until well coated.

Place rolls on baking sheet and bake in hot oven (400°) about 10 minutes, or until browned. Makes 12 rolls.

HOT CRUSTY LOAF

This buttery, crisp-crusted, downright delicious bread takes 20 minutes from package to table.

BUTTERFLAKE BREAD

Let everyone break off his own serving

1 pkg. refrigerator butterflake rolls
1 tsp. sesame seeds

On ungreased baking sheet place 2 rolls side by side, slightly overlapping. Place the next 2 rolls so that they overlap the first 2 rolls a little and also overlap each other. Repeat until all 12 rolls are used. Sprinkle with sesame seeds.

Bake in moderate oven (350°) 15 minutes. Makes 1 loaf.

Quick French Bread

It's disappointing not to find French bread in your store when you want it. Nine chances out of ten, you don't have time to bake the conventional crusty loaf. And your heart may be set on serving garlic bread as a part of a spaghetti or other dinner. We have a solution. Make a quick French bread.

NEW-WAY FRENCH BREAD

You can make a small loaf with a can of biscuits but you'd better bake two

2 cans refrigerator biscuits
1 egg white, slightly beaten
1 tsp. poppy seeds (optional)

Place biscuits on ungreased baking sheet, press together lightly, shaping ends to form a long loaf. Brush with egg white, sprinkle with poppy seeds.

Bake in moderate oven (350°) until rich, golden brown, 30 to 40 minutes. Makes 1 (14″) loaf.

GARLIC BREAD: Slice New-Way French Bread and spread with Garlic Butter. Heat in oven a few minutes. Serve hot.

To make Garlic Butter: Crush 2 or 3 garlic cloves, peeled, and add to ½ c. butter. Let stand at room temperature while baking the bread, stirring occasionally. Remove garlic.

PARMESAN ROLLS

You can get them ready hours ahead to brown at last minute

½ c. butter
½ c. grated Parmesan cheese
½ tsp. onion salt
¼ tsp. paprika
1 tblsp. chopped parsley (optional)
12 dinner rolls

Combine butter, cheese, onion salt, paprika and parsley.

Split rolls. Spread with butter mixture. Place on a baking sheet.

Bake in hot oven (425°) a few minutes until cheese melts. (Or slip under hot broiler to melt cheese.) Serve hot. Makes 12 servings.

Variations: Use hard rolls or buns instead of soft rolls. Substitute garlic salt for onion salt.

BUTTER-PECAN DOUGHNUTS: Slice plain doughnuts from the bakery in half, crosswise. Spread cut sides with soft butter or margarine and sprinkle with brown sugar and chopped pecans. Spread in shallow pan and bake in hot oven (400°) about 5 minutes. Serve with coffee or for dessert alongside canned pears or other fruit.

Made with Loaf Bread

BUTTERY HOT BREAD

So good they'll think it's freshly baked bread

1 (1 lb.) loaf white bread
¼ c. butter or margarine

Spread bread slices on one side with softened butter; put back in shape of loaf. Cut in lengthwise halves and tie with string.

Wrap loaf in foil and heat in moderate oven (375°) 20 to 25 minutes. Unwrap, cut and remove string and serve piping hot. Makes 10 to 12 servings.

more

TEA-PARTY CHOCOLATE TOAST: Instead of cinnamon toast, make the teatime treat this way: mix together ½ c. cocoa, 6 tblsp. soft butter, 1 tsp. cinnamon and 6 tblsp. sugar. Spread on hot toast and serve at once with tea or coffee.

SESAME TOAST STICKS: Spread slices of whole-wheat bread, crusts removed, with equal amounts of butter or margarine and honey, mixed. Sprinkle with sesame seeds. Cut bread slices in finger lengths and place on baking sheet. Toast in very hot oven (450°) until crisp and browned, about 6 minutes. Serve with fruit salad or with tea or coffee.

WAFFLED FRENCH TOAST

Instead of standing alone over a sizzling skillet while the rest of the family is gathered around the table, sit down in a chair, plug in the waffle iron and do your cooking in the family circle. Toast cooks faster this way

- 2 eggs
- 1 c. milk
- ¼ tsp. salt
- 2 tblsp. salad oil
- 10 slices bread

Beat eggs slightly; blend in milk, salt and oil. Pour into shallow pan.

Dip bread in egg-milk mixture, coating both sides.

Bake in hot waffle iron until steam no longer appears and bread is brown. Serve at once with honey, syrup or jam. Makes 5 servings.

Quick Yeast Breads

MADE WITH ROLL MIX

If you like the yeasty flavor in coffee breads, here are recipes you will use often. There's no kneading and little work. These treats are so inviting you will want especially to share them with family and friends around the kitchen table at mid-morning on a wintry day. Cups of steaming coffee complement them. But also serve them with chilled canned fruits for desserts that satisfy and please.

APPLE KUCHEN

Why not serve this modern version of an old-fashioned bread at your next coffee party? Bake it ahead, freeze and then quickly reheat it in the oven

- 1 pkg. hot roll mix
- ¾ c. warm (not hot) water
- 1 egg
- 1 tblsp. melted butter
- 3 c. peeled, sliced apples (3 medium apples)
- ½ c. sugar
- 1 ½ tsp. cinnamon

Prepare roll mix with water and egg as directed on package. Spread in greased pan (13″ × 9″ × 2″). Brush with butter. Arrange apples in rows over dough, pressing in slightly. Sprinkle with sugar and cinnamon, mixed.

Let rise until almost doubled, 30 to 45 minutes.

Bake in moderate oven (375°) until deep golden brown, 40 to 45 minutes. Makes 12 servings.

SPICY SUGAR CAKE

A big panful of light, tender coffee bread, but it disappears like magic

- 1 pkg. hot roll mix
- 1 c. warm (not hot) water
- 2 eggs, unbeaten

2 tblsp. sugar
¼ tsp. salt
¼ c. sugar
1 tsp. cinnamon
1 tblsp. butter or margarine
¼ c. walnuts, chopped
¾ c. sifted confectioners' sugar
3 to 4 tsp. milk

Prepare roll mix with water as directed on package. Stir to dissolve yeast. Blend in eggs, 2 tblsp. sugar and salt. Add flour mixture, blend, then beat about 50 strokes.

Spread in greased pan (13″ × 9″ × 2″). Let rise in warm place until almost doubled, 1 to 1½ hours.

Sprinkle with mixture of ¼ c. sugar and cinnamon and nuts; dot with butter.

Bake in moderate oven (375°) 30 to 40 minutes. Drizzle with mixture of confectioners' sugar and milk. Serve warm. Makes 12 servings.

QUICK SALLY LUNN

Just over an hour from mixing to eating for this light bread

1 pkg. hot roll mix
1 c. warm (not hot) water
3 tblsp. soft butter or margarine
1 tsp. sugar
1 egg, beaten

Prepare roll mix with water as directed on package. Stir to dissolve yeast. Add butter in small pieces, then sugar and egg. Blend and stir the stiff batter with a spoon for 5 minutes, until it is smooth and pulls up long strands that drop in big blobs.

Spread batter evenly into well-greased 9″ tube pan or loaf pan (9½″ × 5¼″ × 2¾″). Cover. Let rise in warm place, 85° to 90°, until double in size, 30 to 60 minutes.

Bake in hot oven (400°) 15 minutes; reduce heat to moderate (350°) and bake 10 to 15 minutes to even golden brown. Turn out of pan. Cool slightly. Serve warm with butter and marmalade. Makes 12 servings.

Sally Lunn Muffins: Mix batter and spoon into well-greased muffin-pan cups (3″ × 1½″), filling half full. Let rise until double. Bake in hot oven (400°) 15 minutes. Makes 12 muffins.

CHEESE BUNS

The time-saver is the roll mix; the unusual flavor comes from cheese

1 pkg. hot roll mix
1 c. warm (not hot) water
1 egg, unbeaten
⅔ c. shredded sharp Cheddar cheese

Prepare roll mix with water as directed on package. Stir to dissolve yeast. Blend in egg and cheese. Add flour. Blend, then beat 50 strokes.

Drop dough into 18 well-greased muffin-pan cups. Let rise in warm place until light and almost double in bulk, 30 to 60 minutes.

Bake in moderate oven (375°) 15 to 20 minutes or until golden brown. Makes 18.

Pizza American Style

If you decide to have pizza for a family or company meal, the remainder of the menu will be a snap to fix. All you need is a bowl of green salad, fruit or sherbet for dessert and something to drink. Melon makes a refreshing dessert when in season. Just chill and cut it. Top it with scoops of lime or lemon sherbet if you wish.

We give you a choice of pizza recipes. One is a from scratch version that takes a little longer to fix. You can save work and time by using a packaged roll mix or an assembled ready-to-bake pizza mix. And you can bake the pizza in the oven or in an electric skillet. It takes about 3 minutes to make the sauce and about that long to add a topping like sardines, anchovies or salami.

PIZZA

An excellent from scratch recipe

1 pkg. active dry yeast
1 tsp. sugar
1 c. warm water
3 c. flour
½ tsp. salt
2 tblsp. salad oil
1 lb. Mozzarella, Muenster, process Swiss or American cheese
Pizza Sauce (recipe follows)
1 (3 ¾ oz.) can sardines, drained
½ c. Parmesan cheese (about)
Orégano

Dissolve yeast and sugar in warm (not hot) water. Beat in half the flour; add salt, oil and remaining flour. Mix well; knead until smooth, adding more flour if needed. Place in lightly oiled bowl; turn dough to oil top. Cover; let rise in warm place (85° to 90°) until double.

Divide dough in half; roll each half into circle about 13″ in diameter. Place on oiled pizza pan; fold edge under and build up rim slightly. (Or bake on oiled baking sheet in two 8″ × 12″ rectangles, building up pizza edges.) Brush with oil.

Divide remaining ingredients in half. Shred half the Mozzarella cheese; sprinkle on dough. Spread on half the sauce; top with remaining cheese, sliced, and sardines. Sprinkle with Parmesan cheese and orégano.

Bake in very hot oven (450°) 20 to 25 minutes (until crusty on bottom). Cut in 6 or 8 wedges. Serve hot.

Repeat with other circle of dough and remaining ingredients. These ingredients make 3 pizzas if you bake them in an electric skillet (see Quick Pizza for directions for baking in skillet).

PIZZA SAUCE

1 clove garlic
1 tsp. salt
1 (6 oz.) can tomato paste
1 (8 oz.) can tomato sauce
½ tsp. sugar
⅛ tsp. pepper
½ tsp. orégano
1 tblsp. salad oil
Dash red pepper (optional)

Put garlic through garlic press or mash to a pulp with salt. Combine with remaining ingredients. Do not cook. Makes 1 cup, enough for 2 (12″) pizzas.

PIZZA TOPPINGS: Use chopped or whole anchovies . . . Italian sausage or salami or cold cuts, cut in strips . . . or ground beef (½ lb. to each pizza), seasoned lightly and sautéed in butter. Circle top of any pizza before baking with slices of fresh or canned mushrooms . . . Sprinkle with chopped chives or parsley, or garnish with chopped stuffed green olives or strips of ripe ones . . . Decorate top with pattern of raw-onion or green-pepper rings dipped in oil.

QUICK PIZZA: Prepare 1 (15½ oz.) pkg. assembled ready-to-bake pizza mix (contains yeast, flour mixture, sauce and cheese) as directed on package. (Or use roll mix, following directions for pizza on package.) Fit dough into an oiled, unheated 11″ or 12″ electric skillet; slightly build up pizza edge. Add sauce, cheese and chosen topping. Cover, set dial at 300° to 320° (low to medium) and bake with vent closed until dough is set, about 30 minutes. Dough browns on bottom of pizza. Slide out with spatula; cut in squares. Serve hot. Makes 4 to 6 servings.

Toasted English Muffins—Hot and Buttery

English muffins are not always easy to locate in some of the smaller food stores. You need not deprive your family of them if they enjoy toasted muffins with strawberry jam or some other fruity spread. You can make them with packaged roll mix.

Bake a batch of these yeasty muffins some day when you have spare time. Cool and freeze them. Then you can split, toast and butter them in a jiffy when you're getting a special breakfast, lunch or supper. And if you have drop-in guests, you can toast the muffins and open the fruity spread while you make coffee.

The traditional method of splitting muffins for toasting cannot be surpassed. Break them apart with a fork. Then the surface you toast will be attractive and rough. You cannot get the same effect by cutting with a knife.

BUSY WOMAN'S ENGLISH MUFFINS

Electric skillet is ideal for baking this delicious bread

1 pkg. hot roll mix
2 tblsp. light corn syrup
¼ c. cornmeal

Prepare roll mix as directed on package, adding syrup with water.

Place dough on lightly floured board and knead a few strokes to make smooth, adding only enough flour to prevent hands from sticking to soft dough.

Roll about ½″ thick; cut in 3″ circles with floured cookie cutter.

Sprinkle half of cornmeal on greased cookie sheet. Place rounds of dough about 3″ apart on sheet. Scatter remaining cornmeal on dough. Cover loosely with waxed paper and let rise in a warm place until doubled in bulk, about 1 hour.

Lightly grease an electric skillet, set temperature at 340° and let heat. Cook four muffins at a time, about 10 minutes on each side. Split cooled muffins in half to serve, toast and butter. Makes 10 muffins.

Note: You can bake muffins on a lightly greased, hot griddle.

STRAWBERRY ROLLS

Festive pinwheels pretty enough for a coffee party and to win compliments

- 1 pkg. hot roll mix
- ¾ c. warm (not hot) water
- 1 egg, unbeaten
- 1 c. strawberry preserves
- 1 c. coconut, flaked or shredded
- 1 c. sifted confectioners' sugar
- 4 to 5 tsp. milk

Prepare dough with mix, water and egg as directed on package. Roll out on well-floured surface to a 20″ × 15″ rectangle. Spread with preserves. Sprinkle with coconut. Roll, starting with 20″ side, like jelly roll. Seal seam. Cut into 18 slices.

Place slices, cut side down, in 2 greased (9″) round pans. Let rise in warm place until almost doubled, 30 to 40 minutes.

Bake in moderate oven (375°) until golden brown, 30 to 45 minutes.

Mix confectioners' sugar with milk until smooth and spread on rolls. Makes 18 rolls.

Variation: Substitute peach, apricot or pineapple preserves for strawberry.

Batter Breads Are Easy

Some busy, minute-conscious cooks omit loaf yeast breads from their baking schedules. The reason is apparent: there is no known way to make them rise fast.

But the batter breads are less time-consuming. You skip the kneading and shaping and have no floured board to clean. And the kitchen has that same warm, yeasty aroma that invites everyone in.

The cook who bakes batter breads the first time may be alarmed that the dough is sticky. She needn't be—this is one of its characteristics. For success, be careful to spread the dough evenly in the pan and don't let it rise longer than necessary.

It's a good idea to slice batter breads slightly thicker than other breads. A serrated knife and a sawing motion give excellent results when the loaf is cool.

Try toasting and buttering batter breads for something especially good to eat.

One farm woman suggests, "If you are looking for a hobby, baking breads may be the answer. It will also give pleasure to family and friends."

ANADAMA BATTER BREAD

Takes half as long to make as standard yeast bread—good toasted

- ¾ c. boiling water
- ½ c. yellow cornmeal
- 3 tblsp. shortening
- ¼ c. light molasses
- 2 tsp. salt
- 1 pkg. active dry yeast or compressed yeast
- ¼ c. water
- 1 egg
- 2 ¾ c. flour

In large mixer bowl, blend water, cornmeal, shortening, molasses and salt; cool to lukewarm.

Sprinkle dry yeast over warm water (110°), or crumble compressed yeast into lukewarm water (85°).

Add yeast, egg and half the flour to cornmeal mixture; beat 2 minutes, medium speed on mixer, or 300 strokes by hand; scrape bowl frequently; add remaining flour; mix until well blended.

Spread in greased glass pan (8½"× 4½" × 2¾"). Sprinkle with 1 tblsp. cornmeal and ¼ tsp. salt. Cover; set in warm place until doubled, about 1½ hours.

Bake in slow oven (300°) 45 minutes. Immediately remove bread from pan to cooling rack. Brush top with melted butter. Cool. Makes 1 loaf.

Note: The dough for this bread requires no kneading and no shaping.

OATMEAL BATTER BREAD

Crust is deep brown—puts homemade flavors and variety on bread plate

- ¾ c. boiling water
- ½ c. regular or quick-cooking rolled oats
- 3 tblsp. shortening
- ¼ c. light molasses
- 2 tsp. salt
- 1 pkg. active dry yeast or compressed yeast
- ¼ c. warm (not hot) water
- 1 egg
- 2 ¾ c. flour

In large mixer bowl, stir together boiling water, rolled oats, shortening, molasses and salt. Cool to lukewarm.

Sprinkle dry yeast over warm water (110°), or crumble compressed yeast into lukewarm water (85°) and add it, egg and half the flour to the lukewarm mixture. Beat 2 minutes on medium speed or 300 strokes by hand. Scrape sides and bottom of bowl frequently. Add remaining flour and stir with spoon until flour is blended thoroughly into dough.

Spread dough evenly in a greased loaf pan (8½"×4½"×2¾").Smooth top of loaf with floured hand. Cover and let rise in warm place until batter reaches top of pan, about 1½ hours.

Bake in moderate oven (375°) 50 to 55 minutes. Remove from pan at once and brush top with butter. Cool on rack out of draft. Makes 1 loaf.

WHOLE WHEAT BATTER BREAD

Use for sandwiches—and you'll have a special treat that will win praise

- 1 pkg. active dry yeast or compressed yeast
- 1 ¼ c. warm (not hot) water
- 2 tblsp. honey or brown sugar
- 1 c. unsifted whole wheat flour
- 2 c. white flour
- 2 tsp. salt
- 2 tblsp. soft shortening

Sprinkle dry yeast over warm (110°) water, or crumble compressed yeast into lukewarm water (85°). Add honey, half the white flour, salt and shortening. Beat 2 minutes on medium speed, or 300 vigorous strokes by hand, scraping sides and bottom of bowl frequently. Blend in remaining flours with spoon. Cover and let rise in a warm place until doubled, about 30 minutes.

Stir batter down and spread it evenly in a greased loaf pan (8½" × 4½" × 2¾"). Smooth top of loaf with floured hands. Let rise until batter reaches ½" from top of pan, about 40 minutes.

Bake in moderate oven (375°) 45 to 50 minutes or until brown. Remove from pan at once, brush top with butter and cool on rack before cutting. Do not place in direct draft. Makes 1 loaf.

Muffins—Plain and Fancy

Muffins lift simple, plain meals above the commonplace. They are a snap to make. And the cook's imagination is the limit to the variety in this hot bread. If you ever are lucky enough to have left-over muffins, cut them in crosswise halves, butter and toast them. They're delicious. Here are country-favorite muffins you'll want to try.

CRANBERRY-CORN MUFFINS

Delightful with poultry, ham or pork

1 (7 oz.) can jellied cranberry sauce
1 (8 oz.) pkg. corn-muffin mix

Cut cranberry sauce into ¼" cubes.

Prepare muffin mix as directed on package. Fold in cranberry sauce. Fill paper-lined muffin-pan cups half full and bake as directed on package. Makes 12 muffins.

PINEAPPLE-ORANGE MUFFINS

Have this hot bread for Sunday breakfast and everyone will be on time

1 (14 oz.) pkg. orange-muffin mix
¼ c. pineapple preserves

Prepare muffin mix as directed on package. Place in 12 muffin-pan cups and spoon about 1 tsp. pineapple preserves on top.

Bake in hot oven (400°) until golden brown, about 20 minutes. Serve hot. Makes 12 muffins.

Variations: Substitute apricot, peach, pineapple-apricot, or strawberry preserves for pineapple preserves.

SPICED RAISIN MUFFINS

Raisins are cut in no time with scissors

2 c. biscuit mix
¼ c. sugar
½ tsp. ground cinnamon
1 c. finely cut raisins
1 egg, slightly beaten
¾ c. milk

Combine biscuit mix, sugar, cinnamon and raisins (if you cut them with scissors in mixing bowl, raisins distribute better).

Blend together egg and milk; add to dry ingredients. Stir until batter is just moistened. Bake in hot oven (425°) about 15 minutes. Makes 12 muffins.

SPICY MUFFINS

Just shake hot muffins in sugar and cinnamon to coat them

1 (14 oz.) pkg. muffin mix, any desired kind
½ c. butter or margarine, melted
1 tsp. cinnamon
½ c. sugar

Prepare and bake muffins as directed on mix package.

Dip hot muffins into melted butter. Shake in paper sack with cinnamon and sugar. Makes 12 to 16 muffins.

MUFFIN STRATEGY

One of the most successful tricks busy cooks use to avoid meal monotony is to change the shape of familiar foods. Muffins are a classic example. Here are 2 ways to give them a new look and to cut down on time—no paper liners or pouring of batter into lots of muffin-pan cups. The baking is quicker, too. Use your favorite muffin mix, like orange, raisin-bran, blueberry or corn.

MUFFIN FINGERS: Prepare batter with 1 (14 oz.) pkg. muffin mix, using 2 envelopes, as directed on package. Pour into greased pan (13″ × 9″ × 2″). Bake in hot oven (400°) 15 minutes. Cut in half lengthwise, then in 8 crosswise strips. Makes 16 muffins.

MUFFIN SQUARES: Prepare batter from ½ (14 oz.) pkg. (1 envelope) as directed on muffin-mix package. Pour into greased pan (9″ × 9″ × 2″). Bake in hot oven (400°) 15 minutes or until top is lightly browned. Cut in squares to serve. Makes 9 (3″) squares.

Note: You can bake Muffin Squares from 1 (14 oz.) pkg. muffin mix, using 2 envelopes, in a greased pan (9″ × 9″ × 2″). Increase baking time to 20 to 25 minutes. The muffins will be thicker and their tops will brown more.

CORN LIGHT BREAD

Sweeter than most Southern corn bread, but it's a favorite there

- 1 c. sifted flour
- ¼ c. sugar
- 1 tsp. salt
- 1 tsp. baking soda
- 1 tsp. baking powder
- 2 c. cornmeal
- 2 c. buttermilk
- 3 tblsp. melted shortening

Sift together flour, sugar, salt, soda and baking powder; stir in cornmeal.

Mix buttermilk and shortening; add to dry ingredients. Stir until smooth.

Pour into greased pan (9″ × 5″ × 3″); bake in moderate oven (350°) 1 hour (crack forms in top during baking).

SPANISH CORN BREAD

Mighty good and mighty filling—good with baked beans, chicken or pork

- 1 (12 oz.) pkg. corn-muffin mix
- 1 (12 oz.) can Mexicorn
- ½ tsp. dry mustard
- 1 small onion, finely chopped
- 1 egg, beaten
- ⅔ c. milk

Combine muffin mix, Mexicorn, mustard and onion. Add egg and milk; blend according to package directions.

Spread in greased square baking pan (8″ × 8″ × 2″); bake in hot oven (400°) about 20 minutes or until corn bread tests done. Serve warm. Makes 9 to 10 servings.

CRANBERRY NUT BREAD

A quick bread that makes chicken or turkey sandwiches extra tasty

- 3 c. flour
- 1 ½ tblsp. baking powder
- 1 tsp. salt
- 1 ¼ c. sugar
- 1 c. milk
- 3 tblsp. melted butter or margarine
- 1 egg, beaten
- ½ c. chopped nuts
- 1 ½ c. frozen Cranberry Relish, partially thawed (see Index)

Sift together flour, baking powder, salt and sugar.

more

Combine milk, butter and egg; add to dry ingredients; beat until flour is just moistened.

Fold in nuts and relish. Pour into greased loaf pan (9¼″×5¼″×2¾″). Bake in moderate oven (350°) 1 hour and 15 minutes. Remove from pan to rack immediately. Makes 1 loaf.

OVEN-BAKED PANCAKES

If you have trouble keeping up with the appetites of the people who are eating pancakes, let the oven take over the work. Here's how to make pancakes that require no turning.

BAKED PANCAKES: Prepare 2 c. pancake mix as directed on package. Pour into well-greased jelly-roll pan (15″ × 10″ × 1″). Bake in hot oven (425°) until top is lightly browned, 15 to 20 minutes. Cut in rectangles and serve at once with butter and syrup or jam. Makes 4 servings.

Note: This is an easy way to bake pancakes for a family of four. To feed more people, you will need 2 jelly-roll pans.

COUNTRY KITCHEN PANCAKES: Make batter as directed on pancake-mix package. Add ½ c. each canned whole-kernel corn, drained, and cooked ham, cut in small pieces. Bake and serve hot with butter and syrup.

MEAT-IN-A-PANCAKE

Inviting, new way to dress up luncheon meat—provides quick change

1½ c. milk
1 egg, beaten
1 tblsp. salad oil
½ c. yellow cornmeal
1½ c. pancake mix
2 (12 oz.) cans luncheon meat, sliced ¼″ thick

Blend milk, egg and oil; add cornmeal and pancake mix; stir until smooth. Dip meat in batter; brown on preheated griddle. Makes 24 cakes.

PANCAKES ORIENTAL

Main dish to fix from foods kept on the cupboard shelf

1 (12 oz.) can luncheon meat, cubed
3 tblsp. shortening
1 c. chopped celery
1 (1 lb.) can bean sprouts, drained
3 tblsp. chopped parsley
12 (4″) pancakes (from mix)
Gravy

Brown meat in shortening; add celery, bean sprouts and parsley; heat through.

Serve mixture between 2 warm pancakes; pass gravy. Makes 6 servings.

Gravy

Stir 2 c. clear chicken broth into 2 tblsp. cornstarch and 1 tsp. salt. Cook until thickened and clear; add 1 tblsp. soy sauce. Serve hot.

BACON–PEANUT BUTTER WAFFLES

Stretches bacon most successfully

4 c. pancake mix
1 c. peanut butter
1 c. crisp-cooked bacon, crumbled

Mix waffle batter according to package directions.

Blend in peanut butter. Fold in bacon. Bake as directed. Makes 6 (9″) square waffles or 4 (12″) square waffles.

PANCAKE WAFFLES

A combination main-dish dessert—for a heartier meal, serve extra bacon

- 3 c. pancake mix
- 3 c. milk
- 3 eggs, beaten
- ½ c. melted shortening
- 3 tblsp. crumbled, cooked bacon

Combine pancake mix, milk and eggs; beat with rotary beater until fairly smooth; blend in shortening and bacon.

Bake in preheated waffle baker. Serve with Apricot Fluff (recipe follows). Makes about 6 (11″ × 6″) waffles.

APRICOT FLUFF

Beat ½ c. butter until fluffy; beat in ½ c. apricot preserves. Makes 1 cup.

Top with Bread Crumbs

Smart young cooks who like short cuts discover fast ways to fix bread crumbs to sprinkle over casseroles and to use in a hundred other dishes. There are about as many favorite ways as there are cooks. But freezer owners agree on one point: it's handy to keep a plastic bag or air-tight container of bread crumbs frozen to add to foods in a hurry. Try separating layers of crumbs in jars with waxed paper for easy removal.

Some busy homemakers say it pays to buy packaged bread crumbs at their food markets. Other women prefer to make their own. The electric blender makes quick work of this chore.

A farmer's wife explains how she fixes dry bread crumbs. "I really make the sparks (crumbs) fly," she says. "I use the Indian technique of rubbing two pieces of dry bread together over a paper bag, partly torn open, to catch the crumbs. It's mighty convenient when I'm trying to get the casserole in the oven before the men, coming in from the field, reach the house."

Some speedy cooks admit they don't bother to butter the crumbs. They just dot them, once they're atop the dish, with butter or margarine. Others follow this conventional method: melt ⅓ c. butter or margarine in a skillet, add 1 c. bread crumbs and stir constantly until crumbs are golden brown.

Busy women who plan ahead frequently stick to the traditional method: putting dry bread through the food chopper, using the fine blade. This is a chore they tuck into a day when there's a little free time. They store the crumbs in the freezer, often buttering them first. And as one thoughtful woman added, "Be sure to tie a paper bag over the blade end of the chopper to catch the crumbs. Then you can pour them into a container in a jiffy—without spilling."

Whatever system you develop or adopt, be sure to use bread crumbs when the recipe so specifies. They add crunchy texture, attractive brown, and delightful flavor atop a casserole. They help sell the dish.

CHAPTER 13

RELISHES AND SAUCES

Today's clever country cooks, like their mothers and grandmothers, serve relishes and sauces to pick up plain-Jane meals. It's second nature to them to open a jar of pickles or a glass of strawberry jam or to pour glossy chocolate sauce over ice cream or pudding. And the more rushed they are at mealtime, the greater their faith in what these extras will do. Or, as one busy farmer's wife puts it, "Relishes and sauces are to a meal what jewelry is to a costume. They add interest, color and glamour."

It takes some sleight of hand to make relishes quickly, but the recipes in this chapter show how busy women do it. A few examples: cottage cheese with fresh cucumbers from the garden folded in, canned fruits quickly spiced, jewel-like jellies to fix in midwinter from canned, bottled and frozen juices and a cranberry-orange-apple relish to blend and freeze for use long after the cranberry harvest ends.

In a timesaving cookbook many of the sauces are built into the recipes for meat, poultry, fish and vegetables. They are American–distant cousins of the tedious French sauces. Many of them start with a can of soup. Don't miss the fish fillets poached like eggs in canned, frozen cream of shrimp soup. It's a gourmet dish most everyone raves over.

But sauces served over foods deserve attention–cheese sauce to make in less than five minutes and use in a hundred ways, quick custard and a praline sauce made without cooking from a pudding mix, shared with us by a Nebraska farm woman.

Heed generations of experience in country cooking and punctuate your meals with easy-on-the-cook relishes and sauces. You'll find intriguing recipes for them in this chapter.

Farm-style Relishes and Sauces

They're flavor boosters

Really Good Relishes

SPICY APPLE RELISH

Chili sauce adds spice—cook relish in a skillet about 10 minutes

4 medium apples
2 tblsp. butter or margarine
1 tblsp. honey
1 c. chili sauce

Cut unpeeled apples in wedges, removing cores.

Melt butter in skillet, add honey and chili sauce, mix thoroughly and heat. Add apples, coating them with the chili-sauce mixture, and cook until slightly soft, about 10 to 12 minutes, turning occasionally to baste fruit. Serve hot or cold as meat relish and garnish. Makes 6 servings.

GLAZED APRICOTS

Serve on platter of chicken or meat—bright garnish and super-fine eating

1 (1 lb.) can apricot halves
1 tblsp. butter or margarine
1 tblsp. brown sugar
1 stick cinnamon

Drain syrup from apricots. Add butter, sugar and cinnamon to syrup and boil 3 minutes. Gently add apricots. Reduce heat and simmer 5 minutes. Serve hot with poultry or meat. Makes 6 servings.

A Country Cook Says:

"You'll get a Grand Hotel taste by stirring 1 tsp. fennel seeds into 2 c. applesauce. Serve with pork sausage or chops. The seeds give that anise-like flavor."

PICKLED BEANS

No work to fix old-time relish this modern way—there's no cooking

2 (15½ oz.) cans whole green beans
1 c. sweet-pickle juice
1½ tsp. celery seeds
½ c. sweet-pickle relish
1 hard-cooked egg, chopped

Drain beans. Spread them in a dish.

Combine remaining ingredients and pour over the beans. Cover and let stand in refrigerator overnight or 8 hours. Makes 8 servings.

Colorful Cranberries the Year Round

Cranberries harvested in autumn match the season's leaves in brilliant color. Then many country women take a day off to make ruby-red relish to freeze for use throughout the year. Partly thawed, it tastes just right in summer with Golden Fried Chicken (see Index). And it glorifies countless other desserts and salads.

CRANBERRY RELISH

Adds a color sparkle and sweet-tart taste to many dishes

4 medium oranges, seeded
2 lbs. cranberries
4 medium unpeeled apples, cored
4 c. sugar

Peel the yellow rind from orange; trim off and discard white part. Put orange pulp and yellow rind, cranberries and apples through food grinder. Add sugar and mix well.

Cover and refrigerate. Or pour into glass jars, leaving ½" head space. Seal and freeze. Makes 4 pints.

Note: Cranberry Relish has many uses in the kitchen. It is an ingredient in the following recipes in this cookbook (see Index): Cranberry Coffee Cake, Fruited Fantan Rolls, Molded Cranberry-Relish Salad, Cranberry Mincemeat Pie, Cranberry Nut Bread and Cranberry Topping.

GLISTENING CRANBERRY SAUCE

An Oregon farm woman sent her prized cranberry-sauce recipe to us with this comment: "The berries stay almost whole and they have a pretty, glazed look." Note how quick and simple they are to fix.

OREGON CRANBERRY SAUCE

Shiny red cranberries that are no trouble to fix. There's no sieving

1 lb. cranberries (4 c.)
2 c. sugar
2 tblsp. water
Dash of salt

Wash cranberries and lift from water into large saucepan. Add sugar, water and salt. Stir to mix sugar and berries.

Cover saucepan and set on heat. Cook only until berries start to pop. Remove lid and lightly stir, using care not to crush berries. Cook 2 minutes. Let the mixture boil up; then boil 1 minute longer. Makes about 3½ cups.

Note: The chilled cranberry sauce, served in dessert glasses and topped with puffs of whipped cream, a little grated orange rind folded in, makes a delightful, colorful dessert.

COTTAGE-CHEESE RELISH

Makes a refreshing salad served atop pineapple rings on lettuce

1 large peeled cucumber
½ c. mayonnaise
1 tsp. celery seeds
½ tsp. salt
1 qt. small-curd cottage cheese

Cut cucumber into small cubes (about ¼") and mix it and all the other ingredients into cottage cheese. Chill in refrigerator.

Serve as relish, garnished with diced cucumber or parsley. Makes 10 to 12 servings.

Variations: Substitute dairy sour cream for mayonnaise. Add a few sliced green onions if they are in season. And if your cucumber is fresh out of the garden, wash it, but do not peel. The green of the cucumber rind adds attractive color.

GARLIC OLIVES: Almost fill a pint jar with drained, canned ripe olives. Add five garlic cloves, sliced, and two thin lemon slices. Pour on enough olive or salad oil to cover, put lid on jar and chill 1 to 2 days. Drain to serve (strain oil and use to make French dressing for tossed salads.)

STUFFED CELERY: Fill celery stalks with peanut butter for the children. They'll like it fixed this way. Or add 2 tblsp. drained crushed pineapple to 1 (3 oz.) pkg. cream cheese and press in celery stalks. You can speed up the preparation by using a pineapple-cheese spread.

Winter Jellies

Choose a day when there's frost on the kitchen windowpanes to make jelly. When the day's over, you'll find that everyone will enjoy looking at your display and tasting the summertime flavors they hold.

Jelly-making in January is easier than in June. No picking of fruit or berries and no washing, peeling, coring, chopping or straining. And no stained jelly bags to empty and wash! That's because you start with bottled or canned fruit juices.

Delicate, coral-pink apple jelly can be varied in many ways. We give you a few favorites of good country cooks.

JANUARY APPLE JELLY

Makes wonderful glaze spread over baked ham for last ½ hour of baking

- 1 qt. bottled or canned apple juice
- 5 drops (about) red food color
- 1 (1 ¾ oz.) pkg. powdered-fruit pectin
- 5 ½ c. sugar

Combine juice, color and pectin in large saucepan; bring to a full boil.

Add sugar; stir until dissolved. Return to boil; boil 2 minutes.

Remove from heat; skim. Pour into hot, sterilized jars; seal. Makes about 7 pints.

VARIATIONS

You can start with the January Apple Jelly recipe and make seven wonderful jellies. Omit the food color. Then follow these directions.

CINNAMON-APPLE: Add ⅓ c. red cinnamon candies with sugar.

CRANBERRY-APPLE: Use equal parts bottled cranberry and apple juices.

SPICED-MINTED APPLE: Add about 5 drops green food color to apple juice; tie 1 tblsp. whole cloves in muslin bag; add to juice with pectin. Remove after cooking; add ½ tsp. peppermint extract.

GERANIUM: Lay a washed rose geranium leaf in each jar before pouring in the hot jelly mixture.

GRAPE: Use bottled grape juice for apple juice.

GRAPEFRUIT-LEMON: Use unsweetened canned grapefruit juice for apple juice; add juice of 3 lemons and about 10 drops yellow food color.

CRANBERRY: Use bottled cranberry juice for apple juice.

SPICY PEACH PICKLES

They bring fancy prices in gourmet shops but are easy to fix at home

1 (1 lb.) can peach halves
1 (3") stick cinnamon
1 tsp. whole cloves
1 tsp. whole allspice
¼ c. white vinegar

Drain syrup from peaches into saucepan. Add spices and vinegar. Simmer 5 minutes.

Pour over peaches, cover and refrigerate overnight, at least 8 hours. Serve as relish with chicken or meats. Makes 6 to 8 servings.

Note: Save the syrup after peaches are served. Heat and pour over more drained canned peaches, apricots, pears or pineapple. Chill.

4-VEGETABLE RELISH

Excellent with fried chicken. A summer substitute for salad

3 large tomatoes, peeled and cut in wedges
½ c. chopped green pepper
½ c. grated cucumber, peeled
1 tblsp. grated onion
½ tsp. seasoned salt
½ tsp. salt
⅛ tsp. pepper

Combine all ingredients. Chill ½ hour or longer to blend flavors. Makes 6 servings.

Dessert Sauces and Toppings

APPLESAUCE À LA MODE: Serve it on unfrosted spice cake or caramel cake or gingerbread. Spoon the applesauce on the dessert and top with a scoop of vanilla or nut ice cream. Sprinkle lightly with cinnamon.

TOPPING FOR APPLE PIE: Fold ¼ c. crushed peanut brittle and ½ tsp. grated orange rind into 1 c. lightly sweetened whipped cream. Top each serving of pie with spoonful of the topping. Also try this on pumpkin pie.

BLUEBERRY SAUCE

The blend of blueberry and pineapple flavors works like magic

1 (10 oz.) pkg. frozen blueberries
½ c. unsweetened pineapple juice
¼ c. water
⅔ c. sugar
2 tsp. cornstarch
Dash of salt

Combine all ingredients in saucepan. Cook, stirring, over medium heat until sauce thickens. Cool and chill. Makes about 2 cups.

Variation: Substitute 1½ c. fresh blueberries for the frozen ones.

CAKE COCONUT TOPPING: When you have a left-over slice of white cake, combine ¾ c. cake crumbs and ¼ c. shredded coconut. Spread on a baking sheet and toast in moderate oven (350°) until light golden brown. Serve over vanilla or chocolate ice cream.

EGGNOG FOR SAUCE

Pour this over the children's cereal for a change—they'll like it

1 egg, beaten
1 c. milk

Pastry basket, made from pie crust mix, holds red-ripe strawberries for company dessert. Jelly glaze adds flavor and sparkle, gives a professional look. An easy-to-make glamorous pastry (recipe page 134).

Cranberry Relish (page 190) is the flavor secret of Cranberry Mincemeat Pie, Cranberry Topping, spread over and between layers of angel food cake, Cranberry Coffee Cake and other exciting dishes in this book.

2 tsp. sugar
¼ tsp. vanilla

Combine ingredients thoroughly. Makes enough for 2 servings on cereal or puddings.

HONEYED CRANBERRY TOPPING

Make it ahead and refrigerate so flavors mellow—on the tart side

2 oranges, quartered
4 c. cranberries (1 lb.)
1 c. honey

Put unpeeled oranges, seeds removed, and cranberries through food chopper. Fold in honey. Cover and place in refrigerator. May be made several days ahead. Makes about 4 cups.

For dessert, spoon cranberry-orange mixture over vanilla ice cream.

CHOCOLATE SAUCE

Keep a supply in the refrigerator handy for dressing up ice cream

1 (15 oz.) can sweetened condensed milk
2 (1 oz.) squares unsweetened chocolate
⅛ tsp. salt
1 c. hot water
½ tsp. vanilla

Place condensed milk, chocolate and salt in top of double boiler. Cook over rapidly boiling water, stirring frequently, until thick, about 10 minutes. Remove from heat.

Slowly add hot water, beating with a rotary beater.

Cool, add vanilla and chill. Serve over ice cream, cake or pudding. Makes about 2½ cups.

SHORTCAKE POUR-CREAM

Tops for peach and berry shortcakes

1 c. heavy cream, whipped
2 egg yolks
3 tblsp. honey
2 tblsp. lemon juice

Whip cream until slightly thick. Add egg yolks one at a time and continue beating. Slowly drizzle in honey and lemon juice. Sauce will be thick and creamy. Pour over shortcakes. Makes about 1¼ cups.

CRANBERRY TOPPING

An eye-catcher—gives plain cake a fancy look, adds vivid color

1 c. heavy cream, whipped
½ c. sugar
1 (8½ oz.) can crushed pineapple, drained
1½ c. Cranberry Relish (see Index), partly thawed and drained

Whip cream, adding sugar slowly, until stiff.

Fold in pineapple and relish, but do not blend completely. Serve on angel food cake slices or use as filling and topping for angel food and other cakes. Refrigerate frosted cakes until served. Makes about 1 quart.

Variation: To make Frozen Cranberry Salad, freeze Cranberry Topping in 1 qt. mold. Serve on lettuce.

EASY CUSTARD-TYPE DESSERT SAUCE

Comes in handy when you're in a rush —it's made with pudding mix

1 (3 ¼ oz.) pkg. vanilla-pudding mix
2 ½ c. milk

Combine pudding mix and milk in saucepan. Heat, stirring constantly, until mixture comes to a full boil. Serve sauce warm. Makes 2¾ cups.

Variation: Add a few drops of almond flavoring after removing sauce from heat.

Note: If you chill this sauce, it thickens.

CUSTARD SAUCE

Uses left-over egg yolks

3 egg yolks, beaten
¼ c. sugar
⅛ tsp. salt
2 c. scalded milk
1 tsp. vanilla

Combine egg yolks, sugar and salt. Slowly stir into scalded milk.

Cook over hot (not boiling) water, stirring constantly, until mixture thickens and coats a metal spoon, about 5 minutes.

Remove pan immediately from hot water and place in pan of cold water to cool quickly. When cool, add vanilla and chill. Makes about 2½ c.

Note: Overcooking causes custard to curdle. Do not let water in double boiler come to a boil. Beating a slightly curdled custard with a rotary beater will help repair the damage, but the sauce will be thinner.

HARD SAUCE

Keep in freezer handy to serve on warm puddings and desserts

½ c. butter or margarine
1 c. sifted confectioners' sugar
½ tsp. vanilla

Beat butter and sugar with electric mixer until fluffy and creamy. Beat in vanilla. Chill or freeze. Makes 1 cup.

Variations: Shape Hard Sauce in balls and roll in grated lemon or orange rind. Or sprinkle Hard Sauce with a touch of nutmeg before serving.

LEMON HARD SAUCE

You'll like what tangy lemon and buttery-rich flavors do to spice cake

¼ c. heavy cream
½ c. butter or margarine
1 ¼ c. confectioners' sugar
1 tsp. grated lemon rind
1 tblsp. lemon juice

Whip cream; set aside.

Cream butter with same beaters. Add sugar; beat until light and fluffy. Add lemon rind and juice.

Fold in whipped cream. Chill. Serve spoonful on each square of gingerbread or on spice cakes. Makes 2 cups.

ICE-CREAM SAUCE: Serve vanilla ice cream, softened until it resembles whipped cream, over desserts. Or stir a little chocolate, butterscotch or other ice-cream topping you buy at your food store through vanilla ice cream for Rippled Ice Cream Sauce.

MELBA SAUCE: Blend 1 cup frozen red raspberries, thawed, 1 tsp. sugar and

1 tsp. cornstarch. Cook over low heat, stirring, until clear. Strain through a sieve. Cool. Serve over vanilla ice cream; or, for the Classic Peach Melba, serve over drained, canned peach halves, their centers filled with vanilla ice cream. Professional chefs add ½ cup currant jelly to the sauce to enhance its flavor and to add sparkle.

A farm woman in Nebraska sent us her favorite recipe for an ice-cream topping. It has that wonderful molasses-butter-pecan flavor blend suggestive of New Orleans. You won't want to miss trying this topping for ice cream. It's good on cake and puddings, too.

NO-COOK PRALINE SAUCE

You couldn't improve on this if you spent hours instead of minutes

1 c. light corn syrup
2 tblsp. molasses
1 (4 oz.) pkg. instant butterscotch-pudding mix
⅔ c. chopped pecans
2 tblsp. water

Blend together syrup and molasses; stir in pudding mix. Add nuts and water. Chill ½ hour. Stir before using. Makes about 2 cups.

PEANUT-CHOCOLATE SAUCE

You start with pudding mix

1 (4 oz.) pkg. chocolate-pudding mix
¾ c. water
¾ c. corn syrup
¼ tsp. salt
1 tblsp. butter or margarine
⅓ c. peanut butter
½ tsp. vanilla

Empty package contents into saucepan. Gradually add water, mixing until smooth. Add corn syrup and salt; mix well.

Cook over medium heat, stirring constantly until mixture comes to a boil.

Remove from heat and add butter, peanut butter and vanilla; stir until melted. Serve warm or cold over ice cream. Makes 1¾ cups.

BANANA-CREAM TOPPING

Bananas and fluffy whipped cream—unusual topping for spice cakes

1 (3 oz.) pkg. cream cheese
½ c. heavy cream
3 tblsp. sugar
Dash salt
2 large, ripe bananas
2 tsp. lemon juice

Beat cheese until smooth. Gradually add cream, beating only to keep mixture smooth. Add sugar and salt.

Mash bananas with fork; add with lemon juice to creamed mixture. Blend thoroughly. Cover and refrigerate. Makes 2 cups. (Use within 2 or 3 hours.)

FRUIT AND HONEY CREAM

Whipped cream, honey and fruit on gingerbread—makes it company fare

1 c. heavy cream, whipped
¼ c. honey
1½ to 3 c. drained fruit

Top each gingerbread serving generously with whipped cream. Drizzle on about 1 tsp. honey; add spoonful of drained fruit cocktail or pineapple chunks.

Variation: Substitute peeled, cored and diced fresh pears for the canned fruit.

ORANGE-MARSHMALLOW SAUCE

This fluffy sauce makes simple gingerbread a company special

4 c. miniature marshmallows
½ c. water
2 to 3 tsp. orange rind
1 ¼ c. orange juice
2 tblsp. lemon juice
Dash salt

Heat marshmallows and water to boiling in small saucepan. Remove from heat; stir to melt marshmallows.

Add rind, juices and salt. Chill until mixture congeals.

Beat with rotary beater until airy and light. Chill. Makes 2¼ cups.

Sauces for Meat, Fish, Vegetables

APPLE-HORSE-RADISH SAUCE

Good with ham, ham loaf and pork

2 c. applesauce or 1 (1 lb.) can
¼ c. prepared horse-radish
⅛ tsp. basil (optional)
½ tsp. salt
⅛ tsp. pepper

Combine ingredients. Makes 2¼ cups.

BACON-KETCHUP SAUCE

Extra good over cooked cauliflower

¾ c. chopped onion
1 tblsp. butter or margarine
8 bacon slices
2 tblsp. flour
1 ¾ c. milk
1 tblsp. ketchup
¼ tsp. salt
Worcestershire sauce

Sauté onion in butter until soft.

Snip bacon with scissors directly into pan. Mix with onion and cook until crisp (about 5 to 6 minutes).

Sprinkle flour over mixture in skillet. Gradually stir in milk and cook, stirring until smooth. Season with ketchup, salt and a dash of Worcestershire sauce. Makes 6 servings.

A Country Cook Suggests:

BROWN BUTTER-CRUMB SAUCE: Delicately brown ¼ c. fine, dry bread crumbs in ¼ c. butter. Add another ¼ c. butter and melt over low heat. Use to top cooked green beans or cauliflower. Try both white or rye bread crumbs.

SPEEDY CHEESE SAUCE

You'll like it on vegetables, fish and in casseroles. Try it on burgers

1 c. undiluted evaporated milk
1 ½ c. cut-up process American cheese
¼ tsp. dry mustard
½ tsp. Worcestershire sauce
Few drops Tabasco sauce

Heat milk over low heat. Add cheese

and continue cooking, stirring constantly, until cheese melts. Add seasonings. Serve hot. Makes about 1½ cups.

NOBBY CHEESE SAUCE

Perfect over eggs on toast—scrambled, poached or hard-cooked and sliced

- 4 tblsp. butter or margarine
- 4 tblsp. flour
- 2 c. milk
- 1 tsp. salt
- ¼ tsp. pepper
- 1 tsp. Worcestershire sauce
- 1 c. (¼″) sharp Cheddar cheese cubes

Melt butter in heavy skillet over low heat; add flour and blend, but do not brown. Remove from heat; add milk and stir to blend. Add salt, pepper and Worcestershire sauce.

Return to low heat and cook, stirring, until mixture is smooth and thickens. Just before serving, stir in the cheese. Makes about 2 cups.

Variation: To make Deviled Cheese Sauce, add 1 tsp. dry mustard and 1 tsp. grated onion.

Creamy Curry Sauce for Hamburgers or Meat Loaf: Blend 1 c. dairy sour cream with ½ to 1 tsp. curry powder. Season with salt to taste. Serve at room temperature with hot meat.

Note: This sauce also may be served with hot vegetables.

Easy Hollandaise Sauce: Cream thoroughly ½ c. butter or margarine; gradually beat in 3 egg yolks, 1½ tblsp. lemon juice, ½ tsp. salt, dash paprika and few grains cayenne pepper; blend well. Slowly stir in ¼ c. boiling water. Place in top of double boiler. Cook over 1½″ boiling water (so water doesn't touch top part of double boiler) 5 minutes, stirring constantly. Remove from heat; beat 1 minute.

Mock Hollandaise Sauce: Blend ½ c. mayonnaise or salad dressing, ½ c. heavy cream and 2 tblsp. lemon juice.

OLD-FASHIONED KETCHUP

You can prepare vegetables for this spicy, red sauce in the blender

- 48 medium tomatoes (about 8 lbs.)
- 2 ripe, sweet red peppers
- 2 sweet green peppers
- 4 onions
- 3 c. white vinegar
- 3 c. sugar
- 3 tblsp. salt
- 1½ tsp. allspice
- 3 tsp. dry mustard
- 1½ tsp. cloves
- 1½ tsp. cinnamon
- ½ tsp. hot red pepper

Quarter tomatoes; remove stem ends. Add peppers, seeded and cut in strips, and onions, peeled and cut in eighths. Mix.

Put vegetables in blender container, filling jar ¾ full. Blend at high speed 4 seconds; pour into large kettle. Repeat until all vegetables are blended.

Add vinegar, sugar and spices, tied loosely in thin muslin bag. Simmer, uncovered, in slow oven (325°) or in electric saucepan until volume is reduced one half. Remove spices.

Seal immediately in hot, sterilized jars. Makes 5 pints.

more

Variation: Add 2 c. thick applesauce to the cooked ketchup and mix thoroughly for Tomato Apple Ketchup.

MUSTARD BUTTER SAUCE

Pour this zippy sauce over boiled or broiled fish just before serving

- ¼ c. butter
- 1 tsp. prepared mustard
- 1 tsp. lemon juice

Heat butter until light brown; stir in mustard and lemon.

ORIENTAL SAUCE

Complements delicate-flavored pork

- 1 tblsp. dry mustard
- ½ tsp. curry powder
- ½ c. ketchup
- 1 tblsp. vinegar
- 1 tblsp. soy sauce

Combine ingredients and bring to a boil. Serve hot with pork. Makes about ½ cup.

BASIC RED SAUCE

Keep in refrigerator or freezer—we give you several ways to use it, and you'll think of more

- 1 c. finely chopped onion
- ⅓ c. salad oil
- 1½ c. ketchup
- ½ c. water
- ½ c. lemon juice
- ¼ c. sugar
- ¼ c. Worcestershire sauce
- 2½ tsp. salt
- ½ tsp. pepper
- 4 drops Tabasco sauce

Cook onion in hot oil until soft and golden. Add remaining ingredients; simmer 15 minutes. Cool and store in refrigerator or freezer. Makes about 1 quart.

Variations: For a more tart sauce, use an additional 2 tblsp. lemon juice. For a hotter sauce, add more Tabasco sauce to suit taste.

Note: The following recipes are made with Basic Red Sauce: Better Burgers, Lamb Balls in Red Sauce, Nippy Cheese Dip, Vegetables in Foil, Short-cut Salad Dressing and Shrimp Creole (see Index).

SPICY TOMATO SAUCE

Decorative on meat loaves

- 1 can condensed cream of tomato soup
- 1 tblsp. prepared mustard
- 2 tblsp. prepared horse-radish
- ⅛ tsp. pepper

Combine ingredients. Heat and serve over meat loaf. Makes about 1½ cups.

TARTAR SAUCE: Combine 1 c. mayonnaise, 2 tblsp. pickle relish, 1 tblsp. chopped onion, 1 tblsp. snipped parsley and 1 tblsp. chopped pimiento. Makes 1¼ cups.

Spreads for Breads

ORANGE HONEY BUTTER

Lifts hot waffles and pancakes into the gourmet class

½ c. butter or margarine
⅔ c. honey
1 tblsp. orange juice
1 tsp. grated orange rind

Combine ingredients and beat until blended. Makes about 1¼ cups.

Variation: Add 1 tsp. lemon juice with orange juice.

HERB BUTTER

Keep it in freezer to make Herb-flavored Bread

½ c. soft butter or margarine
½ tsp. salt
¼ tsp. paprika
¼ tsp. dried savory or 2 tsp. chopped parsley
½ tsp. dried thyme
Few grains red pepper

Cream butter with salt, paprika, savory, thyme and red pepper. Makes enough for 1 (13 to 16 oz.) loaf French bread.

HERB-FLAVORED BREAD: Cut French bread diagonally, almost through to bottom crust, in 12 equal slices. Spread Herb Butter between slices. Wrap loaf snugly in foil. Heat in hot oven (400°) about 15 minutes. Makes 6 servings.

Variation: Omit paprika, herbs and red pepper in Herb Butter and add 3 tblsp. minced onion.

OTHER SEASONED BUTTERS FOR FRENCH BREAD

Use them instead of Herb Butter to make other flavored breads; follow directions for Herb-flavored Bread. You also can wrap the loaf in foil and place on a grill over hot coals for heating. Turn it frequently and heat 20 to 25 minutes.

BASIC RECIPE

Soften ½ c. butter or margarine by creaming in mixing bowl. (Makes enough to spread one loaf French bread.) Add and mix well:

ONION-PARSLEY: 4 tblsp. each minced onion and parsley.

CHILI-KETCHUP: ½ tsp. chili powder, 2 tblsp. ketchup and 2 crushed garlic cloves. (Garlic press may be used.)

MUSTARD: 2 tblsp. prepared mustard.

GARLIC: Crush 3 or 4 peeled garlic cloves. Add to butter or margarine. Let stand at room temperature 1 or 2 hours, stirring occasionally.

CURRY: ½ tsp. curry powder.

SMOKE: ½ tsp. smoke salt.

BLUE-CHEESE: ¼ c. crumbled blue or Roquefort cheese.

SWISS-CHEESE: ½ c. coarsely shredded Swiss cheese.

SAGE: ½ tsp. powdered dry sage.

THYME: ½ tsp. powdered dried thyme.

SAGE AND THYME: ¼ tsp. each.

BLENDER BUTTER: Pour 1 c. heavy cream into blender's container. Blend at high speed 15 seconds or until cream is whipped and starts to thicken around blades. Add ½ c. cold water and 1 crushed ice cube. Blend at high speed 2 minutes. Spoon sweet butter into small bowl; work with a wooden spoon to extract liquid (save to use in baking, as in making biscuits). Salt butter if you wish. Makes 6 ounces.

Note: Peel a small clove of garlic or use half a large one. Add with cold water and crushed ice cube to Blender Butter. Spread on top of sizzling steaks for delightful aroma and flavor.

WHIPPED BUTTER: Let ½ lb. butter (unsalted, if available) stand at room temperature until soft, about 1 hour. Beat with electric mixer on low speed until smooth. Then beat on high speed until light and fluffy, about 10 minutes. The butter takes on a lighter color. Store in refrigerator. Let whipped butter soften at room temperature before serving with hot breads, pancakes and waffles. Makes about 1½ cups.

CHAPTER 14

APPETIZERS AND SNACKS

Appetizers are to meals what frostings are to cakes—decorative and tempting. Their role, in contrast to that of cakes, is not to satisfy appetites, but to serve just before a meal to stimulate with the promise of good food to follow. They set the pace.

Snacks need to satisfy hunger when someone in the family arrives home too late for a meal. When company comes, they promote sociability. Good food and good talk are country comrades. That's why the coffee break is so popular with farm people.

Appetizers and snacks are on common ground in the minds of many busy women. Often they eliminate the former and serve whatever they have on hand, with no previous planning, for the company snack.

Smart short-cut cooks call the easy-to-fix meal starters and snacks that follow "sure-fire compliment catchers." The snacks especially tempt the young crowd, but people of all ages enjoy them.

Don't overlook the ability of fast-fix Spiced Fruit Cocktail to give company dinners and banquets a bright send-off. You make it ahead; the flavors mellow while it chills. Or do as more and more busy hostesses are doing: let the family and friends sip fruit juices in the living room while you put the finishing touches on a meal. Makes the time pass pleasantly and quickly. Some blustery winter evening, surprise everyone with one of the fun-making dips for dunking. Try Swiss Dip with crusty bread.

Use all the appetizers and snacks in this chapter to make people happy—to keep hospitality alive at your house in these hectic times. Don't forget the 4-H boys and girls. Pass popcorn balls so easily made in new ways. Take your pick of the two recipes in this chapter. Or stir up a batch of homemade candy by melting sweet chocolate and adding walnuts. Place in the refrigerator to cool in a hurry. Or let them fix pralines with a butterscotch taste. And remember that sugared Orange Walnuts are a nibbler's delight.

Company Appetizers and Snacks

They add the gala, friendly touch

Meal Starters

The best way to get the company meal off to a good start is to serve a tasty, colorful appetizer. It's a forecast of what will follow. Here are some excellent choices.

SPICED FRUIT COCKTAIL

Surprise flavor delight. You can make it a day ahead

- 2 (1 lb. 1 oz.) cans fruit for salad or fruit cocktail
- 1 (1 lb. 1 oz.) can light cherries
- 2 tblsp. lemon juice
- 1 (6″ piece) stick cinnamon
- 1 tsp. whole cloves
- ⅛ tsp. salt

Drain syrup from fruit into saucepan. Add juice, cinnamon and cloves (tied in cheesecloth bag) and salt. Boil 5 minutes. Remove spices. Pour over fruit. Chill several hours or overnight.

Serve in sherbet glasses. Garnish each serving with a sprig of mint. Makes 6 servings.

FRUIT AND SHERBET COCKTAIL

Bright color contrasts make appetizers pretty as nosegays at each place

- 1 (1 lb. 14 oz.) can pineapple chunks, chilled
- 1 (10 or 11 oz.) can mandarin oranges, chilled
- 1 pt. lime sherbet

Drain fruits. Half fill glasses with pineapple chunks; top with scoop of sherbet. Fill around sherbet with orange sections. Makes 6 servings.

3-IN-1 FRUIT JUICE COCKTAILS

RUBY PUNCH: Combine 4 c. cranberry-juice cocktail, 1 c. pineapple juice and 1 c. orange juice. Garnish each drink with a quarter of thin slice of orange. Makes 8 (6 oz.) glasses.

PINEAPPLE GLOW: Combine 3 c. apple juice, 3 c. pineapple juice, ¼ c. maraschino-cherry juice and ¼ tsp. almond extract. Garnish each drink with a maraschino cherry and a sprig of mint. Makes 8 (6 oz.) glasses.

ROYAL ADE: Combine 3 c. apple juice, 3 c. grape juice, 2 tblsp. fresh lime juice and ¼ tsp. nutmeg. Garnish with lime slices. Makes 8 (6 oz.) glasses.

MELON-BOAT COCKTAIL

Refreshing in summer when melons reach their flavor peak

- 1 large cantaloupe
- ½ c. Fresh Mint Syrup (recipe follows)
- 1 ½ to 2 c. pineapple chunks and sliced strawberries

Cut cantaloupe into sixths; make a crisscross pattern in wedges. Spoon about 1 tblsp. Fresh Mint Syrup over each. Heap fruit in center. Makes 6 servings.

Variations: Use honeydew melon instead of cantaloupe, or pour Fresh Mint Syrup over servings of melon cubes; a combination of fresh and frozen fruits like pineapple, orange and grapefruit; strawberries, raspberries or blueberries; drained, canned fruit cocktail or other fruits. To step up color and flavor, add scoops of lime, orange, lemon or raspberry sherbet.

FRESH MINT SYRUP

Good to keep in refrigerator to serve over melons and fresh fruits

- 1 c. sugar
- ⅔ c. water
- ½ c. chopped mint leaves
- ¼ c. lemon juice
- ½ c. orange juice

Combine sugar and water in small saucepan; boil 3 minutes. Add mint; cool. Strain.

Add juices; chill. Makes 1½ cups.

TOMATO JUICE IN PUNCH BOWL

A country hostess who likes to entertain many friends at a time often serves tomato juice in her punch bowl. "It keeps everyone in the living room out of the way while I arrange the food on the buffet," she says, adding, "I usually freeze a ring of ice for a garnish."

Here is how she fixes it a few days before her party. She uses a ring mold that fits into the punch bowl. On the bottom of it she arranges thin lemon, cucumber and radish slices, pours on ¾" cold water and puts it in the freezer. When frozen, she fills the mold about three-fourths full of water and returns it to the freezer.

To turn out the decorative ring in the punch bowl, she quickly dips the bottom of the mold in warm water. She pours on the chilled tomato juice, seasoned as the spirit moves. The gala ring floats in the red juice, festive side up.

Good Meal Send-offs

ASPARAGUS-CLAM SOUP: Combine 1 (5½ to 8 oz.) can of undrained minced clams, 1 can condensed cream of asparagus soup and 1 soup can of milk, light cream, or half-and-half milk and cream. Mix well and heat. Makes 4 servings.

CLAM CHOWDER UNIQUE

Yellow cheese floats on top

- 1 can frozen condensed clam chowder
- ½ c. grated Cheddar cheese

Prepare clam chowder according to directions on package. Ladle into bowls. Top with cheese and serve with crackers. Makes 3 servings.

TOMATO BOUILLON

Float thin lemon slices in hot or chilled bouillon for an attractive garnish

- 1 (16 to 17 oz.) can tomato juice
- 1 can condensed beef broth
- ¼ tsp. seasoned salt

Combine all the ingredients and heat. Serve piping hot with crisp crackers. Makes 6 servings.

more

Variation: Instead of heating Tomato Bouillon, chill and serve in juice glasses.

TOMATO-HAM CANAPÉ

Here's a salad that gives a meal the right start

3 medium tomatoes
⅓ c. salad dressing (French type)
1 (4 ½ oz.) can deviled ham
6 lettuce leaves
2 hard-cooked eggs
1 tblsp. chopped chives

Cut tomatoes into 2 thick slices. Marinate them in salad dressing in refrigerator several hours.

Drain. Spread tomato slice with deviled ham; place on lettuce leaf. Sprinkle top with chopped egg and chives. Makes 6 servings.

Nibblers' Delights

PIZZA SNACKS

Custard cup makes rim on biscuits for a professional touch

½ lb. Italian sausage
1 (6 oz.) can tomato paste
1 tsp. mixed Italian herbs
1 pkg. buttermilk biscuits
1 c. shredded sharp cheese
¼ c. grated Parmesan cheese

Brown sausage; drain off fat. Stir in tomato paste and herbs.

Flatten biscuits on greased baking sheet with bottom of floured custard cup. Leave rim cup makes.

Fill centers with sausage mixture. Top with shredded cheese; sprinkle with Parmesan cheese. Bake in hot oven (425°) for 10 minutes. Makes 10 pizzas.

Variations: Use sliced wieners, chopped brown-and-serve sausages or hamburger for Italian sausage.

NIPPY CHEESE DIP

Set a bowl of this out for guests who like to dunk and nibble

1 (8 oz.) pkg. cream cheese
¼ c. Basic Red Sauce (see Index)

Soften cream cheese at room temperature.

Whip cheese with electric mixer or wooden spoon. Add Red Sauce gradually, beating after each addition, until light and fluffy.

Serve with snack-style crackers, potato chips or corn chips.

JIFFY CHOCOLATE-NUT DROPS

Candy to fix in the twinkling of an eye. Keep ingredients on hand

2 (9 ¾ oz.) sweet chocolate bars
2 c. chopped walnuts

Melt chocolate over hot water. Stir in nuts. Drop by teaspoonfuls onto waxed paper. Makes 3 dozen.

Note: Chill the candy in the refrigerator when in a hurry.

CHOCOLATE-MARSHMALLOW CANDY

You melt the chocolate, stir in nuts and marshmallows—presto, it's candy

2 (9 ¾ oz.) sweet chocolate bars

3 c. miniature marshmallows
2 c. chopped walnuts

Melt chocolate over hot water. Stir in marshmallows and nuts. Drop from teaspoon on waxed paper. Makes 4 dozen.

ORANGE WALNUTS

Keep in freezer for drop-in guests

1 ½ c. sugar
½ c. orange juice
Few drops yellow food color (optional)
1 tsp. grated orange rind
½ tsp. vanilla
3 c. walnut halves

Combine sugar and orange juice in saucepan. Cook to soft-ball stage (240°) on candy thermometer. Tint a delicate orange with food color.

Remove from heat; add rind, vanilla and walnut halves. Stir until syrup begins to look cloudy. Before it hardens, drop by spoonfuls on waxed paper. Separate nuts. Makes about 1 pound.

PANCAKE ROLL-UPS

The young crowd will enjoy dunking this snack in cheese sauce

2 eggs, thoroughly beaten
⅔ c. milk
½ c. pancake mix
¼ tsp. salt
1 tsp. sugar
1 tblsp. melted shortening
3 (2 ¼ oz.) cans deviled ham
¾ c. pickle relish, drained
Pimiento-stuffed olives
Pineapple chunks

Combine eggs and milk; stir in pancake mix, salt, sugar and shortening; beat until smooth.

Lightly grease preheated (380°) 10″ electric skillet. Pour in ½ c. batter; tip to let batter run over bottom. Bake until browned and top is set; brown other side. Place in warm oven until all cakes are baked.

Spread each cake with 1 can ham and ¼ c. relish; roll like jelly roll. Insert picks each ½″ to hold edge; slice between picks. Garnish picks with olives and pineapple chunks; serve warm with piping-hot cheese sauce. Makes about 4 dozen roll-ups.

MARSHMALLOW POPCORN BALLS

Marshmallows do the work—they sweeten and hold kernels in balls

1 c. popcorn
1 tsp. salt
¼ c. butter or margarine
½ lb. marshmallows

Pop corn; sprinkle with salt.

Melt butter in skillet. Cut marshmallows in quarters. Alternate layers of popcorn and marshmallows in skillet.

Cover; heat slowly until marshmallows are partially melted. Mix well; form into balls. Makes 9 (2″) popcorn balls.

CHEESE POPCORN: To freshly popped, hot, salted popcorn add ¼ c. melted butter and ⅓ c. shredded or grated Parmesan cheese. Toss to mix.

POPCORN BALLS

Only a kettle and measuring cup to wash. Pop the corn and add syrup

½ c. light corn syrup
½ c. sugar
½ tsp. salt
½ tsp. vanilla
¼ c. salad oil
½ c. popcorn

Mix syrup, sugar, salt and vanilla.

Heat oil in large kettle (4 qt.) about 3 minutes. Add corn, cover loosely and shake over the heat until popping stops.

Pour syrup mixture over corn and stir over medium heat until corn is completely coated.

Shape corn into small balls (about 1½"). Makes 16 balls.

QUICK PRALINES

A new version of the famous New Orleans candy—so easy and so good

1 (4 oz.) pkg. butterscotch-pudding mix
1 c. sugar
½ c. brown sugar, firmly packed
½ c. evaporated milk
1 tblsp. butter
1 ½ c. pecans

Combine pudding mix, sugars and milk in a saucepan. Add butter and cook, stirring frequently, over low heat until mixture reaches the soft-ball stage (236°). Add nuts and remove from heat.

Beat just until mixture begins to thicken. Drop by spoonfuls onto waxed paper. Makes 2 dozen pralines.

POPSICLES

Keep on hand—a treat for the children

1 (3 oz.) pkg. orange-flavor gelatin
1 (⅝ oz.) pkg. grape-flavor drink powder
1 c. sugar
2 c. boiling water
1 ¾ c. cold water

Dissolve gelatin, drink powder and sugar in boiling water. Stir in cold water. Freeze in ice-cube tray. (You may insert wooden sticks or picnic spoons in mixture when partly frozen.) Makes 18 cubes.

Variation: Substitute other flavors of gelatin and drink powder for the orange and grape ones.

Hot Dips for Dunking

When friends drop in on a chilly evening, serve them hot dips. Set the dip bubbling hot on the table along with a plate of crusty bread cut in 1½" cubes. Be sure every piece of bread has some crust. You can use French, Italian or Vienna bread, or hard rolls. Provide everyone with a fork and plate.

Start the fun by spearing a piece of bread on your fork through the soft part to the crust. Dunk the bread in the dip and transfer it to your plate—then eat it. Ask everyone to join in.

Be sure to keep the dip piping hot. You can serve it in a chafing dish or a heavy casserole over a candle warmer. Make it in a double boiler. Or, still easier, make and serve the dip in an electric skillet (see recipe for Swiss-

Cheese Dip which follows). The skillet will keep it at just the right heat.

You also can serve these dips in a meal—supper or lunch. Just spoon them over toast.

SWISS-CHEESE DIP

Thick and creamy—adapted from an old-time Swiss recipe

- 1 tsp. salt
- ½ tsp. garlic salt
- 2 tblsp. flour
- 1 ½ c. milk
- 1 lb. natural Swiss cheese, coarsely grated (about 4 ⅓ c.)
- 1 tblsp. vinegar
- 2 tsp. mustard
- ½ tsp. Worcestershire sauce

Combine salt, garlic salt and flour. Add ¾ c. milk; blend well. Add remaining milk; blend. Pour into electric skillet; heat to simmering point (200°), stirring constantly.

Drop cheese by cupfuls into milk to melt; stir with fork after each addition.

Add remaining ingredients; stir well. Serve from skillet (do not reduce heat) or other cooking utensil. Makes 3 cups.

MUSHROOM-BACON SUPREME

This is a meal in itself

- 2 tblsp. butter or margarine
- 2 tblsp. flour
- 1 ½ c. milk
- ¼ tsp. salt
- ¼ tsp. pepper
- 1 tsp. lemon juice
- ½ tsp. Worcestershire sauce
- 1 c. crisp-fried bacon, crumbled finely
- ½ c. finely chopped mushrooms

Melt butter over low heat. Add flour; mix until smooth and bubbly. Remove from heat; stir in milk. Heat to boiling, stirring constantly, and let bubble one minute.

Add remaining ingredients and heat thoroughly. Makes 2 cups.

HOT DEVILED HAM

Spicy and satisfying

- 3 (4 ½ oz.) cans deviled ham
- 3 tblsp. cornstarch
- 1 tblsp. mustard
- ½ tsp. ground red pepper
- 3 tblsp. minced onion
- 3 tblsp. chopped green pepper
- ¾ c. dairy sour cream

Heat ham; drain off fat. Add cornstarch and thicken over low heat.

Add remaining ingredients, except sour cream, and heat thoroughly.

Fold in sour cream; heat just to simmering; serve hot. Makes about 2 cups.

TUNA TREAT

Also good without cheese

- 2 cans cream of chicken soup
- 3 tblsp. lemon juice
- ¾ c. coarsely grated process American cheese
- 2 (7 oz.) cans tuna, drained
- ¾ c. chopped stuffed olives

Heat soup; add lemon juice and cheese. Stir until cheese melts.

Add tuna, shredded, and olives. Heat thoroughly. Makes 4½ cups.

CHAPTER 15

BEVERAGES

Sipping beverages is an old farm custom. The coffee break started in the farm kitchen. And the habit of afternoon tea is firmly established in many homes. Children drink milk when they return hungry from school, as they always have. People of all ages drink milk for a pickup.

But other drinks also have enthusiastic following, as recipes in this chapter indicate. Hot cocoa, milk specials and festive fruit punches are typical examples. Fruit beverages often lead a dual life. They appear at parties when there are guests and, like hot coffee and iced tea, go to the field to sustain workers on sultry afternoons when they can't get away to come to the house. They're taken on motor trips for roadside enjoyment and to picnics and community meals.

You'll want to get acquainted with Steamers, our new hot-milk drinks, and our flavored milk Coolers. The recipes were developed in our Countryside Kitchens. Do try creamy Peach Milk Shakes on a hot day.

Ice cream and sherbets in beverages often serve as dessert or between-meal refreshment. Don't overlook the pretty pink Cherry Sodas to fix in your kitchen for the children and their friends. And be sure to try Hot Apple Punch, one of FARM JOURNAL's most popular recipes. It came from a Utah farm woman. Its tantalizing, spicy fragrance and fruity taste almost guarantee the success of a party. You'll also find some excellent chocolate drinks in this chapter–farm people are chocolate fans.

Remember, too, that a good meal has contrast–in flavors, texture, temperature, color and in solid and liquid foods. Read this chapter and you'll see how easy it is to fill refreshing glasses.

Cheerful Country Beverages

They promote hospitality

Milk Steamers and Coolers

Serve them hot in mugs or cups or serve them frosty cold in glasses. These good-for-you drinks are refreshing either way. The weather often decides for the cook which one will have the greatest appeal at the moment.

SPICED STEAMER

Keep some of the syrup on hand in refrigerator to speed up the making

2 qts. milk
1 c. Spiced Syrup (recipe follows)
⅛ tsp. salt
Marshmallows or whipped cream

Heat milk in double boiler, covering to prevent skin from forming. Stir hot milk into syrup. Add salt. Serve hot in mugs, topped with marshmallows. Makes 8 servings.

SPICED SYRUP: Mix in saucepan 2 c. water, ¼ c. whole cloves, ½ c. red cinnamon candies and ½ c. sugar. Simmer 15 minutes, stirring occasionally. Strain. Use 2 tblsp. for a cup of milk.

Variations

Omit Spiced Syrup, salt and marshmallows for the following:

COFFEE-COCOA: Mix 3 tblsp. instant coffee, 3 tblsp. instant cocoa and 1 tblsp. sugar. Stir into hot milk. Pour into mugs; top with whipped cream. Serve at once.

BUTTERSCOTCH: Add ¼ c. butter and ½ c. dark brown sugar to hot milk. Blend; serve at once, sprinkled with cinnamon.

Note: You may use dry milk in steamers. Either reconstitute it and heat or slowly stir dry milk into hot water. If you prefer a sweeter drink, use whole milk with extra dry milk added.

CHOCOLATE-BANANA MILK

Children and grownups alike enjoy this substantial luncheon or supper drink

3 c. milk
3 medium, ripe bananas
½ c. instant chocolate mix

Blend half of ingredients in blender 1 minute. Pour into pitcher. Blend second half of ingredients 1 minute. Add to pitcher. Makes 4 servings.

Note: For a South-of-the-Border touch, add ½ tsp. cinnamon to chocolate mix.

HONEY-PEANUT FOAM

Add coffee for a grownup's treat

1 tblsp. honey
2 tblsp. peanut butter
1 c. milk
2 tblsp. dry milk

Combine ingredients and whip in drink mixer or blender until well blended and foamy. Pour over frozen milk cubes. Makes 1 big (10 oz.) glass.

Variation: Blend ¼ c. honey and ½ c. peanut butter in your electric mixer. Slowly add 1 qt. milk, continuing to beat; scrape mixer bowl often. Add ½ c. dry milk and (for adults) 1 tsp. instant coffee; whip until foamy. Pour over frozen milk cubes. Makes 4 (10 oz.) glasses.

FROZEN MILK CUBES: Pour reconstituted dry milk into ice-cube tray and freeze.

LEMON COOLER

Smooth, thick, tangy

1 qt. milk
1 ½ c. fresh lemon juice
¾ c. sugar
½ c. dry milk
Dash of salt
½ pt. vanilla ice cream

Combine ingredients. Whip until ice cream is well blended. Serve immediately. Makes 8 (8 oz.) glasses.

LOW-CALORIE PICKUP

If there's mint in your garden, use sprigs of it as a garnish

¾ c. frozen pineapple-juice concentrate
1 qt. reconstituted dry milk, chilled
Green food color
Frozen milk cubes (see recipe above)

Combine pineapple concentrate and milk; whip until foamy.

Add food color for a minty green tint.

Pour mixture over frozen milk cubes. Serve at once. Makes 6 (8 oz.) glasses.

Variation: If you prefer, use half whole milk and half reconstituted dry milk.

PEPPERMINT FLUFF

Perfect summer twosome: pretty pink drink and chocolate cookies

3 c. milk
¾ c. crushed peppermint candy
¼ c. cold water
1 ½ tsp. lemon juice
½ tsp. vanilla
¼ c. dry milk
1 tblsp. sugar

Scald milk in double boiler. Add candy and stir until dissolved. Chill.

Combine water, lemon juice, vanilla and dry milk in deep bowl. Beat with electric beater about 6 minutes or until stiff. Gradually add sugar. Beat 1 minute or until blended. Chill.

When ready to serve, whip peppermint mixture until foamy. Fold in half of whipped dry-milk mixture. Pour into glasses.

Use remaining whipped dry milk to top each drink, about ¼ c. per glass. Sprinkle with bits of crushed peppermint candy. Makes 4 (10 oz.) glasses.

ORANGE EGGNOG

Pretty enough for the punch bowl at a hot-weather party

3 c. water
1 ½ c. dry milk
6 eggs, separated
½ c. sugar
1 tsp. vanilla
1 pt. orange sherbet
Red and yellow food colors (optional)
Nutmeg

Mix water and dry milk. Chill thoroughly.

Beat egg whites until stiff; gradually add ¼ c. sugar, continuing to beat.

Beat egg yolks until very light; add remaining sugar and vanilla. Fold in egg whites.

When well blended, gradually pour into milk mixture, folding as you pour.

Add sherbet and whip until foamy. If desired, add red and yellow food colors to tint a deeper orange. Pour into punch bowl or glasses. Sprinkle with nutmeg. Makes 2½ quarts.

Variation: To make eggnog in electric drink mixer, blender or mixer, combine and blend ¾ c. water and ⅓ c. dry milk. Add 1 egg, ⅛ tsp. vanilla and ½ c. orange sherbet; whip until foamy. Pour into glass. Sprinkle lightly with nutmeg. Makes 2 (8 oz.) glasses.

STRAWBERRY FROST

Tempting and rewarding

1 qt. milk
3 tblsp. strawberry instant soft-drink mix
½ c. strawberry ice cream

Combine ingredients; beat until foamy. Makes 4 (10 oz.) glasses.

Variations: Substitute 3 tblsp. strawberry-flavor rennet dessert powder for soft-drink mix. If you do not have ice cream, fold ½ c. whipped dry milk into drink just before serving.

Ever-welcome Fruit Drinks

HOT APPLE PUNCH

A famous FARM JOURNAL *recipe*

2¼ c. sugar
1 qt. water
2 (2½") sticks cinnamon
8 whole allspice berries
10 whole cloves
1 whole piece ginger root (about size of quarter)
1 qt. orange juice (fresh, canned or reconstituted frozen)
1 pt. lemon juice or a 16 oz. bottle
2 qts. apple cider or juice

Combine sugar and water and boil 5 minutes. Remove from heat; add spices. Let syrup stand, covered, 1 hour. Strain.

Just before serving, combine syrup, fruit juices and cider; bring quickly to a boil. Remove from heat; serve at once. Makes 4½ quarts.

3-CITRUS FRUIT DRINK

Just the punch to sip on hot days

1 (6 oz.) can frozen orange-juice concentrate
1 (6 oz.) can frozen lemonade concentrate
1 qt. cold water
2 (7 oz.) bottles carbonated water
1 pt. lime sherbet

Blend together orange and lemonade concentrates and 1 qt. water. Pour over ice cubes in pitcher. Carefully pour in carbonated water; stir gently. When ice thoroughly chills mixture, fill glasses ¾ full. Top with spoonfuls of lime sherbet. Makes 6 servings.

Note: You may substitute 2 c. plain cold water for carbonated water.

EASY SPARKLING PUNCH

For a party, serve with frosted and coconut-sprinkled cupcakes

1 (6 oz.) can frozen orange-juice concentrate
¼ c. lemon juice, fresh, frozen or canned
¼ c. corn syrup
1 qt. ginger ale

Prepare orange juice as directed on can. Stir in lemon juice and syrup. Slowly pour in ginger ale. Serve in ice-filled glasses. Makes about 2 qts.

JIFFY FRUIT PUNCH

Open cans and bottles to make this

1 (6 oz.) can frozen orange juice
2 (6 oz.) cans frozen limeade
1 (6 oz.) can frozen lemonade
1 (46 oz.) can pineapple juice
1 pt. cranberry-juice cocktail
2 to 4 c. cold water
2 qts. ginger ale, chilled
1 qt. plain soda water, chilled
Strawberry Ice Cubes (see Index)
Mint for garnish

Empty frozen juices, pineapple and cranberry juice and water into large container or bowl. Thaw; stir well.

Pour mixture into punch bowl. Add Strawberry Ice Cubes. Just before serving, gently pour in ginger ale and soda water. Top with sprigs of mint. Makes 30 servings.

HOLIDAY FRUIT PUNCH

A Merry Christmas drink, but also good at other seasons

1 (6 oz.) pkg. or 2 (3 oz.) pkgs. lime-flavor gelatin
1¼ c. sugar
3½ c. boiling water
2 (5¾ oz.) cans frozen lemon-juice concentrate, thawed
1 (46 oz.) can pineapple juice
6 c. cold water

Dissolve gelatin and sugar in boiling water. Stir in lemon juice, then pineapple juice and cold water.

Pour over ice cubes in punch bowl. Serve in punch cups. Makes about 4½ quarts.

LEMON ICED TEA

Tea bags do the straining

12 tea bags
1 qt. boiling water
2 qts. cold water
1 (6 oz.) can frozen lemonade concentrate

Steep tea in boiling water 5 minutes. Remove tea bags. Stir in remaining water and lemonade concentrate. Serve in ice-filled glasses. Makes 12 servings.

LIME COOLER

Tart and refreshing with a cool look

1 (6 oz.) can frozen lemonade concentrate
½ c. lime juice
1 (7 oz.) bottle ginger ale
Few drops green food color

Prepare lemonade as directed on can. Add lime juice, ginger ale and food color.

Serve over ice in glasses. Garnish with thin lime slices. Makes 6 servings.

MULLED APRICOT NECTAR

Heat this spicy treat after guests arrive —they'll enjoy its aroma and taste

- 1 (46 oz.) can apricot nectar
- ½ lemon, sliced
- 2 (2½") sticks cinnamon
- 15 whole cloves
- 8 whole allspice berries

Combine all ingredients in heavy saucepan and bring to boiling point. Simmer gently 5 minutes.

Remove from heat; cover; allow to stand 30 minutes.

Strain. If you wish, sweeten to taste with honey or sugar. Heat before serving. Makes about 5 cups.

Good idea: Pass a plate of fudge.

RASPBERRY FLOAT

Frozen citrus juices speed the cooling of this sparkling punch

- 3 (3 oz.) pkgs. raspberry-flavor gelatin
- 4 c. boiling water
- 1½ c. sugar
- 4 c. cold water
- ½ c. lime juice
- 2¼ c. orange juice
- 1¼ c. lemon juice
- 1 qt. ginger ale
- 2 (10 oz.) pkgs. frozen raspberries
- Raspberry Ice Cubes (see Index)

Dissolve gelatin in boiling water; add sugar, cold water and juices; cool, but do not chill or gelatin will congeal. (If you let it congeal, heat just enough to bring back to liquid state.)

When time to serve, pour punch into punch bowl. Add ginger ale and frozen raspberries. Stir until raspberries break apart and are partially thawed. Add ice cubes. Makes about 4 quarts.

SPICED TOMATO JUICE

Make ahead if more convenient—then reheat at serving time

- 1 (46 oz.) can tomato juice
- 6 tblsp. brown sugar
- 6 whole cloves
- 2 (2½") sticks cinnamon
- ½ lemon, sliced

Combine all ingredients in saucepan. Bring to a boil; simmer 5 minutes. Strain; serve hot. Makes 5½ cups.

Tips from a Smart Country Cook:

Summer Orange Lemonade: For the picnic or motor trip, slightly thaw 1 (6 oz.) can frozen concentrate for lemonade and 1 (6 oz.) can frozen concentrate for orange juice. Pour into a 2 qt. jar, fill with ice cubes and add all the cold water jar will hold. Seal. Set jar in two paper bags, one inside the other, for insulation. You can carry this refreshing drink in your car for 4 to 6 hours. It still will be cold.

Winter Orange Lemonade: Fill the jar as directed, seal, and let stand unrefrigerated until ready to serve.

Variations: Substitute frozen grape-juice concentrate for the orange juice. Or substitute frozen concentrate for strawberry, raspberry or pineapple lemonade or canned frozen concentrate for limeade for the lemonade.

STRAWBERRY ICE CUBES: Prepare 1 (6 oz.) can frozen strawberry-lemon-punch concentrate as directed on label. Pour into ice-cube tray and freeze. Fill glasses with ice cubes. Add bottled lemon-lime carbonated beverage.

Variation: Substitute frozen raspberry-lemon-punch concentrate for strawberry-lemon-punch concentrate.

Children's Specials

COCOA FLOAT: Make 4 c. hot cocoa with instant cocoa mix as directed on label. Serve in cups, topping each with a scoop of vanilla ice cream. Dust with cinnamon if desired. Serve at once. Very refreshing on a cold day. Makes 8 to 10 servings.

GINGER-ORANGE FLOAT: Put a scoop of orange sherbet in each glass and fill with chilled ginger ale.

CHILDREN'S ROOT BEER: Pour ¾ c. chilled, liquefied dry milk in each tall glass. Stir in ¼ c. chilled root beer. Add a big spoonful of vanilla ice cream to each glass.

PEACH MILK SHAKES

It's both dessert and drink

1 c. diced fresh peaches
¼ c. honey
½ tsp. vanilla
1 ½ c. milk
1 pt. vanilla ice cream

Mix peaches and honey. (Honey keeps peaches from darkening as well as sweetening them.) Add remaining ingredients and mix in blender to a smooth cream. Serve in tall glasses. Makes 4 servings.

Variation: Substitute ice cream of other flavors for the vanilla ice cream. Try coffee ice cream.

Note: Never keep honey in refrigerator; cold temperatures encourage it to crystallize. When crystallized, set the container of it in warm water to liquefy it. Honey must be at room temperature to blend with milk.

CHERRY SODAS

Just right for the Fourth of July—welcome on any warm day

1 (⅝ oz.) pkg. cherry-flavor drink powder
1 c. sugar
2 c. milk
1 qt. carbonated water
Vanilla ice cream (about 1 ½ pts.)

Blend together drink powder, sugar and milk. Slowly pour in carbonated water.

Put generous scoop of ice cream in each glass. Pour cherry-beverage mixture over ice cream. Makes 6 servings.

Country Coffee Specials

COFFEE-BUTTERSCOTCH FOAM

A drink that's also dessert

4 tsp. instant coffee
½ c. boiling water
1 ½ c. cold water
¼ c. butterscotch topping
½ pt. (1 c.) vanilla ice cream

Dissolve coffee in hot water; add cold water. Combine with remaining ingredients in blender or large bowl of electric mixer. Blend or beat until frothy. Pour into tall glasses. Sprinkle with cinnamon if desired. Makes 3 servings.

COFFEE, SWEDISH STYLE: Bring 2 qts. water to boil. Combine 1 c. regular grind coffee with ¼ c. cold water and 1 egg, beaten. Pour boiling water over coffee mixture; cover and let stand 12 to 15 minutes in warm spot on grill, but do not let boil. Makes 8 servings.

CHAPTER 16

MENUS FOR SHORT-CUT MEALS

Every woman's mental conversation includes this question at one time or another: "What'll I get for dinner?" This chapter has 40 answers for you. We asked homemakers, members of FARM JOURNAL's Family Test Group, how they plan meals. Their blueprint helped us decide on the sequence of chapters in this cookbook and plan the menus that follow. Use this system and you can plan hundreds of other quick and easy meals from the recipes in this cookbook.

These experienced cooks select meat or the main dish first–unanimously. Next they choose the vegetables. Then the salad. And now the dessert. Bread comes in for consideration at this stage, although sometimes, in short-cut meals, sandwiches are the main dish, in which case the bread choice comes earlier.

The majority of homemakers think of relishes next. They may be accessories, but country cooks rely on them to glamorize meals with their bright colors and piquant flavors. Appetizers are next in line; in many farm homes they appear only on special occasions. Soups are more likely to be valued as hearty main dishes, and fruit cocktails for dessert.

Beverages are planned last, and "rightly so," one farm woman says, "because they are so easy. At our house we have coffee, tea, milk or milk drinks at mealtime, fruit beverages at parties and between meals." Instant makings for beverages are appearing in many farm kitchens.

Successful short-cut cooks use menus as the foundation on which to build the meal–it's the combination of foods that really counts.

Forty menus for 30-minute and 60-minute meals follow. All of them feature short-cut recipes in this cookbook. Let them start you planning many other speedy menus with the recipes in this collection.

Meals That Bring Compliments

No one will guess they're so quick

Meals You Can Get in 30 Minutes

Some women work faster than others. The menus in this chapter are for meals which cooks of average speed can get in 30 minutes, and in 60 minutes. They are mostly dinner menus, although you'll note suggestions that some also make good suppers.

If you want more substantial dinners, add a quick vegetable (see Chapter 6). And you can supplement many of the desserts with cookies or ice cream. Or maybe you'd like to pass candy or sugared nuts after dessert (see Chapter 14). You may also add to our dinner menus by starting off with canned or frozen soup with crackers—such first courses take only a few minutes to heat.

Keep your eye on the clock, or your ear tuned to the timer, when you try these menus to find out whether you are faster or slower than the average busy cook. And don't let these 40 menus stop you from putting hundreds of other short-cut dishes in this cookbook together in quick and easy meals.

Timesaver: Dishes for which recipes are in this book are followed by the page numbers.

Supper Ham and Eggs (24)
Herb Potato Chips (87)
Hot Biscuits
Fruit-Salad Wheel (100)
Rocky-Road Chocolate Pudding (156)

Make the pudding first. When you take the biscuits from the oven, reduce heat and put the potatoes in to heat. They will be ready by the time you get the other food on the table. If you do not have hard-cooked eggs in the refrigerator for the main dish, substitute Tuna-Egg Scramble. (59) Add cookies from the freezer, or a package, for a more substantial meal.

Fish Poached in Shrimp Soup (48)
Buttered Peas Rice
Country-Style Cucumber Salad (103)
Parmesan Rolls (177)
Minted Grapefruit (146)
Cookies

Use precooked rice. Spoon the liquid in which the fish cooked over it. You also can use this menu for supper or lunch. A Friday favorite!

Baked Deviled-Cheese Sandwiches (68)
New Orleans Succotash (91)
Lettuce Slaw (105)
Pear Shortcakes (146)

Fix the succotash first, then the sandwiches. Shred lettuce before baking sandwiches. Make shortcakes just before serving, using canned chocolate sauce. If the men are meat-and-potato fans, serve this for supper instead of dinner. Or add Herb Potato Chips (87) to make meal more substantial for them.

California Minute Steaks (14)
Italian Green Beans with
Sour Cream (79)
Carrot Sticks
French Bread
Nut-crested Cake (126)

Put the cake in the oven to bake. It will be ready by the time the main course is eaten.

Grilled Turkey Sandwiches (73)
Jellied Cranberry Sauce
Sliced Tomatoes Pickles
Cinnamon-Peach Cobbler (158)
Cream

Put the cobbler in the oven. Use cooked turkey from the freezer or canned boned turkey.

Tuna-Potato Pie (52)
Pimiento Green Beans (78)
Grapefruit-Beet Salad (105)
Banana Sundae (150)

Assemble and put Tuna-Potato Pie in oven. Cook the frozen beans.

Corn Chowder (96)
Waffled French Toast (178)
Lettuce with Blue-Cheese
Dressing (108)
Peach Melba (194)

Make the chowder. Then fix the salad. Make the French toast at the table. A good supper choice.

Italian Hamburgers (67)
Cheese French Fries (88)
Tomato Salad
Sour-Cream Dressing (110)
Pineapple Sherbet

Serve cookies with the dessert for a crisp texture and to make meal more substantial.

Speedy Pancake Roll-ups (28)
Buttered Applesauce (28)
Jiffy Ambrosia (144)
Cocoa Float (214)

Add celery and radishes for texture contrast in this menu.

Homemade Chili con Carne (18)
Pineapple-Cucumber Salad (102)
Corn Chips
Royal-Purple Sundae (151)

If you think making the chili will hurry you too much, use Chili with Hominy. (18)

Farmhouse Oyster Stew (50)
Assorted Crackers
Lettuce with Cream Dressing (108)
Quick Apple Pie (133)

First get the pie in the oven to bake. It will be ready by the time the main course is eaten. Top it with vanilla ice cream from freezer. You may like this menu for supper.

Supreme of Liver (15)
Cream Gravy (15)
Lima Beans with Celery (84)
Tomato-Salad Platter (106)
French Bread
Honeyed Applesauce (144)

Prepare the food in this order: lima beans, tomatoes, liver and gravy, Honeyed Applesauce. Cookies will complement the dessert.

Barbecued Steak Sandwiches (70)
Elegant Green Beans (78)
Celery
Cherry-Peach Dumplings (153)

Bake the dumplings at the table if you have an electric skillet.

Curried Frankfurters (32)
Short-cut Zucchini (93)
Fruit-Salad Wheel (100)
Toasted Rolls
Topsy-Turvy Cake (125)

Put the cake in the oven first. It will be ready by the time the main course is eaten.

Double-Quick Bean Bake (82)
Cabbage Salad Bowl (103)
Rye Bread
Upside-down Chocolate Cake à la Mode (115)

Give the cake first attention. It will be ready before the main course is eaten. For a quicker dessert, if you have an unfrosted chocolate-cake layer in freezer, spread top with cream cheese and spoon on canned cherry-pie filling. Wonderful flavor blend!

Macaroni and Cheese (62)
Beets in Cream (77)
Toasted Rolls
Carrot Sticks or Celery
Broiled Apples (160)

Serve crisp cookies or small pieces of cake with the dessert for a more substantial meal. Try this menu for luncheon. . . . For dinner, you can use a heartier dessert like Cherry-Pudding Dessert (153), made in advance.

Company-Broiled Ham (24)
Hasty Creamed Carrots (81)
Buttery Hot Bread (177) Jelly
Carolina Autumn Salad (103)
Frosted Pineapple (146)

If you prefer a vegetable salad, use tossed greens.

Spoonburgers (67)
Buttered Broccoli
Sliced Tomatoes
Ginger-Apple Fluff (144)

Another good dessert to serve with this meal is Lemon-Pear Velvet. (145)

Tomato Soup
Skillet Tuna Sandwiches (72)
Celery
Jellied Strawberries (150)
Cookies

Make the Jellied Strawberries first, then the sandwiches. Use packaged cookies if you do not have a supply in the freezer.

Chicken Newburg on Toast (44)
Tangy Green Beans (78)
Peach Salad with
Pink-Cloud Dressing (110)
Honey-Nut Sundae (160)

Use cooked chicken from the freezer, or canned chicken.

Meals You Can Get in 60 Minutes

Italicized dishes are those you prepare or partly prepare in advance. (In some cases you may have purchased the rolls or other prepared food.)

Beef-Cheese Casserole (12)
Pronto Saucy Cauliflower (80)
Fiesta Vegetable Salad (106)
Hot Rolls
Raspberry Crunch (154)

Use rolls from your freezer or bakery. Heat them in the oven at the last minute. Fix the casserole first, then the Raspberry Crunch. They bake together.

Lamb Balls in *Red Sauce* (29 and 198)
Squash-Pineapple Casserole (94)
Mixed Vegetable Salad (106)
Brownie Pie (137)

Make the pie first, then the squash casserole. Bake them at the same time. Use Basic Red Sauce in fixing and seasoning the lamb.

Pork Chops with Apple Jelly (25)
Cinnamon-Candied Sweet
Potatoes (95)
Lettuce Slaw (105)
Orange-Banana Tapioca (157)
Cookies

Make the pudding, then get the pork chops on to cook; the sweet potatoes are next in line for attention.

Veal Patties (31)
Southwestern Green Beans (79)
Tossed Salad
Butterflake Rolls
North Pole Cherry Pie (135)

The rolls are from the refrigerator. If you want to fix Cheese Rolls, (171) you will have plenty of time.

Pan-broiled Steak (22)
Hash-brown Onion Potatoes (89)
Tomato Salad
Corn-Kernel Biscuits (170)
Angel Food à la Mode (112)

Peel and cube potatoes first; put them on to cook. Make the biscuits and bake them while you pan-broil the steak. Get the angel food cake ready to broil, but toast it just before serving.

Oven-fried Fish (49)
French-fried Potatoes (frozen)
Sunshine Fruit Salad (100)
Dill Biscuits (172)
Chocolate-Bar Pie (138)

Set the table first. Put the salad on the table. This meal moves fast. While the fish cooks, get the biscuits ready to put in the oven when the fish comes out. Serve the meal, passing the hot biscuits last.

Meat Balls in Buttermilk Sauce (13)
Red and Green Rice (94)
Swedish Cabbage (80)
Tomato Herb Salad (105)
Pineapple Supreme (147)

Make the meat balls and gravy first and put them in the oven while you fix the other dishes. Add cookies to the menu if you like.

Ham-Asparagus Casserole (24)
Buttered Mexicorn
Raspberry-Applesauce Mold (99)
Raisin Griddle Cookies (167)

Either bake the cookies in an electric skillet at the table or just before you sit down to dinner. Keep them in a very low oven if you want to bake them before serving the meal. You then can serve them hot.

Chicken Crunch (41)
Asparagus with Herbs (76)
Pineapple-Cheese Mold (102)
Fruited Fantan Rolls (172)
Lemon Sherbet
Crunchy Chocolate-Chip Cookies (164)

Put the chicken casserole, previously assembled, in the oven to bake. Fill the refrigerator rolls so they will be ready to bake when the casserole comes from the oven. The sherbet is from the freezer. Have the cookies ready to bake while the main course is eaten. Or if you prefer, make them in advance.

Baked Lemon Steak (14)
Speedy Stuffed Potatoes (95)
California Broccoli (80)
Tomato Salad
Peach Islands (148)

Put the steak in the oven; make the Peach Islands, then put the potatoes in their foil shells ready to heat at the last minute.

Hearty Italian Spaghetti (20)
New-way French Bread with Garlic Butter (177)
Tossed Salad (106)
Broiled Peaches (147)

Bread takes the most time to bake. So start with it. The spaghetti is double quick. You'll have no trouble getting this dinner on the table in an hour.

Tomato Juice
Frankfurter-Egg Sandwiches (67)
Potato-Cheese Balls (87)
Overnight Bean Salad (102)
Apricot Pie (133)

When the pie is in the oven, get the Potato Cheese Balls ready for the oven. Bake pie, then the potatoes.

Party Crab Bake (50)
Buttered Peas
Celery Olives
Crusty Rolls
Danish Raspberry Pie (140)

This is an easy meal to get. Try it for a women's luncheon or supper. Use rolls from bakery or freezer.

Company Pork Chops (26)
New Orleans Succotash (91)
Hot Onion Bread (175)
Garden Lettuce with
Cream Dressing (108)
Frozen Pumpkin Pie (136)

Start the pork chops first; then the onion bread. The rest is easy.

Succotash Chowder (96)
Cheese Rye Loaf (68)
Pear Salad with
Fruit-Juice Dressing (109)
Mocha Dream Cake (124)

Fix the Cheese Rye Loaf first. Bake it while you heat the chowder.

Hot Potato Salad in
Bologna Cups (107 and 35)
Broccoli with Brown Butter-
Crumb Sauce (80 and 196)
Hard Rolls
Open-faced Peach Pie (134)

Such a speedy menu that you have ample time to bake the pie within the hour if you like it warm. This is a good supper menu, but it answers for dinner, especially if you start off with chilled tomato juice.

Barbecued Turkey (45)
Buttered Peas
Hot Rolls
Frozen Cranberry Salad (98)
Black-Walnut Chocolate Pie (136)

The turkey slices are cooked, from the freezer. This is a quick menu, so you can move with leisure during the hour, especially if you have a baked pie shell on hand.

Hasty-Tasty Rarebit (62)
Green Beans with Almond Butter (77)
Olives Pickles Radishes
Ice Cream with *Blueberry Sauce* (192)

A good supper menu. Some cooks can get this meal in 30 minutes. If your men must have potatoes, try Oven-fried Potato Slices. (88)

Tuna-Cornbread Casserole (52)
Creamy Cabbage (80)
Lettuce-Cucumber Salad
Apple-Orange Dessert (144)

Get the casserole in the oven. The rest is quick. If you have ready-to-bake cookies in the freezer, you will have time to bake enough for dessert. Or try Speedy Scotch Shortbread. (167)

Potato-Sausage Skillet (27)
Hasty Creamed Carrots (81)
Cheese Rolls (171)
Spicy Applesauce Mold (99)
Oven-baked Scones (166)

Once the Potato Sausage is in the skillet over heat, there will be plenty of time. If tomatoes are in season, slice them for a nice addition.

CHAPTER 17

FOOD TO MEET THE OCCASION

What farm woman hasn't answered the telephone to hear: Will you bring potatoes to the church supper next Wednesday? . . . Will you folks be home this evening, we'd like to come over? . . . Will you take the chairmanship of the food committee for the Home Demonstration Club Achievement dinner? Once you've said yes, your thoughts turn to food.

What kind of potatoes shall I take? . . . What can I fix this busy day for refreshments tonight? . . . What new and interesting dishes can I suggest to the food committee?

To help women, pinched for time, make these and other food decisions fast, we add this final chapter to the cookbook. We've given you a start by pointing out some of the special-occasion dishes in this cookbook. You'll find many others.

Next to superior flavor, the most outstanding virtue of the special-occasion foods listed in this chapter is how easily and speedily you can fix them. And many of them, especially the salads and desserts, are showy enough to attract admiring eyes. But we include others for different reasons: Italian beans are new enough in many areas to make people wonder what the broad green beans are; the potato dishes depart just enough from the traditional to awaken curiosity. Almost every dish we mention has a surprise.

Don't be afraid to depart from the usual–say, with ice cream. Let everyone have a choice of sauces for it, or of ice creams to fill cones. Pour deep-purple frozen grape juice, partly thawed, over vanilla ice cream. And for snacks, how about hot dips and crusty bread to dunk in them?

Do use the Index to find the recipes in a jiffy. That's the first and best way to save time!

Melting marshmallows float atop Spiced Steamer, a hot milk drink sweetened with Spiced Syrup (recipe page 209). Keep a supply of this syrup in your refrigerator for speedy use. See Chapter 15 for other Milk Steamers.

Milk-made coolers, pale green Low-Calorie Pickup, Honey-Peanut Foam and pink Peppermint Fluff, tempt lagging summer appetites (recipes pages 209, 210). Frozen milk cubes add frosty note without diluting drink.

Country Hospitality Flourishes

Friendliness and good food foster it

We asked a group of busy farm women, "What are the most important social occasions for which you prepare and serve food?" Their answers selected the "Big Five" for us to present in this chapter:

1. Covered-dish meals
2. Company home meals
3. The coffee break or party
4. Evening refreshments for friends in for a visit
5. Women's group luncheons

So many busy cooks mentioned two other less frequent, but all-important, social affairs, however, that we give a menu for a wedding reception and a winter-evening reception for a large group of people.

WEDDING RECEPTION

Informal Wedding Cake
Jiffy Fruit Punch

Our mix-made three-tier wedding cake is gorgeous. Marshmallows made the simple but gala decoration (see picture). And we have recipes for several punches in Chapter 15 which you can use with great success. We suggest Jiffy Fruit Punch, made with frozen and canned juices, chilled by pretty pink Strawberry Ice Cubes or Raspberry Float. This has an inexpensive raspberry-flavor gelatin base and uses frozen raspberries for garnish.

WINTER-EVENING RECEPTION

Hot Apple Punch
Coconut-Nutmeg Cookies
Mexican Chocolate Crinkles

Hot Apple Punch, served in a punch bowl, is a wonderful selection. Just watch the appreciative sniffs when people notice the aroma of the steaming, spicy fruit juice. We mention a couple of cookies from the chapter filled with cookie recipes, but you can select others if you like.

Women short on time will want to bake the cookies in advance and freeze them, fix the drink and then reheat it just before serving.

What to Take to Covered-dish Meals

Dishes that travel successfully

Covered-dish suppers are here to stay —for the way they multiply time, if for no other reason. All the families that gather round the table have a finger in fixing the food and in contributing it. Farm people always have felt that meals brought from home kitchens taste better and cost less than those that many commercial establishments serve. A real compliment to country cooks!

MAIN DISHES TO TOTE

Most busy women search continuously for out-of-the-ordinary main dishes to tote—something guaranteed to bring compliments after people help themselves and taste. There are dozens of recipes for this kind of dish in this cookbook, but we are suggesting a baker's dozen for a sampler.

SPECIALS FOR THE BEEF EATERS

If beef is your choice, here are five excellent recipes to use. The first three bake, travel and come to the table in casseroles. You can assemble the ingredients in advance and refrigerate until time to cook just before leaving for the social gathering, so your dish can be hot. The meat loaf bakes in foil. Leave the silver jacket on, as an insulator, until you are ready to serve it.

Beef-Cheese Casserole
Green Bean-Burger Bake
Lasagne Casserole
No-mix Meat Loaf
Baked Lemon Steak

HOT HAM AND PORK PARTY TREATS

Ham and pork potluck dishes have an enthusiastic following. We are suggesting a quartet of them. The Easy-to-Serve Ham has been a first choice in many neighborhoods ever since the recipe appeared a few years ago in FARM JOURNAL. We have had many letters of praise about it. None of these meats requires carving. That means they are easy to serve.

Easy-to-Serve Ham
Potluck Ham Casserole
Barbecued Pork Chops
Pork Chops with Apple Jelly

CHICKEN FROM COUNTRY KITCHENS

Chicken, of course, is a standby at community gatherings. We've sorted out some of the unusual poultry dishes in this cookbook. But certainly some of the oven-fried chicken recipes deserve consideration—especially those perked up by pour-on barbecue and other sauces. Cooked turkey may be used in the casseroles instead of chicken. And, by the way, our Chicken Casserole Supreme contains noodles and asparagus as well as chicken.

Chicken Casserole Supreme
Chicken-Corn Casserole
Chicken Crunch

GIVE SEA FOOD A TRYOUT

Why not change the pace at a group meal with a sea-food dish? Our selections: a crab casserole for luncheon, oyster stew for supper.

Party Crab Bake
Farmhouse Oyster Stew

Many country communities are rediscovering the charms of an old-fashioned oyster supper. It fits cold, snowy winter evenings so well. It's a good idea to carry the stew, all but the oysters, in a vacuum jug. Add the oysters at the place where supper is served and heat in portable electric ovens. Buffet style of service is best. Let one person fill the bowls, and just to be sure everyone gets his quota of oysters, let a second person ladle them into the bowls from another roaster. All you need to complete the feast is crackers, celery, pickles and a dessert toted from home kitchens.

VEGETABLES TO TOTE

Potatoes come first. "Don't serve covered-dish supper without potatoes," one country cook warned the committee planning the menu. "All the men in our neighborhood think the vegetable kingdom is three-fourths potatoes." That's just another way of saying farmers are meat-and-potato men. We have sorted out, from the many potato recipes in this cookbook, five classics:

Baked Creamed Potatoes
Two-step Potatoes
Potato-Clam Scallop
New Potatoes in Casserole
Speedy Stuffed Potatoes

Unless you can run the Speedy Stuffed Potatoes in an oven a few minutes before serving them, you'd better save them for home meals. You can pass the dairy sour cream instead of plopping it on the spuds, to cut down on time. Or, better still, pass, on a tray, bowls of sour cream with chives (you can buy it ready-to-go), with crumbled crisp bacon, grated cheese and butter or margarine, melted—if you have facilities for melting it. All people do not like the same potato dress-ups. Give everyone his choice.

OTHER VEGETABLES

Here are a few dishes featuring vegetables which you will be proud to take to a covered-dish supper. Also proud to pass to admiring friends:

Mixed Vegetables Mornay
Cinnamon-Candied Sweets
Squash-Pineapple Casserole
New Orleans Succotash
Italian Green Beans
Curried Onions

AN INNING FOR BAKED BEANS

Baked beans are a common must for covered-dish suppers. "They're wonderful 'filler-uppers' for hungry boys and they always make a hit," one mother of four sons vows. Church suppers are her specialty. We have four bean dishes you'll be interested in, but you'll find several others in this book. The limas start frozen; the other beans come from cans. The limas have a smoky "outdoors" flavor. Serve the beans in a homey bean pot—it gives them appetite appeal. And it's easy to heat and carry them right in the pot.

Baked Beans with Pineapple
Boston Baked Beans
Baked Kidney Beans
Baked Lima Beans

TAKE-ALONG SALADS

Most salads for covered-dish suppers are molded. There are at least two good reasons why: their bright color and sparkling beauty; and they're easy to carry. But there are other kinds of "covered-dish" salads that make a nice change. Our Chili Mac teams perfectly with fried chicken; Overnight Bean Salad pleases the men and boys, especially. And you can't go wrong on a well-made green salad. Here are some good salads to help you get ready for the next covered-dish supper:

Overnight Bean Salad
Country Salad Bowl
Country-style Cucumber Salad
Tomato Salad Platter
Tossed Salad in a Hurry

FRUIT SALADS TWO WAYS

Mandarin-Orange Salad and Overnight Fruit Salad are refrigerator-made and delightful spooned on crisp lettuce. The following salads are molded:

Apricot Salad
Sunshine Fruit Salad
Raspberry-Apple Salad
Spring-Fling Salad
Cranberry-Relish Salad
Pineapple-Cheese Salad

DESSERTS TO TOTE

Let's face it: it's the dessert at the covered-dish supper that most people, even the calorie watchers, praise the most. Not surprising—those made in country kitchens are so luscious.

CONSIDER CAKE

Many of the cakes in this cookbook would add an accent to any covered-dish meal. It's hard to make a choice. But do consider the four lard cakes made by the meringue method, not only because they are tender and tasty, but because every farm woman who tastes them will want your recipe. They'll make conversation in any place where farm people gather. We think they're the best lard cakes we ever tasted. Do use the frostings and toppings specified in the recipes.

Chocolate Lard Cake
Yellow Lard Cake
Orange Lard Cake
Feather Spice Lard Cake

There are other marvelous cakes in this cookbook—on the unusual side with distinctive, rewarding flavor blends:

Apple Spice Cake
Cherry Crown Cake
Surprise Angel Food
Chocolate Mound Cake
Nut-crested Cake
Crumb Cake
Ambrosia Cake Dessert

PIES PLEASE EVERYONE

Pies are easy to carry and to serve: they make a hit with the men. This cookbook has recipes for so many good ones that we are hard put to select the best. But possibly you should omit the frozen ones unless you can keep them in a freezer or refrigerator while the first part of the supper is served. But do consider the following (if you choose Quick Apple Pie, you'll want to take along whipped cream to top it—or ice cream):

Open-faced Peach Pie
Apricot Pie
Quick Apple Pie
Easy Pecan Pie
Hawaiian Pineapple Pie
Black-Walnut Chocolate Pie
Chocolate-Bar Pie
Frozen Mincemeat Pie
Frozen Pumpkin Pie
Peachy or Strawberry Ice-Cream Pie
Danish Raspberry Pie

RELISHES TO TOTE

Maybe it's because country women bring their Sunday-best food to covered-dish suppers—anyway, even though our menus are better planned with fewer dishes, something about the meals suggests the feasts our grandmothers used to load on tables for company dinners. Maybe relishes are the link—old-fashioned cooks opened cans and jars generously. Today's short-cut farm cooks, even though they have to make relishes quickly, seldom serve a meal without them. Just try toting these favorites to a community supper:

Glazed Apricots
Spicy Apple Relish
Pickled Beans
Glistening Cranberry Sauce
Cranberry Relish
Cottage-Cheese Relish
Spicy Peach Pickles
4-Vegetable Relish

None of these tempters are seasonal except the 4-Vegetable Relish: it requires fresh-from-the-garden vegetables. And possibly the Cottage-Cheese Relish, which contains cool chunks of cucumber. You can freeze the cranberry relishes to enjoy the year round.

ICE CREAM TO TOTE

You know that almost everyone likes ice cream, but the only question is how to keep it frozen until serving time. So you'll use your judgment, depending on whether there's a freezer to keep it in until ready to serve.

Speedy, glamorous trims are so easy to add: just spoon ruby-red Honeyed Cranberry Topping over vanilla ice cream, for instance. Or use the dessert sauces in this cookbook to provide the homemade touch to commercial ice cream. You won't go wrong on:

Royal-Purple Sundae
Make-Your-Own Sundae
Party Ice-Cream Cones
Honeyed Cranberry Topping
Orange-Marshmallow Topping

APPETIZERS TO TOTE

Spiced Fruit Cocktail heads the list of appetizers that carry well, but it would be short-sighted not to mention the easy-to-pour canned fruit juices. Chill them in the cans and open just before serving, or, if easier, open them at home and tote in vacuum jugs. Busy farm women make extensive use of canned and frozen blended juices.

How about serving tomato juice in a punch bowl? People are so relaxed when they gather round to sip and talk. Look in the Index for:

Spiced Fruit Cocktail
Tomato Punch Bowl
Ruby Punch
Pineapple Glow

When Company Comes

Choose Stay-at-Home Dishes

All the dishes to tote are admirable choices for home company meals as well. But there are exceptional recipes in this cookbook for foods that do not travel successfully—those that spill easily, that need to hurry from the oven, saucepan, refrigerator or freezer to the table. They're too good to pass up.

STAY-AT-HOME MAIN DISHES

Broiled steaks and chops wait on no one, yet nothing on the platter pleases more. Ditto for broiled chicken and fish! Chicken with biscuits on top is another direct-from-kitchen-to-table dish. And cheese pie, especially suited for guest lunches and suppers, requires speedy transition from oven to serving plates. Meat balls in lots of rich, brown gravy wait patiently, but they are likely to spill if carried to a group supper. So be sure to try these splendid foods in home guest meals:

Broiled Steak
Oven-roasted Steak
Meat Balls in Buttermilk Sauce
Broiled Chicken
Chicken with Bran Biscuits
Lamb Grill
Veal in Sour Cream
Ham Balls with Peaches
Baked Swiss Fondue
Cheese-Bacon Pie
Broiled Ham

SERVE-AT-HOME VEGETABLES

Good country cooks agree that some of the simplest and tastiest vegetable dishes should waste no time between kitchen and guest. Take French fries, so popular with men, for instance. Or deep orange carrots, shaved with the potato peeler and cooked fast—in a few minutes—their fluffiness disappears if they wait. And new peas in cream, tiny green beans from the garden and roasted corn rapidly lose their delicacy. All the following vegetable dishes are most succulent when served immediately after cooking:

New Peas in Cream
Asparagus with Bacon
Hasty Creamed Carrots
Parsley Carrots
Buttered Tomatoes
Roasted Corn in Foil
New Potatoes in Cream
Broiled Potato Slices
Oven French Fries
California Broccoli
Saucy Cauliflower
Cauliflower in Sour Cream

STAY-AT-HOME SALADS

Many of the salads in this cookbook are the make-ahead kind. Busy farm women prefer kinds they can fix in advance and chill to bring out to company at the last minute. Most of the recipes they sent us were that kind. However, we give you here three examples of salads that need to be served in home meals:

Lettuce Slaw
Frozen Sherbet Salad
Cabbage Salad Bowl

STAY-AT-HOME DESSERTS

Just about all the cakes in this cookbook are company specials. So are the pies. But here are a few you'll want to serve at home to guests:

Pink Party Pie
Buttermilk Pie
Ice-Cream Cookie Pie

Among the other stay-at-home desserts that wind up company meals happily are the following:

Butterscotch Dessert Waffles
Ice-Cream Sandwiches
Pear Shortcakes
Maple-Jelly Cake
Pineapple Supreme
Whipped Jellied Strawberries
Minted Grapefruit
Clover Leaf Cherry Tortes
Lemon-Pear Velvet
Broiled Peaches
Cinnamon-Peach Cobbler
Peach Islands
Frozen Lemon Torte

Coffee's Ready—Pull Up Your Chair

Coffeetime in the country is delightful. Busy women find that "one something" to eat is adequate to serve with the coffee, but this one something must be extra special. "The secret," one farm homemaker advises, "is to serve different kinds of coffee go-withs to friends who are frequent guests. I search for new accompaniments worthy of fine coffee–and I never stint on variety. My freezer makes this possible."

You can serve a different coffee go-with every day for a month using recipes in this cookbook.

BREAD RATES AS THE MAINSTAY

Breads are farm-favorite coffee go-withs. Sometimes the country cook has only loaf bread on hand, but that's no hurdle. She gives it a speedy dress-up and heats it in the oven. Often she serves sparkling jelly or marmalade with it. She buys plain doughnuts at the bakery-goods counter and dolls them up in a jiffy. And she uses brown-and-serve rolls with unlimited possibilities for her own touches of talent. Examples:

Buttery Hot Bread
Butter-Pecan Doughnuts
Maple-Nut Stickies
Crunchy Orange Rolls

Hot biscuits are country regulars and the basis of many exciting coffee breads. Some tempters start as refrigerator biscuits. You can add your own trademark by fashioning coffee cakes with them or baking them in the waffle iron–simple enough, but effective. And coffee cakes made with biscuit mix are little trouble to fix and so well received. Many of them contain fruits that supply color, flavor and a festive look. Try:

Waffled Biscuits
Orange Sugar Bread
Quick Crumb Cake
Caramel-Nut Cake
Apricot Coffee Cake
Strawberry-Swirl Coffee Cake
Apple-Cherry Ring

Yeast breads also rate as coffee favorites. Many busy women keep at least one yeast coffee cake in the freezer ready to serve. Other hostesses pin their faith and reputation as cooks on freezing English muffins and the batter breads to slice, toast and butter. Good choices:

Busy Woman's English Muffins
Anadama Batter Bread
Oatmeal Batter Bread
Whole-Wheat Batter Bread
Apple Kuchen
Spicy Sugar Cake
Strawberry Rolls

Muffins, made from different kinds of mixes, tossed with sugar and cinnamon in a paper bag or baked in cake pans to cut in different shapes are typical farm coffee accompaniments. So are fruited muffins. Make:

Spicy Muffins
Pineapple-Orange Muffins
Cranberry Muffins
Muffin Fingers
Muffin Squares

Cookies, of course, are perfect with coffee—or tea. Turn to Chapter 11 and take your pick. Coffeetime cookies on the farm often are baked in substantial he-man sizes. Bake and freeze them or make the dough and freeze for quick baking. We name only a few—you can find others quickly. Here are samples:

Coconut-Nutmeg Cookies
Butter-Pecan Crisps
Speedy Scotch Shortbread
Brownies
Raisin Griddle Cookies
Oven-baked Scones
Mincemeat Bars

When the church group, Home Demonstration Club or some other committee meets with you, make a special coffee cake with date-bar and biscuit mixes. It's so simple. And the bread is so tasty that everyone present finds that plans and decisions come easy. And every woman enjoys meeting in your home:

Date-Streusel Coffee Cake

Delicious Evening Refreshments

The hallmark of good cooks

Farm custom dictates that you bring out refreshments when friends come over for the evening. The food may be simple, but it must be tempting. And to many clever country cooks, it must be something to make everyone take notice. The menu is in two parts—food and beverage.

SWEET REFRESHMENTS

Why not surprise everyone with waffles? When time is at a premium for cooking, take frozen waffles from the freezer, add a luscious topping and broil. Or bring out old-fashioned gingerbread, cut in squares and add a topping. Unfrosted cake layers have possibilities. Spread a chocolate layer with cream cheese and spoon canned cherry-pie filling on the servings. Try:

Butterscotch Waffles
Cherry-Cheese Topping
Tropical Gingerbread
Applesauce à la Mode
Banana-Cream Frosting

All ice-cream pies are excellent evening refreshment selections, but for something out of the ordinary, serve ice-cream "pie" shells that hold tasty fillings:

Cranberry-Nut Ice-Cream Pie
Chocolate Peppermint Ice-Cream Pie

Or how about a pie with refrigerator cookie crust and ice-cream filling? Fruit sauce on ice cream? Or an unusual sundae?

Ice-Cream Cookie Pie
Peach Melba
Blueberry Sauce
Banana Sundae

SUBSTANTIAL REFRESHMENTS

Sometimes it's refreshing to pass up sweet-type dishes and serve something quite different. Make pizza with a mix in your electric skillet. Or set out a hot dip and crusty bread to dunk in it:

Quick Pizza
Pizza Snacks
Swiss-Cheese Dip
Mushroom Bacon Supreme
Tuna Treat

ON THE LIGHTER SIDE

The country is filled with nibblers. The hostess who caters to their pleasure has a treasure trove in our chapter containing snack recipes. Here are a few suggestions:

Cheese Popcorn
Jiffy Chocolate-Nut Drops
Chocolate-Marshmallow Candy
Pralines
Orange Walnuts

DRINKS OF THE EVENING

Among the splendid suggestions are coffee, tea, frozen and canned fruit juices, cocoa and other drinks made with instant mixes. Hot milk, flavored and sweetened, is a new country favorite. And some of the carbonated bottle beverages are highly favored. Do freeze Strawberry Ice Cubes for praise-winning remarks—try them in bottled lime-lemon carbonated beverage and in fruit juices.

Cherry Soda
Children's Root Beer (grown-ups like it)
Milk Steamers
Cocoa Float
Ginger-Orange Float
Lemon Iced Tea
Lime Cooler

Your Turn to Have Club?

Make the women's lunch color-bright

When busy country women entertain club members or other groups of friends at luncheon, they depend on color in foods to set the tone. "If the food is pretty and cheerful to look at," one farmer's wife suggests, "it helps put everyone in a festive mood."

Many of the dishes in this cookbook are just right for a women's luncheon. We give four luncheon menus composed of a few of them.

Party Crab Bake
Asparagus with Herbs
Celery Olives Pickles
Strawberry Basket

The casserole has a red and yellow top (tomato slices and cheese). And if you'll serve the dessert at the table, everyone will wonder who your French chef is. It's showy—straight rows of strawberries, pointed ends up, with glistening glaze over all. This easy-to-make pastry, an open-faced "pie," baked over the back of a cake pan, is a work of art.

Hot Tuna Bake
Pimiento Green Beans
Fruit-Salad Wheel
Butterflake Bread
Ice-Cream and Sherbet Bouquets

Individual casseroles of hot tuna salad are flattering–everyone has a serving fixed just for her. Pimiento splashes the green beans with brightness. Rings of canned pineapple topped with round slices of canned, jellied, tart cherry sauce on lettuce make the world's simplest salad–colorful and extra tasty. And what could be more appealing than scoops of different flavors of ice cream and sherbet in a big bowl just out of the freezer? Frost coats the bowl, adding to the dessert's beauty.

Women's Luncheon Sandwiches
Celery Radishes Cranberry Relish
Frozen Sherbet Salad

The hot corn bread and ham sandwiches are almost a meal. So it's easy to serve a salad that also answers for dessert. If you must have a vegetable, buttered peas are an excellent choice.

Chicken Casserole Supreme
Glazed Apricots
Fruited Fantan Rolls
Melon-Boat Cocktail

Glazed apricots, shiny and golden, substitute for the salad. The dessert features melon and fruits for flavor accent. No vegetables–the casserole contains asparagus. The rolls provide crispness.

INDEX

Recipes in this cookbook are of three types—make-ahead, no-watch and last-minute. Symbols tell you at a glance in which of these groups a dish belongs. Some two-step dishes are partly made ahead and completed at the last minute. On these we used both symbols.

† Make-ahead
‡ No-watch
§ Last-minute

† Make-ahead, ‡ No-watch, § Last-minute

† Make-ahead, ‡ No-watch, § Last-minute

† Make-ahead, ‡ No-watch, § Last-minute

† Make-ahead, ‡ No-watch, § Last-minute

† Make-ahead, ‡ No-watch, § Last-minute